DATE DUE

JUN 1 0 1989	
JUN 2 6 1992	
MAY 2 6 1993	
June 9	
SEP 1 5 1993	
NOV 0 6 1995	

SCHEDULING
HOME HEALTH CARE
PERSONNEL

SCHEDULING HOME HEALTH CARE PERSONNEL

LOUISE WOERNER

President
HCR
Washington, D. C.

with

KAREN CASPER FELDSTEIN

Assistant to the President
HCR
Washington, D. C.

WILEY

A Wiley Medical Publication

JOHN WILEY & SONS

New York / Chichester / Brisbane / Toronto / Singapore

Copyright © 1988 by John Wiley & Sons, Inc.

All rights reserved. Published simultaneously in Canada.

Library of Congress Cataloging in Publication Data:

Woerner, Louise.
  Scheduling home health care personnel / Louise Woerner with
  Karen Casper Feldstein.

  p.   cm. — (A Wiley medical publication)
  Includes bibliographical references and index.
  ISBN 0-471-63497-2
  1. Home health aides—Time management. 2. Medical appointments
and schedules. I. Feldstein, Karen Casper. II. Title. III. Series.
  [DNLM: 1. Home Care Services—manpower—United States. 2. Patient
Care Planning. 3. Personnel Management—methods. WY 115 W843s]

RA645.3.W64   1988   88-5584
362.1'4'068—dc19   CIP
DNLM/DLC
for Library of Congress

Printed in the United States of America

10 9 8 7 6 5 4 3 2 1

In memory of my mother,
who gave me vision.

Preface

Home health care is a rapidly changing as well as a growing component of the health care industry. Health care itself is expanding. In 1970, the United States spent $7.5 billion on national health, which was 7.4% of the gross national product (GNP). In 1985, the United States spent $425 billion in this category, or 10.7% of the GNP.[1]

The portion of the health care industry devoted to noninstitutional care is increasing both in dollars and in numbers of clients. Estimates of expenditures for home health care services by all payers show a growth from $6 billion in 1985 to an estimated $6.8 billion in 1988, $10.5 billion in 1990, and $14.2 billion in 1995.[2] In addition, over 1.5 million people received home health care services through Medicare in 1984, while only 392,700 people were served in 1974.[3]

---

[1]U.S. Health Care Financing Administration, *Health Care Financing Notes*, September 1986.

[2]National Association for Home Care, *Basic Statistics on Home Care*, August 1987.

[3]C. Helbing, W. Kirby, and V. Latta, "Medicare Use and Cost of Home Health Agency Services, 1983–1984," *Health Care Financing Review*, Vol. 8, No. 1, Fall 1986, p. 94.

Home care businesses, unlike large institutions, can be started with relatively minimal investments. Possibly for that reason, and also because it is only recently that the industry opened to for-profit companies (Omnibus Reconciliation Act of 1980—Public Law 96-499), home care has experienced rapid growth. The number of Medicare-certified home health agencies grew from 1,753 in 1967 to 5,877 in 1987.[4]

However, while home care agencies have been started in large numbers, they tend to be small, although the systems of which they are a part are large and complex. It is incumbent on the agency administrator, therefore, to understand the keys to success in order to survive and prosper in this complex and competitive environment. The single most important procedure is scheduling home care. It is the one which has the greatest influence on quality of care and profitability.

The scheduling of home care services is an art as well as a science. This task involves making decisions which crucially influence the quality of care and profitability of a home health agency. It is, therefore, appropriate that a book on home care be devoted to this complex topic.

Scheduling Home Health Care Personnel is presented as a manual which can be used by home health care agency administrators and scheduling managers to strategize their personnel departments by training individuals who perform the key tasks of scheduling services to recognize aspects and procedures in scheduling that will enable them to perform more successfully. In writing this book, my intent was to describe various aspects of successful scheduling of home care services so that the home care professional can understand not only what to do but also the rationale for the procedures. Examples are included to help the reader better understand the concepts, so that they can be understood and applied more easily.

The objective of scheduling is to minimize the amount of scheduling work. If the process of scheduling is approached with a thorough understanding of the concepts and an ideal in mind, the schedule which is planned and assigned will better meet the needs

[4]National Association for Home Care, *Basic Statistics on Home Care*, August 1987.

of clients and employees, and changes, which are time-consuming and costly, will be minimized.

This book is based on experience gained in starting and operating a growing and profitable home health care agency over a period of 10 years. During that time, many internal and external changes occurred in the business and industry. The successful development of our business within the context of these changes leads me to believe that the information presented here will prove useful as a guide and helpful as a basis for each agency to formulate the business plan it will need for success.

As the health care environment continues to change, there will be growing concern regarding cost and quality of care; home health agencies will be faced with increased demand for service and, at the same time, competition. Scheduling of home health services is changing as rapidly as the health care industry. Agencies, as they gain their market niches, will begin to experience the effects of increasing shortages of health care personnel. At that time, the focus of scheduling and delivering home health services may change from the client to the worker. The concepts presented in this book will form a basis for the shift in emphasis from patient diagnosis to manpower issues, while quality and costs are maintained.

The techniques described in this book form the basic tenets upon which future work in scheduling will be built. Part 1, consisting of Chapters 1 and 2, describes the roots of scheduling in theories of operations management and discusses the time and personnel factors that influence scheduling.

Part 2 consists of chapters exploring the critical significance of careful planning and development of systems for scheduling. Chapter 3 describes the importance of communication in the scheduling process. Procedures for determining times of service that maximize the benefits of home care for the client and best meet employee preferences are found in Chapter 4. Chapter 5 provides procedures for aspects of scheduling related to personnel management. Chapter 6 discusses the selection and assignment of personnel, detailing the careful process of matching workers to clients and cases.

Part 3 presents procedures for developing a schedule. Chapters 7 and 8 explain the mechanics of scheduling for manual and computer systems, respectively. Chapter 9 provides guidelines for monitoring and adjusting the schedule as necessary to maximize cost-effectiveness and quality of care.

Part 4, which includes Chapters 10 and 11, covers documentation and the development of alternative approaches to scheduling. Chapter 10 provides the necessary procedures for developing record-keeping practices to document all care provided and ensure compliance with applicable regulations. Chapter 11 describes an innovative approach to scheduling, first developed under a Small Business Innovation Research (SBIR) grant from the Health Care Financing Administration and since replicated with significant cost savings, known as Shared Care. This system, in accordance with the legislative intent of the SBIR program, has been commercialized by HCR for replication by other agencies to achieve significant cost savings and increases in productivity.

All of us who work in home health care have a contribution to make. I hope that mine is to organize the personnel activities that comprise the task of scheduling into a useful structure which, when applied, will improve quality of care and delivery of home health care services to those in need.

LOUISE WOERNER

*Service mark pending, HCR.

Acknowledgments

I would like to acknowledge gratefully the assistance of a few individuals who have promoted effective strategies for managing and delivering home care services. Mr. Gabe Russo, Commissioner of Human Services, Monroe County, New York; Mr. Gary Merritt, Director, Office on the Aging, Monroe County, New York; Mr. W. Burton Richardson, Director, Department of Social Services, Monroe County, New York; and Ms. Lorraine Cappellino of the Monroe County Department of Social Services have supported the efforts of home care providers in Monroe County in identifying cost-effective innovations. I would like to thank former New York Congressman Barber Conable for his avid support for and work in home health and long-term care. In addition, New York State Assemblywoman Audre "Pinny" Cooke of the 132nd District, a leader in encouraging quality care for the disadvantaged and disabled, and Doris E. Hanson, Ph.D., President of HomeCall, Inc., helped me understand the essentially nonmedical nature of many home care job tasks so that they could be reorganized. The ongoing support of Dr. Helen Schwartz, author of *Interactive Writing*, and Dr. Willard I. Zangwill of the University of Chicago, author of *The Theory Z Approach to Management*, is greatly appreciated. I would also like to thank

Joseph Halbach and Barbara Robinson, Vice Presidents of HCR;
Lee VandenBos, formerly a Vice President of HCR; and David Fiore,
Assistant to the President of HCR, for their support. I would also like
to express my appreciation to HCR's dedicated staff, including
Helen Munier, P.H.N., the staff nurses, and the untiring home care
workers, who developed and implemented many of the techniques
described in this book.

LOUISE WOERNER

Contents

PART 1

1. The Theory of Scheduling   3

Beyond Manufacturing, 5
Structuring the Approach, 6

2. Factors in Scheduling Home Health Care   21

The Scheduling Plan, 24
Factors in Scheduling, 27

PART 2

3. Communication   45

Types of Communication, 48
Quality and Accuracy in Communication, 58
Common Communication Problems, 63
Improving Communication, 66
Round-the-Clock Communication, 71

4. Determining Times of Service   **73**

Evaluating the Need for Service, 75
Analyzing Activities, 80
Assigning Days and Times, 87

5. Evaluating Personnel   **93**

Evaluating Skill Level, 95
Evaluating Personal Qualities, 104
Evaluating on a Continuing Basis, 111

6. Selecting and Assigning Personnel   **119**

Selecting Personnel, 120
Assigning Personnel, 130

PART 3

7. Manual Scheduling   **139**

Scheduling Tools, 140
Organizing the Schedule, 146
Creating the Schedule, 148
Checking the Schedule, 151
Changing the Schedule, 152
Scheduling Supervisory Visits, 154
Anticipating Problems, 158

8. Computer-Assisted Scheduling   **161**

Choosing to Schedule Electronically, 163
Developing a Computer-Based System, 164
Computerized Operations, 170

9. Monitoring and Schedule Adjustment   **181**

Types of Monitoring, 183
Organizing a System of Monitoring, 190
Adjusting the Schedule, 195

PART 4

10. Documentation 201

Record Keeping, 203
Tools, 205
Verification, 215
A Note on Confidentiality, 219

11. An Alternative Scheduling System of Sharing Services 221

The Need for Alternative Approaches, 225
The Shared Care System, 228
Benefits of Sharing Care, 230
The Model Shared Care Program, 233
Results of the Program, 240
Parameters of the System, 241
Implementing a Shared Care Schedule, 242
Monitoring in a Shared Care System, 244
Record Keeping and Billing for Shared Care, 247

INDEX 257

PART **1**

1

The Theory of Scheduling

This chapter describes the theoretical framework within which home health care services fall. Scheduling is discussed in the context of business management concepts so that the reader can better understand how to analyze issues that affect efficiency and cost elements when designing a schedule for home care services. In home health care, the scheduling of services is usually the responsibility of the personnel department. However, in the business literature, the theory of designing a schedule does not fall under the disciplines of personnel or organizational behavior, but rather under production management. The intent of this chapter is to increase awareness of operations techniques that can be applied beneficially to home health.

Many of the theoretical issues concerning the management of a company's human resources, such as how to set standards that ensure quality of care or how to motivate and supervise employees, appropriately fall under management or personnel administration theory. These are concepts with which most home care professionals are familiar. The business theories to be discussed in this book are therefore limited to those that form the basis of the design of home health care schedules for services. Those concepts fall within the management science related to work (or production) flow. This chapter describes the application of production management theory to scheduling home care services, with the goal of clarifying how the application of concepts that form the basis of cost-efficient work flow can ensure efficient use of scarce health care personnel.

Managers of agencies that provide social or medical service, like heads of other businesses, must be able to understand and apply management theories, particularly in times of limited resources. Economic reality forces both not-for-profit and for-profit companies to maximize their efficiency in order to survive. The worst possible outcome of poor management is the inability to support the goals of the company. With this outcome, the company is unable to provide any care at all.

Knowledge of operations management theories and how they can be applied to home health care will enable the scheduler to provide the best possible schedule of services, therefore ensuring the best quality of care. By applying the theories described in this chapter, the scheduler will also be able to provide the maximum amount of care allocated within the cost limit. Maximizing the amount of care delivered within the cost limit minimizes the periods when no care is being provided. That is, improvements in scheduling can improve the frequency and length of care, thus improving the quality of care.

BEYOND MANUFACTURING

The application of the theories of production and operations management to a service industry such as home health care requires that we examine the components of a schedule. A schedule is a way to process work. It is necessary to analyze each component of this process, keeping in mind that maximum efficiency is the objective.

There are a variety of ways to set up the flow of work. Some simple types of businesses, such as those that organize goods for distribution between wholesalers and retailers, can be described with one or two models of work processing. However, scheduling home health care is too complex to fall into this category. A schedule for home care involves several concepts and models of production management.

Because the theories were first developed and applied in the factory, production and operations management have been linked to this setting. In the late eighteenth century, Eli Whitney pioneered the concept of interchangeability of parts in the manufacture of guns. This principle was soon applied to the manufacture of other items. In the early twentieth century, Henry Ford developed the assembly line to facilitate the production of automobiles. Henry Gantt, a theorist of the early nineteenth century, realized that a process was a combination of operations and developed methods for sequencing operations.[*]

Operations research received a boost in its development as a field of management during World War II. At that time, the United States and Britain were recruiting scientists from various fields to assist the Allies in solving complex problems of logistics and military strategy. After the war, nonmilitary applications of operations research were developed.[†]

[*] M. K. Starr, *Operations Management*, Prentice-Hall, Englewood Cliffs, N. J., 1978, p. 593.
[†] *Ibid.*, p. 595.

As the U.S. economy shifted toward the service industries, the same theories of production and operations management were applied off the factory floor. Managers came to realize that their work systems were production processes, and they applied production and operations techniques to their businesses.

Retail department stores provide good examples of businesses which apply production and operations techniques. Directing the flow of customers through the store is a primary objective, with the idea that maximum customer exposure to merchandise will increase sales and therefore profitability. Managers achieve maximum customer exposure by placing staple goods that are routinely needed away from the main traffic flow area, forcing customers to walk through other areas to reach them. Goods often purchased on impulse are located near the high-traffic areas, with the expectation that the customer will spot and buy them.

Food service establishments have also applied the concepts of production and operations management, particularly in the facilities layout. Depending on the particular type of place (fast food place, college cafeteria, or elegant restaurant), a different facilities layout and production system is required to ensure efficient operation. The flow of food production in the kitchen must be coordinated with the flow of people through the dining area. The production and flow system design must be structured so that fluctuations in demand can be accommodated.

Airport facilities are also designed with efficiency in mind to minimize the distance that will have to be walked and the cost of handling passengers and baggage. They are designed with the ability to handle different volumes of passengers and anticipated population growth.

STRUCTURING THE APPROACH

The application of management theories to scheduling home care is schematically represented in Figure 1.1. The client at home is at the center of the diagram, symbolizing the focal point of the scheduling effort and forming the basis of the fixed-position layout configuration (to be explained in the next section).

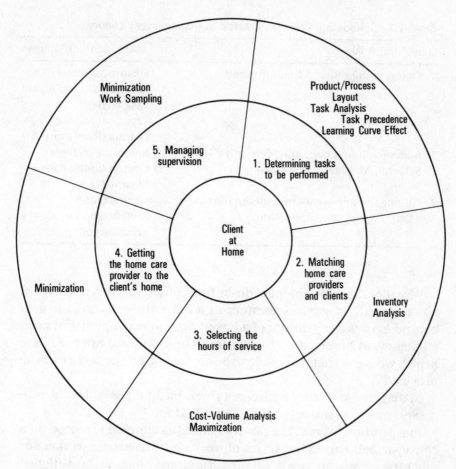

Figure 1.1. Fixed-position layout. Scheduling tasks are arranged in the second circle, management theories in the outer circle.

In Figure 1.1, the tasks directly related to scheduling home health care circle the client and are organized in order, moving clockwise from the top center. The outer circle shows selected management techniques and theories applicable to each task in the scheduling process. Note that some management theories are applicable to more than one scheduling task.

Table 1.1 relates each scheduling task to the applicable theories of production and operations management.

Table 1.1   Scheduling Tasks as Related to Management Theory

Scheduling Tasks	Management Theory
1. Determining tasks to be performed	Fixed-position layout
	Product/process layout
	Task analysis
	Task precedence
	Learning curve effect
2. Matching home care providers and clients	Inventory analysis
3. Selecting the hours of service	Cost/volume analysis
	Maximization
4. Getting the home care provider to the client	Minimization
5. Managing nursing supervision	Minimization
	Work sampling

Whether it be placement of desks in an office, kitchen facilities in a restaurant, or service counters in a department store, the goal behind a manager's design of a layout system is to operate at peak efficiency. In home care, the factors to be organized are the home health workers, their schedules, the patients, and the services to be provided.

Management theory addresses three basic types of layout processes: product, process, and fixed-position.

In a *product layout*, the product being assembled is moved on a conveyor belt through a series of work stations, where workers or machines perform work which ultimately creates the finished product. The product, and the operations performed on the product, are standardized and rarely change. The assembly line is a product layout. The product layout is commonly used in the production of automobiles and appliances.

In a *process layout*, the machines or personnel are grouped by the task performed, such that functional departments are formed. The process layout works best when the services to be performed are not always the same for each individual or product. One example might be a custom furniture manufacturer. The process layout also applies to a health clinic, where areas are set up to provide vaccines to children or to receive blood donations.

The operational approach to home health care scheduling can be considered a *fixed-position layout.* In a fixed-position layout, the product or service remains stationary and the capital and labor are brought to the product during the process of transformation from raw materials to finished product. Examples of this layout in manufacturing include home building, ship building, and dam construction. The fixed-position layout is used when the costs of transporting the product from one work station to another are high. The fixed-position layout is not as frequently found in manufacturing companies as product and process layouts and is, therefore, not often discussed in business literature. This chapter offers not only an explanation of that concept but also a new application of the fixed-position production theory, which we think the reader will find useful.

Figure 1.1 describes the fixed-position approach to home care scheduling and offers a new way of looking at the scheduling process. Each of the five major tasks in scheduling will be discussed: determining the tasks to be performed, matching providers and clients, selecting hours of service, getting the caregiver to the client, and managing nursing supervision. Management theories can be applied to each of these tasks to maximize the efficiency of the home care scheduler.

Determining the Tasks to Be Performed

The home health care business may be thought of as a fixed-position layout, in which the product, in this case, the client, is stationary (the care recipient at home), while the capital and labor (home health care aides, nursing supervisors, physical therapists, and their equipment and supplies) are brought to the client's location. The finished product in this analogy is the treated home care recipient.

Although home health care scheduling resembles a fixed-position layout, it also incorporates some aspects of product layout. On an assembly line, managers must decide sequence in which activities have to be performed. Applied to home health care scheduling, task sequence requirements determine the activities to be performed by a caregiver once he or she arrives at the client's home (i.e., at the work station). These tasks are developed from the treatment plan and listed on the client's activity sheet. For example, if a client must take medication on a full stomach, the worker must prepare the meal prior to administering the medication.

Managers must also decide how much time each activity requires. In a factory, managers calculate cycle time, which is defined as the amount of time the product is available at each work station. Once the home care worker arrives at the client's home, the operations can be treated like those of a fixed-position situation. The cycle time would be considered the amount of time the caregiver is in the client's home (i.e., at the work station on the assembly line). In a typical 4-hour case, this would equal 240 minutes.

The total time, in minutes, that the worker spends in the client's home equals the demand per day per client. By definition, in a fixed-position layout, the number of work stations is one (the client's home). The total amount of productive time in an ideal world would be 240 minutes (the exact time of the case). This cannot realistically be expected, since the worker will take breaks. A more accurate estimate of productive time per 4-hour case may actually be closer to 220 minutes. The scheduler must then schedule as many tasks in this 220 minutes as possible.

Another management theory which has application to scheduling home health services is the *learning curve effect*. The learning curve effect dictates that the more times a worker performs a specific task, the more rapidly it will be done the next time. That is, the worker becomes more efficient. There is, however, a limit to the increased efficiency, as the amount of time the worker saves in completing a task decreases with each repetition. For example, a worker may take 20 minutes to perform a given task the first time, 16 minutes the second time, 13 minutes the third time, and 11 minutes the fourth time.

The scheduler must remember that the home health worker will become more proficient at given tasks with practice. This implies that newly trained caregivers should have fewer tasks on their activity sheets than experienced workers, because the new person will take longer to complete them. Conversely, more experienced workers will be able to handle more activities per case. Task scheduling needs to be adjusted to reflect the learning curve effect. Scheduling of tasks for the caregivers must be considered in terms of minutes of working time, not in terms of the actual number of tasks.

By not taking the learning curve into account, the scheduler risks not scheduling enough tasks for the employee to perform during a case. The person may finish tasks more quickly than the scheduler anticipated, resulting in idle time for the aide and decreased productivity. This will also have a negative impact on the entire company, because the client will observe the worker sitting idle. The learning curve will need to be considered in the schedule of each client. An employee will not be as productive or able to do as many tasks the first day on the job as a week later when he or she knows the client, the environment, and the routine better.

Matching the Home Care Provider with the Client

The daily task of the home health care scheduler is to match a list of clients who need home care with a list of home care workers who are available to provide service. It is possible to view this situation as similar to that of a manufacturing plant. In this analogy, the employees available to provide service constitute a supply of goods which have been produced, in the sense that they have been recruited, screened, trained, and medically examined by the home health agency. The home care workers, similar in concept to an inventory of goods, are awaiting shipment to their consumers or clients.

The home health clients constitute the demand for shipments or orders. These are the customers for whose benefit the goods are produced. The demand created by the clients affects the cost and the supply of home care services which should be available in an agency. For example, when there are clients who have to wait in the hospital or who have to go home without care, an agency needs to recruit and train more personnel to match the amount of services available.

Clearly, the increasing demand for home care requires *inventory management theory*. The home care scheduler must ensure a sufficient supply of services to satisfy an unknown demand at any given time. It is the uncertainty of the demand for health care at any particular time that forces the home care scheduler to guard against uncertainty by always having on hand a certain level of services available, or employees on stand-by. In our analogy, it is useful to think of inventory not as boxes of goods, but rather as a pool of home care human resources waiting for an assignment.

In managing an inventory, there are two types of costs: ordering costs and carrying costs. Ordering costs consist of those costs associated with placing an order for more goods, such as supplies, ordering forms, administrative time, and order processing. In a home health care context, ordering costs are those linked to ordering more home health care workers, namely, recruitment, screening and training costs, management time, the costs of medical examinations and inoculations, and special supplies (company uniforms and identification cards). Ordering costs are the costs of increasing the pool of home health workers available to cover cases.

Carrying costs are those related to maintaining (or carrying) the pool (or inventory) of home health workers. These costs include administrative and bookkeeping time associated with setting up employee files, increased workmen's compensation, other insurance, and employee turnover due to lack of work. Some agencies guarantee employees a set number of hours. The time when the employee cannot be assigned would also be considered a carrying cost.

The scheduler must determine, based on client demand, at which times and in what quantities to "order" (recruit, train, and so forth) more home health workers in order to match caregivers with clients. To do so, the scheduler must understand the trade-off between ordering and carrying costs. Depending on whether the bulk of the home care agency's inventory costs are ordering or carrying costs, the scheduler must determine the most cost-efficient combination between placing large orders infrequently and placing small orders frequently, or between recruiting large numbers of employees who may have to be paid some guarantee to stand by until they have a full case load and selecting smaller numbers of employees more frequently.

In the home health care scheduling context, the greater costs are the ordering costs, while carrying costs remain relatively low. This leads to the conclusion that each order should be rather large (because the costs of frequent small orders are so high) but infrequent (because the carrying costs associated with a large inventory are low). Of course, each scheduler must assess the costs associated with ordering and carrying inventory in his or her agency.

It is the responsibility of the scheduler to keep the inventory of home care workers at the optimum level. Less than optimal management of the inventory level can result in adverse conditions for the agency. A balance must be maintained between having too few employees in the pool to fill orders (a situation termed, in inventory management, a *stockout*) and having too many employees whose skills and training are not being put to good use. The costs to the home health agency of either can be detrimental.

The dangers of having too few available workers are clear. First, the clients' needs are not satisfied and no service is provided. This is contrary to the home care agency's purpose. Second, clients may lose faith in the ability of the agency to provide the home care they need. They may turn to another agency or, worse, stop asking for home health service, creating the potential for unnecessary institutional placement.

Another set of problems exists when there are too many home health workers in the pool and insufficient demand for services. In this case, the caregivers have been overproduced and are now a surplus. The consequences in this case are clear. First, the home care agency has invested time and money in training the caregivers. The agency's resources have been expended and there is no return on investment for those unassigned workers, since there is no work for them to do and for the agency to bill. Second, the caregivers are not working, so they have no income and may lose interest in being home care workers. If this situation continues long enough, the employees may quit. Alternatively, if they do finally receive a case, their performance may be poor, leading to dismissal.

Selecting the Hours of Service

The scheduler's task of selecting the hours of service is related to the management technique of *cost/volume analysis*. For-profit companies are assumed to be profit maximizers, and the cost/

volume analysis is a tool for reaching this goal. Not-for-profit companies can employ the same technique to become efficiency maximizers.

The scheduler's first task is to determine the *breakeven point*, which is defined as the number of units that a company must sell or provide in order to break even (no profit, no loss). The breakeven point may be expressed in terms of units (or hours of scheduled home care) or dollars (total dollars billed to clients). Expressed either way, the scheduler knows the volume that must be attained in order to keep the organization viable and to continue helping needy elderly and ill individuals.

The scheduler determines the breakeven point by first separating costs into two categories—fixed and variable. Fixed costs do not change in relation to the number of hours of home care produced by the agency, such as rent, overhead, management salaries, insurance, and utilities. Variable costs go up in relation to the number of hours of home care produced. These include costs for training home health workers, medical examinations, uniforms, payroll (other than administrative) and fringe benefits, recruitment, and nursing supervision.

Second, the scheduler divides the number of units of health care produced into the total variable costs to obtain the variable costs per unit. Third, the scheduler subtracts the variable cost per unit from the selling price per unit (the amount billable to the client for an hour of service) to obtain the contribution margin per unit. The contribution margin per unit is the dollar amount that each unit (hour of home care) contributes to the payment of the agency's fixed costs. The breakeven point is equal to the total fixed costs divided by the contribution margin per unit. The breakeven point expressed in dollars is equal to the breakeven point in units multiplied by the selling price per unit.

Knowledge of the breakeven point (especially in terms of units) permits the scheduler to plan so as to guarantee that the number of hours of service scheduled are sufficient to cover the agency's costs. *Maximization* and *minimization* refer to linear programming techniques designed to assist managers in making decisions. With linear programming problems, the objective is to minimize or maximize some quantity (such as cost or profit) in the presence of constraints which limit the ability to attain the desired objective. In a home health scheduling setting, the objective is to maximize the total hours of coverage.

At the implementation level, this effort involves scheduling the biggest pieces first. This is because more staff time and telephone calls are required to locate four aides willing to work 2 hours each on four different cases (for a total of 8 hours) than to locate one aide willing to work 8 hours on a single case (again, for a total of 8 hours). Scheduling an 8-hour case is preferable to scheduling a 2-hour case and should therefore receive first priority. Furthermore, when a caregiver is assigned to a client for an entire week, the client will usually not require any additional coverage. This frees the scheduler's time to continue covering other cases.

Similarly, emphasis should be placed on covering the permanent cases. The rationale is that the permanent cases need only be covered once, whereas temporary or one-time cases must be covered again tomorrow.

The constraints on this approach require scheduling staff to be aware not only of the objective but also of the negative consequences for clients if they are unable to obtain service. In these situations the scheduler must consider the priority of the care, which, for the purposes of this book, means the life-threatening consequences of lack of service. This would include, for example, clients who need the most skilled nursing services, such as regular insulin injections and medication.

In addition to meeting the goals outlined above, the home health care scheduler has a social-oriented objective that the production manager may not necessarily have. That objective is to maximize the total output of the product (home care service to those who need it) so that the greatest good to society is achieved.

Getting the Home Care Provider to the Client's Home

Similar to the maximization problems in determining the hours of service, linear programming is applied to getting the employee to the client's home. The only difference is that here the scheduler is concerned with minimizing the total distance the employee must travel to get to work.

Because scheduling home care is a patient-driven process, that is, provided at the request of the patient (or the doctor for the patient), the scheduler attempts to minimize the distance that each aide must travel to arrive at the client's home. This is done by selecting employees who live closest to the patient when scheduling coverage, moving outward from the client's location as the nearer employee possibilities become exhausted.

Admittedly, this is not an easy task. The scheduler needs accurate and accessible data on the location of each worker and client. The total number of caregiver-to-client distance combinations is the number of workers multiplied by the number of clients. With accurate data for each caregiver-to-client distance, the scheduler can determine the average distance between a worker and a client. Using this average, the scheduler can verify that the caregiver-to-client combinations being scheduled for that day fall within an acceptable range. This method serves as a measurement standard to ensure minimization of the distance. Because of client and employee turnover, the scheduler must periodically recalculate the average caregiver-to-client distance.

The minimization of distance traveled by workers ensures that the agency pays taxi and bus fares only when absolutely necessary. Another benefit is a positive psychological effect on the employees, since they do not have to travel extensively to reach a case. Finally, travel minimization increases the likelihood of their accepting assignments, as well as their ability to arrive reliably and on time.

Managing Supervision

Like scheduling health care workers, managing supervisory visits presents a situation in which the scheduler wishes to minimize the travel distance between cases. This permits the nurse to visit a maximum number of cases in one day, thereby raising productivity.

Figures 1.2 and 1.3 indicate the five cases that a nurse or other professional may supervise during a typical day. Assuming that the cases can be seen in any order, the scheduler wishes to minimize the total travel distance and thus the transportation costs. The constraint in this problem is that the supervisor is required to start and end at the office. The number of different possible routes that

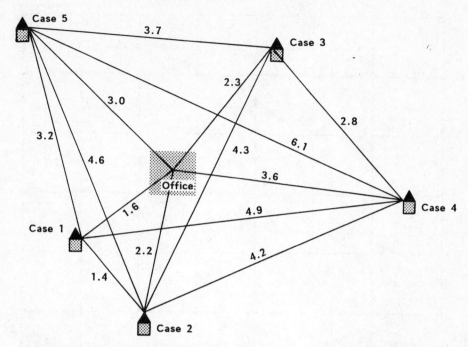

Figure 1.2. *Managing supervision: map showing five cases. Distances shown in miles.*

the supervisor can take is equal to 5! (five factorial), or (5 × 4 × 3 × 2 × 1) = 120 different routes. Each route has a different mileage (although some routes may have the same mileage).

Analysis of the mileage chart reveals to the scheduler that certain routes can be eliminated immediately, thus narrowing the possibilities. For example, it is apparent in Figure 1.2 that case 2 is closest to case 1 and that case 1 is closer to the office than any other case. Therefore, the sequence "office to case 1 to case 2" or "case 2 to case 1 to office" should be configured into the nursing supervisory case visit schedule.

Furthermore, case 2 is closer to case 4 than it is to either case 3 or case 5, so the sequence should be either "office to case 1 to case 2 to case 4" or "case 4 to case 2 to case 1 to office." Similarly, case 4 is closer to case 3 than to case 5, which would provide the sequence of "office to case 1 to case 2 to case 4 to case 3" or "case 3 to case 4 to

	Case 1	Case 2	Case 3	Case 4	Case 5	Office
Case 1		1.4	3.9	4.9	3.2	1.6
Case 2			4.3	4.2	4.6	2.2
Case 3				2.8	3.7	2.3
Case 4					6.1	3.6
Case 5						3.0
Office						

Figure 1.3. Mileage chart.

case 2 to case 1 to office." Lastly, the optimal, efficient sequence of case visits is "office to case 1 to case 2 to case 4 to case 3 to case 5 to office" or "office to case 5 to case 3 to case 4 to case 2 to case 1 to office," both of which total 16.7 miles in distance traveled.

During the supervisory visits, work sampling can be used to estimate the percentage of time that the caregiver is either working or idle. Work sampling is a random set of observations of the employee at work. It can be used as a method of assessing productive and nonproductive time and establishing job content.

Depending on the confidence level and accuracy desired, the sample size of home care providers observed for work sampling will vary. When gathering observations for work sampling, random observation (in terms of both the workers visited and the time of the visit) is necessary to ensure unbiased results. During the observation period, the supervisor records whether the worker was busy or idle. The supervisor records the observations until the desired sample size has been observed.

The supervisor then creates a chart showing the total number of observations when a caregiver was either busy or idle. In the next column, percentages are calculated for both busy and idle time. This information is helpful for the scheduling and supervisory staff because it can be used to monitor the number of activities that the worker is asked to perform for the client.

It cannot be assumed, however, that an employee will work 100% of the time. The agency must allow for breaks and other unproductive periods. This is referred to as the *company allowance fraction.* A company can set its own allowance fraction and readjust it as needed.

Work sampling can be used to determine not only whether the home care worker is busy or idle, but also which tasks the person is performing when the supervisor makes a random observation. For example, the supervisor records the task that the worker is doing when observed, and this information is tallied. The number of observations of each type of task are recorded, and the percentage of the total number of observations for each task is calculated. This information tells the scheduler that, for example, 10% of the employee's time is spent preparing meals or that 25% of the time is spent doing household chores. The scheduler can monitor these work samples against the task activity sheets.

The scheduler's knowledge of idle time takes on even more significance when the agency bills on a per-visit basis, regardless of the length of the case. Per-visit billing provides a strong incentive to the company to decrease allowance fractions for tasks to a minimum.

The issue of operating as efficiently as possible is relevant to the not-for-profit as well as the for-profit company. The theoretical components discussed indicate the best way to set up the systems design for scheduling. That is, it is beneficial to think of scheduling in the home health care organization in the context of production management, if one is to develop the best systems for matching personnel with clients.

It should be noted that many additional issues related to scheduling fall under the discipline of personnel administration, which is not discussed in this chapter. While the importance of that discipline to scheduling is clear, it is important to emphasize the systems requirements of the scheduling plan, which fall under production management and operations management theories that are less frequently discussed in both home care and business research. The reader who has no personnel management background may also want to review that literature.

2

Factors in Scheduling Home Health Care

Staff members who schedule home care consider the same medical and service needs of clients as do physicians, nurses, and administrators in institutions. In addition, scheduling services outside the facilities and resources of an institution requires consideration of factors to fulfill the plan of care and maximize the benefits of home care. Staff members must consider the service requirements of the case, the logistics of providing care (the location of the home or the equipment needs of the client), and the resources and preferences of the client and family in whose home the agency will work.

These additional factors make scheduling home care difficult, but they result in considerably more individualized care than that provided in an institution. Home health care, or medical and support services delivered to individuals in their homes, is provided as an alternative to institutional placement. Clearly, the superior feature of care provided in the home is that it is demand based, that is, tailored to the needs and preferences of the client.

The flexibility that can be designed into an individual's schedule is an aspect of home care that contributes to its being inherently better than institution-based services for most people. For example, one client's schedule could have dressing and feeding times and designated days changed to accommodate a regularly scheduled visit to a physician, such as might be required for chemotherapy. Meal times, the amount of food served, or toileting tasks could vary, as could the intensity of service.

In a 3-week chemotherapy cycle, services could be provided daily for 3 days following the chemotherapy, every other day for the next 4 days, then every 3 days, and then not at all until the next 3-week cycle started. The job tasks could also be adjusted, as could the level of care, if necessary. A schedule with this flexibility would be relatively easy to provide in home care but problematical and costly in an institution, where adjusting the time, frequency, and level of care is more difficult.

Home health services, in addition to maintaining or improving the quality of life for the elderly and infirm, are geared to controlling the costs of health care services, fostering independence, and reforming the family structure. Scheduling, therefore, often incorporates into the care plan activities that the client and the family might perform, as well as those to be performed by the home health worker.

The agency must remember that the primary considerations in scheduling home care are as follows:

1. *Meet the client's needs for medical and supportive services.* All home health schedules must meet the requirements specified in the physician's orders or treatment plan. The services authorized, the amount and frequency of service, and the level of care required (such as skilled nursing, speech therapy, or personal care) must be provided as ordered. In addition, the scheduling staff must consider the equipment and supplies needed to perform the required services. Often a team of professional and paraprofessional workers is required to provide all of the medical and supportive services required for a successful plan of care. Each employee must be scheduled to keep costs to a minimum and maximize interventions.

2. *Be cost-effective.* When home care services cost more than comparable services that can be provided in an institution, home care cannot long be a viable alternative for the client. In addition, to be competitive in the growing home care industry, the agency must increase its efficiency wherever possible to minimize costs so that pricing will be competitive. When an unfavorable cost comparison between home care and institutional care is unavoidable, more efficient scheduling options, like Shared Care, should be explored (see Chapter 11).

3. *Ensure the quality of care.* A well-planned schedule should secure the highest quality and continuity of care. It should ensure that clients receive the support and services they need at the time required. It should ensure the greatest possible supervision and the fewest number of hours in which clients are alone, unsupervised, and without human contact or assistance (hours of no care). It should also ensure that service is provided, wherever possible, according to the preferences of the client.

Overall, the schedule should be responsive to both the needs of the individuals and their preferences regarding care. Service schedules in institutions are driven by personnel factors such as shifts. For example, the meal service in a hospital ward is scheduled to accommodate the dietary and food preparation staff, as well as those who distribute the meals. The meal schedule must also fit other schedules, such as those for physicians' rounds, house-keeping, or laboratory tests. Schedules of home care can be more flexible than those of institutions. Home care should meet the specific needs and desires of the clients and be convenient. This flexibility is an important advantage of home care and should be maximized.

Whether the agency's clientele is large or small, ensuring that the objectives of scheduling are met for all cases requires that the scheduling staff have a scheduling strategy. The objective of scheduling is to minimize the amount of scheduling work. Scheduling times of service and assigning personnel must be a careful and calculated process, although the pressure to service clients seems to generate a countervailing sense of urgency. The scheduler must balance the daily demands for schedule changes or case coverage with his or her own agenda of cases to be covered that day.

To achieve an organized scheduling system that runs smoothly, the home care agency must develop a scheduling plan to help the staff prioritize cases. Once they have decided which cases to schedule, the staff must work systematically, considering each of the factors that comes into play when determining times for service and selecting and assigning personnel.

THE SCHEDULING PLAN

All referrals received by an agency are important, as is every client currently on an agency's schedule. The scheduling staff is often caught between the need to schedule new cases, reschedule existing cases that require changes, and attend to the host of daily problems that seem to require immediate attention. Scheduling staff who spend their days reacting to changes and telephone calls never progress with their own agenda for the day, so that each day results only in coverage of the day's cases.

Scheduling staff, constantly balancing an agenda of unscheduled cases against telephone calls from clients and employees, tend to schedule cases based on which client or referral source is most insistent. In order for scheduling functions to proceed smoothly, however, staff members have to resist the daily pressures of last-minute schedule changes and remain focused, establishing the priority of each request for scheduling or rescheduling and responding accordingly.

Once a case has been accepted, care must be arranged. However, the first element of any plan for prioritizing cases is the urgency of the request. A client's need for medical or other sustaining services, including meal preparation, takes precedence over cases requiring nonskilled care.

Once the most medically urgent cases have been assigned, the order in which other cases are handled can vary, depending on the structure of the agency and the methods used by referral sources in referring clients. In a community where referrals are centralized, for example, and 30 agencies may compete for clients, a referral source may call 6 agencies and explain that whichever agency covers the case first will get the referral. If scheduling staff are already backed up, trying to cover priority cases and emergencies, the agency may decide that it is not worthwhile to try to cover a case when there is only a one in six chance of getting the referral.

In other situations, there are more requests for services than available providers. The agency then makes decisions on accepting cases based on working relationships with referral sources, the length of the case, the appropriateness of the case for available personnel, contract agreements, and other factors.

Regardless of the particular community, management staff should set guidelines to help scheduling staff structure their caseloads. Several issues common in the management policy of agencies are noted below. Others, such as contractual agreements, should be analyzed within the context of the specific business.

1. *Total hours of coverage or number of visits made.* Once the most important cases, in terms of critical care requirements or treatment, have been scheduled, most agencies try to maximize the total hours of coverage or number of visits when choosing between cases to schedule. Thus, assuming that the treatment priority of each case is the same, the scheduling staff schedules the longest cases first. This scheduling strategy requires the least amount of work, since more staff time is required to cover a greater number of short cases than one long case. In addition, because of the cost and

travel time involved, home care employees generally prefer longer assignments. Employees might be able to handle only three 2-hour cases in a day because of travel, compared to working for 8 hours on one full-shift case.

2. *Profitability.* This is an important issue in home care. Both for-profit and not-for-profit agencies provide home care and support services under various funding arrangements. The goal of maximizing profits or ensuring that the agency breaks even is consistent with the objectives of home care, as good-quality care requires a fiscally sound agency. Costs affect the scheduling plan, depending on the structure of the agency or how it handles charity care (such as whether or not the agency receives deficit funding). Even in a not-for-profit agency, the more cost effective a caseload is, the more persons can be served.

Certain cases are more costly to an agency than others, depending on the length of the case, the type of caregiver, or the billing rate. With some exceptions, the longer the case, the more profitable it is (assuming the level of worker is constant). Unless a premium is paid, which is sometimes the case, 2-hour cases are decidedly less profitable than 4-hour cases. By accepting a 2-hour case, the agency foregoes the possibility of assigning the same worker to a 4-hour case (and therefore gives up 2 more hours of billable time). This causes the employee loss of potential earnings and the agency loss of the opportunity for better cases. In addition, many agencies must pay their employees a premium to accept the shorter cases, increasing their costs. The scheduling time for short and long cases is the same, but the payoff may vary significantly. That is, a greater number of hours generates a greater contribution to administrative expenses.

Some agencies also prioritize cases based on the contract under which the case is covered. Some contracts are more profitable than others because the rates set for each type of worker can vary. Thus, if a scheduler has two cases to cover, both involving the same treatment priority, the order in which the cases are covered may be determined on the basis of which contract is more profitable or otherwise advantageous.

3. *Type of case.* Emphasis should be placed on covering permanent cases as opposed to temporary assignments, that is, giving priority to assigning caregivers who would be expected to provide the specified care for the duration of the care plan. Generally, permanent cases need only be covered once; no rescheduling is needed unless a problem arises. This minimizes schedule changes

that are time-consuming and costly. Temporary assignments must be covered with temporary personnel until a permanent schedule can be established.

4. *Duration of coverage.* Cases referred to an agency may be short- or long-term, depending on the client's requirements for care and the payment mechanism. Medicare guidelines, for example, cap the duration of services at specific periods of time. Private pay cases may be long-term, as may cases involving clients with psychiatric or developmental disabilities. Depending on the agency's primary market for services, the duration of the case may be a necessary and important consideration, as less work is needed to schedule one long-term case than several short-term cases.

5. *Desired mix of clients.* An agency should determine its market niche. Many types of services, both paraprofessional and professional, exist in home care. There are specialized types of work from private pay to Medicaid. Home care patients may be children or the elderly. An agency must decide what its place is in the home care industry. One agency might prefer to emphasize more acute care than another, or decide on a certain geographic emphasis within a community.

FACTORS IN SCHEDULING

Once a decision has been made regarding the order in which cases will be covered, a variety of scheduling factors must be considered. Objective factors include the service needs of the client, the availability of appropriate employees, and the location of the client (and caregivers). Subjective factors such as personal preferences are also considered. These factors determine the two most important facets of the schedule: the times when services will be provided and the selection and assignment of personnel to provide the care. They can be divided as follows:

Time Factors	Personnel Factors
1. Service needs	1. Service needs
2. Availability of the client	2. Geography
3. Personal preferences for service	3. Availability of appropriate caregivers
4. Availability of outside support	4. Employee preferences
5. Psychosocial needs of the client	5. Special factors

The times at which services will be provided are usually determined first, based on the activities required in the treatment plan. However, matching clients and caregivers is an important component of home care, and the times selected usually affect the choice of personnel available. Sometimes it is more important to change the time of service in order to get exactly the right person to cover the case than to assign an available employee who is less desirable in other respects, such as having experience with a certain diagnosis. Scheduling requires balancing the best possible times of service and the best possible people to assign. Which factor is more significant depends on the case and must be decided by the scheduling staff.

In balancing time and personnel factors, the staff must first ensure that the needs of the client are met. The time the client is to receive medical and support services is the primary determinant of the schedule. For example, it may be most important that a client be bathed, fed, and assisted with dressing in order to be picked up for an adult day care program. In this case, the services cannot be provided later in the day. When the significance of the time of the service is established, schedulers can make decisions regarding the various permutations and combinations of possible schedules on the basis of cost and quality issues.

When the client's medical and support needs are time specific, the time factors determine the schedule. For example, there is little flexibility in scheduling the case of an emphysema client who requires an oxygen treatment at 7:00 a.m. daily. The time of the service is fixed. In assigning personnel to the case, the scheduling staff would first see who is available at that time. If more than one caregiver is available, the staff would determine who is closest geographically. They would then attempt to match the client and caregiver on the basis of preferences, special factors, and personalities.

When the client's needs are less time specific, there is more flexibility in designing a schedule. For example, the emphysema client described above might be authorized to receive home health aide service twice a week, in addition to the daily nursing service. Although the physician might suggest that the home health aide come while the client is receiving medication from the nurse, the agency could be creative in determining a schedule that might be more beneficial for the client. To be efficient, the staff might consider geography first. At what time is someone nearby? Then the agency could look at other types of support received by the client and the client's preferences for times of service. The scheduling staff might then suggest that, to increase supervision and create more opportunities for the client to have contact with people, the home health aide serve the client in the afternoon rather than in the morning. Alternatively, if it were more cost effective to consolidate a supervisory and treatment visit of a nurse or other health care professional, the combination and coordination of tasks could be planned.

The determination of the schedule will ultimately be based on the service requirements of the client and, to the greatest extent possible, the other factors as well. As described below, information should be gathered on each of these factors for every case being scheduled. The significance of each factor depends on the requirements of the particular case. In some instances, the timing of service needs identified in the treatment plan will be so specific that they become the only factor determining the schedule. In other instances, the agency can use flexibility and creativity, combining several factors to design a schedule that best meets the needs of the client and the availability of personnel and contains costs.

Time Factors

Time issues are central to home care. Some times of service are flexible, others fixed. Home care can accommodate service demand factors, that is, required and preferred times. Meals can be prepared early or late. Unlike the institutional concept of time as shifts, home care schedules can accommodate clients' preferences for service and employees' preferences for working hours. Some workers may prefer a workday that starts and finishes early; others like to work mornings and evenings and have the middle of the day free. This time flexibility is the essential distinguishing characteristic of noninstitutional care.

Service Needs
The client's service needs must be the primary consideration when scheduling home care services. These needs dictate who can be

assigned to deliver services (i.e., the level of worker) and, in many cases, when and how often the services are delivered.

The physician's orders and the plan of care prepared by the community health nurse, social service worker, or client and family (depending on the payment mechanism) authorize the number of hours and frequency of service. They also specify the level of care, which determines the type of employee (registered nurse, therapist, licensed practical nurse, personal care aide, home health aide, homemaker, chore worker, or other home care staff) assigned to the case. These specifications greatly affect how units of service, tasks, and personnel are defined and scheduled.

Determining units of service is the first step in considering the treatment plan. If the physician or nurse who developed the care plan specifies scheduled times for service, the agency should try, whenever possible, to design the schedule accordingly. If not, the agency can, with some flexibility, break the care plan into units of service that will optimize quality of care and efficiency.

If the agency decides to break up the care plan into scheduling units, the staff must first determine the units in which the services can be offered. The basic units used in home care are *visits*, which are defined as the length of time required to perform a specific treatment or group of services, and *hours*, which are usually organized into minimum units of 2 or 4. Many home health agencies have 2- or 4-hour minimum billing units. Alternatively, some reimbursement systems limit care to a specified number of visits. An agency must remain within these limits when determining units of service.

The physician's orders and the care plan developed by the registered nurse or other professional and family are then broken down into job tasks, or the activities that the client requires. In order to make certain tasks into a schedule, the staff must make many decisions, such as on what days, at what times, and for how long the services will be provided. For example, the service ordered could be a nursing visit to change a sterile dressing three times a week. The scheduling staff would allot sufficient time in the schedule for this task to be completed, but it could be done at almost any time that was agreeable to the employee and client.

Appropriate blocks of time for delivering services can also vary with the job tasks required. Some services require a full 8-hour shift and others, such as shopping, chore services, and laundry, can be organized into 8 hours spread over a week without sacrificing quality of care. Other services require delivering care in frequent smaller units, such as visits, or two 4-hour or four 2-hour units. For example, medical treatments, such as intravenous therapy, dressing changes, or administering insulin or medication, require short, frequent visits. Physical therapy often requires several visits per week, while meal preparation or personal care must, of course, be scheduled for at least one visit per day. Services to maintain an individual's environment may be delivered less frequently. Paraprofessional work is more often scheduled in units of time than in visits.

The agency should keep in mind that in determining blocks of time for routine services, the staff can consider the increased quality of care that often results from shorter, more frequent visits. The benefits of more frequent intervention include additional supervision, stimulation, and psychological support. Where there is greater flexibility in planning the duration and frequency of service, these factors should be taken into account, although it is obvious that larger blocks of care are less costly.

Once units are separated by activities, the staff can look at the tasks to be completed and determine appropriate times for service. Often there is flexibility in assigning the exact day or time of service. In scheduling according to the tasks in the care plan, the agency must consider the flexibility with which the job tasks can be performed. While some job tasks are flexible, others are not. A bed bath, for example, can be scheduled somewhat flexibly, while medication which must be given or taken in accordance with a set timetable can determine a patient's schedule.

In addition, examining specific tasks allows a scheduler to know who he or she needs to consult in determining the best times for service. A schedule involving tasks such as administering medication must be set as directed. Service involving other tasks, such as meals or baths, can be scheduled, within reason, as preferred by the client and agreeable to the employee.

After consultation with the physician, case manager, or client, each component of the treatment plan should be evaluated and placed in priority. This process, known as *job task analysis,* is described in detail in Chapters 5 and 11. Essentially, the higher the priority of the task, the less flexibility can be used in scheduling it. Examples of high-priority or time-specific tasks are administering medication such as insulin, providing medical treatments such as dialysis or oxygen therapy, and providing meals or intravenous feeding. Moderate-priority tasks include meal preparation, some types of physical therapy, and exercise. These tasks could be provided at many times during the day but would not be appropriate at certain times. Rigorous or demanding exercises, for example, would not usually be suitable immediately after a meal, just after waking, just before bed, or during the night. Lower-priority, more flexibly scheduled tasks include chore services and grocery shopping.

High-priority, time-specific tasks must be identified first. Medication that must be administered every 8 hours causes more cost problems in home care than in institutional care, as does regular, round-the-clock turning of a patient to avoid bed sores. In home care, the caregiver must remain in the home or come and go, causing increased costs and loss of time in travel. In institutional care the personnel are always available, at least in theory. Similarly, a mobile electrocardiogram, x-ray, or other procedure that can be ordered at home must be scheduled precisely, with little or no flexibility. These tasks therefore determine a client's schedule; other more flexible tasks that can be logically performed before or after the high-priority tasks can then be combined into one unit of time that meets the agency's minimum billing requirement or provides the services that have been authorized.

Availability of the Client or the Family

Not all home care services are provided under Medicare, which requires that the client be homebound. Some patients pay for their services themselves. These clients, and those who receive chore and personal care services funded by state social service programs such as Title XIX (Medicaid) or Title XX of the Social Security Act, for example, have to be scheduled with the idea in mind that the client may have treatments or other commitments outside the home that would preclude home care service during that time.

For example, a client with end-stage renal disease who receives support services at home may be at the hospital for kidney dialysis during specific hours each week, or a cancer victim receiving chemotherapy may go to the hospital for treatment. Scheduling staff would have to know this prior to scheduling.

In addition, a person who is not homebound may attend religious services or even a bridge game regularly. Although this may seem much less important than the home support services the person is receiving, it may be what the person looks forward to most or keeps him or her in good mental health. It may also be the person's only opportunity for socialization outside the home or with peers. With isolation identified as the most significant problem faced by aging persons, socialization is clearly critical to quality care. Clients should, of course, never have to decide between the activities they enjoy and the home support services they need.

Family members or friends often play a most significant role in the schedule. Services may be needed at times when family members are not available to provide them. Another part of home care is training or educating the family in techniques for the care of a family member. For example, the family of an elderly client with diabetes may need to be taught how to administer insulin; new parents receiving pediatric home care need to be taught how to work an apnea monitor to track an infant's breathing or respond to an infant heart monitor. In this case, the agency must also schedule services at a time when the family can be available to watch the nurse and learn the techniques they need to know for ongoing care. While it can be assumed that family members will place the highest priority on learning to accomplish these tasks, they may have jobs or other commitments around which they would prefer to have services scheduled.

Preferences of the Client and Family

The preferences of the client and family influence scheduling. Attention to the preferences of sick clients and to often seemingly insignificant requests can make a world of difference to their emotional well-being, as well as their quality of life. Regardless of what the funding agency or referral source may be, particularly when third-party payers set limits on reimbursable service, the client is the recipient of the services, and attention to his or her preferences and concerns creates a feeling that services are being provided according to personal wishes. Recognizing that preferences may need to be balanced in order to control costs, it is still most useful to try to learn about and accommodate preferences to the extent possible. Clients and families may have specific requests or preferences for times of service. If, for example, a treatment plan includes a bed bath, a task that can be scheduled somewhat flexibly, personal preference can come into play. If a client is to receive both a bed bath and exercise, it may be preferable to give a bed bath after the exercise, when a patient is likely to perspire. On the other hand, the patient may be tired after the exercise and may prefer not to have the additional movement involved.

Similarly, clients may have preferences for hours of service. If, for example, the client is an early riser and feels more alert in the morning, he or she may prefer to have a home care worker early in the day. If the client likes to sleep late and does not require rigidly scheduled medication or treatment, he or she may prefer to receive service later in the day. Demand-based home care, as opposed to shift- or schedule-based institutional care, allows such individualized service. The agency should promote and provide this benefit, as it is a quality that makes home care preferable, even when the cost is comparable to that of institutional care.

Availability of Outside Support

Another factor to be considered in scheduling services is family- or community-based support received by the client. Support, or lack of support, ties in the issues of hours of no care, timing of service, and client preferences. The level of family or outside support received by the client affects how an agency plans the timing and frequency of service.

First, the level of family or outside support may influence the amount of supervision and stimulation that the agency will provide. If a client receives no outside support and has no family, the agency should take into account possible isolation and schedule services over several days, to maximize the intervention, if these small units are allowable or affordable. If the client receives significant family support, and if the care plan permits, service can be scheduled in larger blocks of time.

Outside services received by the client also influence the timing of services. If a client receives service from another agency, such as Meals on Wheels, home health services should be scheduled with this in mind. The agency would not want to interrupt other activities the client receives, and the client would benefit from the greater number of interventions delivered separately. In addition, it would be inconvenient for a client to receive personal care which conflicts with the meal schedule set by Meals on Wheels or activities connected with transportation services or adult day care programs.

Receiving outside support or services can also influence client preferences for scheduling. If clients attend day care programs, for example, they may want personal care service early on those days. In addition, a client may be too tired for physical therapy after a morning at day care, so this service can be scheduled on a day when the client does not attend.

It is important to note that outpatient medical services or treatments, by affecting the physical condition of the client, can also affect preferences for service. Clients who receive dialysis or chemotherapy, for example, may feel physically sick, tired, or emotionally low after returning home. They may wish to have home care workers in their homes on those days or, alternatively, may prefer to be alone. An ability to adjust to personal wishes is one of the aspects of quality care that distinguishes home care.

Psychosocial Needs of the Client

Since the emotional or social needs of clients (such as frequent human contact, companionship, or respite) are not services that are generally reimbursed by the primary funding sources for home care (i.e., Medicare and, in most states, Medicaid), they may not be specified in the plan of care. However, meeting the psychosocial needs of the clients and their families, which are often apparent in their stated requests and preferences, is an important aspect of home-based care and should be addressed in the plan of care and in the schedule, incidental to the skilled aspects of care.

For example, a client who is recently disabled may need greater emotional support and reassurance from the people with whom he or she has contact. In making a schedule, the agency can consider delivering shorter but more frequent units of service in order to increase supervision and interpersonal contact for the client. Timing and pacing of care to increase self-reliance and foster independent living while providing needed services requires careful case planning and sensitivity to changing circumstances. For example, rehabilitation for certain illnesses may have plateaus or steps in levels of attainment. The effects of the rehabilitation programs should be maximized by designing the care plan to move past these plateaus most effectively.

In addition, the family may have psychosocial needs that can be fulfilled with careful and intuitive scheduling. A family that seems to be particularly burdened, physically and emotionally, with the care of a loved one may benefit from support at particular times. Services provided during the day, for example, would enable them to leave their home for a brief period, while services provided in the evening would allow them some rest. An astute scheduling person should be able to understand these needs and incorporate them into the schedule where possible.

Personnel Factors

The personnel who provide home health services are the most important component of service delivery. The selection of caregivers is based on objective factors, such as level of training required, and subjective considerations, such as personality and employee preferences regarding their work schedules. However, the feelings that develop between people, the reactions between them, are often the aspect of care that is most significant in the perception (and usually the reality) of the quality of the care provided.

Service Needs

The level of worker specified in the treatment plan is considered first. Among qualified personnel, the scheduling staff must then look for employees who have the expertise to meet any special requirements of the case. For example, a treatment plan may call for a technological procedure, such as administering home dialysis, that requires specific skills. Other cases may require someone who has significant experience with a particular type of client, such as a terminally ill child or a victim of Alzheimer's disease, or knowledge of a foreign language. The need to use equipment, such as hoyer lifts, and the type of hands-on care required, affects the choice of the worker to be assigned.

Geography

There are many reasons that geography takes on critical significance in home care. One reason is cost. While travel time and transportation expenses between cases or for the benefit of a client must generally be paid, employees must arrive at their first job and go home at the end of the day on their own. High travel costs or long travel time are a disincentive to work, and thus for workers to cover cases. The fact that a case is easily reached reduces the cost for the employee and usually enhances reliability and timeliness.

It is possible to induce employees to cover cases outside their preferred geographic area by supplementing their transportation costs. This may be a useful short-term strategy to cover a case while a more permanent plan is developed. Because of the costs involved, however, this technique should not be used extensively. In addition to being costly, such inducements, when used to excess, tend to make scheduling personnel less creative in recruiting a more geographically suitable worker and indicate to employees that their transportation expenses to the job will be paid.

In addition, few people like a long or difficult trip to work, and home care workers are no exception. Therefore, cases can best be covered when they are close to the employee's home and when travel time between cases, should more than one be scheduled for an employee in a day, is kept to a minimum.

The influence of geography on continuity of care is most significant, and, of course, continuity of care, the worker's ability to arrive at the job reliably and on the days scheduled, is a key factor in quality of care. Most employees have specific geographic preferences. These comments should be weighed heavily when scheduling services.

An agency should be cautious, however, in addressing geographic concerns based on proximity alone. Because of the availability, or lack of availability, of public transportation, simple geographic proximity may not be the way to assess the ease of reaching certain clients. Workers and clients on main bus routes may be closer together than seemingly nearer employees and clients when a walk is required. Because it is necessary to have a car to reach some clients, an agency may decide to charge or pay a premium for cases not accessible by bus or those beyond a certain distance from the employee's home.

The organization of services by geography for ease of access requires a detailed understanding of the agency's service area. Therefore, one of the first reference tools an agency needs is a current and detailed map of its service area. Cases and employees can be identified by placing a pin in the map. Bus or other public transportation routes can then be superimposed on the map. It is then easy to determine the best geographic matches for scheduling.

Service delivery can also be divided on the basis of geography in an automated scheduling system. Public transportation and neighborhood boundaries can be input, as well as the location of employees' homes, and codes assigned to the location of clients' homes during the intake process. Clients and employees can then be matched automatically, using cross-tabulation. These codes could have breakdowns with varying degrees of detail, depending on the size of the patient load or the number of employees. It seems unlikely, however, that such sophisticated systems would be cost effective, except in the very largest agencies.

Even with an automated matching system, such as one that uses zip codes, it is important for scheduling personnel to have a good knowledge of the geography of their locale. Judgment is needed, even in an automated system, when residences fall near borderline areas or when public transportation creates overriding advantages or disadvantages.

Geography is also important not only for proximity but with respect to ethnicity and culture. In studying the service delivery area, the neighborhood concept is useful, as it is often indicative of other special factors that will be helpful in arranging the plan of care. For example, neighborhoods may indicate racial, ethnic, or income factors that may be important in matching the client and the home care worker. In addition, particular neighborhoods may have special social service systems, community service or support systems, or senior centers that could be utilized as part of the program of care.

The neighborhood where a client lives can also influence the scheduling of particular tasks. If the client lives in a primarily residential area or has a park nearby, an exercise program might be designed and scheduled so that some portion of it could be performed outside. If meal preparation is required, ethnicity can be an important consideration. Grocery shopping for items used by the client can also be affected by the availability of these items in the neighborhood and by the pricing or special sales of certain stores.

Availability of Appropriate Caregivers

Scheduling staff members face certain limitations in creating a schedule, one of which is the availability of the appropriate type of worker to cover a case. An agency has set time slots available for its employees; if 20 clients need to see one therapist, the design of those clients' schedules is dependent upon the availability of the therapist. This restriction reduces flexibility in scheduling when an agency's staff is limited.

When a client needs specialized services that require personnel with a particular area of expertise, the agency is more limited in terms of scheduling possibilities. Some employees may be more skilled or more experienced with a particular procedure; for example, one nurse may have more experience with intravenous therapy than another. If the demand for the procedure is too great to be performed by one nurse, another nurse can be trained, increasing the time during which the procedure can be performed. For routine care, however, clients can be accommodated within the professionals' schedules, in accordance with the objective and subjective factors suggested above.

Balancing the number of workers needed against the number of clients is always a problem. The issue of continuity of care is most important. However, in terms of priority of tasks, the agency should keep in mind that an immediate need for an intervention or service by a client may cause an existing schedule to be changed. For example, if an agency receives a referral for a client who is being discharged immediately from a hospital and requires immediate service, the schedule of an appropriate caregiver can be altered to accommodate the pressing needs of the new client. Other clients who were to receive service by that caregiver in that time period must then be rescheduled as soon as possible, and in a way which minimizes disruption and meets all care plan requirements. These alterations depend on the circumstances and may cause changes in the personnel assigned or adjustments in the hours or days of service.

The availability of staff also determines how efficiently services are provided. While client preferences must be kept in mind, the availability of the appropriate employee, including his or her proximity to the client's home, usually must be considered first. Workers must not only have available time in their schedules, but must be nearby in order to deliver services. An exception would occur when a patient is paying privately and is willing to subsidize transportation in order to have a special person or persons provide the care.

Employee Preferences

Accommodation of employees' preferences regarding schedules can greatly increase job satisfaction, leading to greater continuity of care, better work performance, and retention of personnel. When case assignments are made, caregivers can be categorized by the time of day they prefer to work. Schedulers can provide flexible schedules for nurses, therapists, and other home health workers. Consideration of these preferences allows new segments of the work force to enter the field of home care. Part-time workers, including students, housewives, and persons who hold primary jobs in institutions, for example, could all have the same schedule.

In addition to preferences for particular schedules, home care workers may prefer different types of cases in terms of duration, geography, or tasks required. For example, a nurse may prefer to develop experience in technological therapies, while another worker may wish to provide long-term care to developmentally disabled persons. Some individuals may limit the geographic areas in which they are willing to work or may specialize in a particular area. This desire for specialization could be mutually beneficial for the employee and the agency.

Special Factors

Some highly subjective, interpersonal concerns can be very significant in designing a schedule for continuity and quality of care.

These are the factors that ensure that the care provided is completely responsive to the client. When time is well planned and the person assigned meets all subjective requirements, both the patient and the worker will look forward to each visit.

Attention to special, personal factors can also improve quality of care. It is easiest to do a good job when you like what you are doing. The home care worker must like the client and the environment. The client must like the employee. As discussed in Chapter 6, matching employees carefully with clients is a crucial part of the scheduling process. Sometimes the best matches are made accidentally, such as when a new client enters the schedule or a new employee is hired. This is why careful attention to the suitability of client and employee matches is important; when a client and employee appear well matched, the schedule should continue to hold for the duration of the treatments or services.

Personality is a very important factor in assigning workers and matching them with clients. Although compassionate home care workers often overlook difficult client personalities, burnout, absenteeism, or other factors related to stress are more likely to occur when the client is difficult. There are workers, however, who prefer difficult clients, thinking that their ability to continue working in undesirable situations is a sign of strength or professionalism. This match then becomes suitable. The idea that there is someone for everyone should be kept in mind.

The individual strengths and talents of employees are also factors in scheduling home health services. A staff person may have a gift for serving clients with dementia, who are often difficult, physically and emotionally, to serve. Others may be particularly good with clients who are active, encouraging them to participate in their care as much as possible. Still others, with an upbeat attitude, seem to have a positive influence on lonely or depressed clients. These special qualities of employees should be considered as part of the scheduling process.

It is not uncommon for a home care worker to become almost a family member. Many home care workers put in extra time visiting their clients if they are hospitalized or calling during off hours to visit. One home health worker volunteered to stay overnight with a client after the death of a beloved pet. Anyone in home care can cite examples of how a strong relationship between client and caregiver makes the experience more rewarding and beneficial to all involved.

Clients may also have preferences about staff members who deliver services. Some clients may prefer more outgoing personnel, with whom they think they have better rapport; others may prefer someone who is quiet or shy. When an agency has sufficient staff from which to choose, these preferences can be factored into a schedule design.

Sometimes paying attention to the little extras, such as personal interests, can make a placement particularly rewarding and can help scheduling staff to select personnel. Many clients have interests that employees share, such as cooking, sports, or reading. Making an effort to inquire about clients' interests, or asking home care workers about their interests, can help scheduling staff to ensure not only that the client-employee match is acceptable but that it is particularly rewarding for both parties. Employees should be encouraged to use these special interests in performing their duties. Involving a client in helping to wash dishes in warm water after a special cooking project can be very beneficial to a client with arthritic hands.

The home environment of the client is one more factor that comes into play when selecting personnel. Whether or not the client smokes or keeps pets can influence employee satisfaction and, ultimately, continuity of care. Some clients are very attached to their pets; an employee who is allergic or is not a cat or dog lover is certainly a less than ideal match. Clearly, these factors are significant.

The factors described above vary in importance; of course, the first step in scheduling is to make sure that all tasks in the treatment plan are provided and that service is delivered as efficiently as possible. Factoring in the other considerations, however, can help an agency make its schedule, and its services, as pleasant and rewarding as possible for clients and staff.

PART 2

3

Communication

The complex topic of communication pervades every aspect of scheduling. Many concepts regarding communication can be used in scheduling home care. There are also many concepts that are beyond the scope of this chapter. Additional study of communication techniques and practices is recommended for improving the quality of home care.

Good communication consists of conveying information accurately, quickly, and to the right person. It also requires the person who receives the information to understand the points being conveyed. Communication is, therefore, most useful when it occurs in a two-way flow. Communication involves two processes—transmission (sending information through written, verbal, or visual means) and comprehension (the understanding of information by the receiver). The analogy used frequently is that of television transmitters and receivers. This analogy is useful in that it allows us to think of the many aspects of communication.

In home care, two-way communication supports decision making in scheduling. Before making scheduling decisions, communication is used for fact finding or gathering information to determine what the best schedule would be. Explaining the schedule to the employee and client is a second critical aspect of the communication process in home care. Third, after a schedule has been implemented, communication is used for evaluation. The staff may use information reported back to determine whether scheduling decisions were correct or, if not, how to adjust the plan.

Prior to scheduling a case, the scheduling staff must know all the facts regarding the client and available employees. They must be advised of the client's exact requirements for medical and support services by the case manager. The geographic location of the client must be known, with specific directions on how to get there. The staff must also determine the client's preferences for service and the hours an employee is willing to work. They must obtain information about the skills and interpersonal qualities of agency employees from interviewers, training faculty, nursing supervisors, and other staff.

The flow of information once the schedule is in place is equally important. After scheduling decisions are made, communication is used to ensure that services are provided as scheduled and that changes in the schedule or care plan are addressed. The staff must ensure that clients' needs are met, that is, that a case is covered if a caregiver does not report as scheduled. If a client's condition deteriorates after scheduling decisions are made, the staff must be informed and must expand the schedule accordingly. If a personality conflict between a client and caregiver occurs, the scheduling staff must be aware of the problem so that they can attempt to resolve it or assign another caregiver to the case.

Information regarding the above aspects of the schedule and care plan comes from a variety of sources. The client, family, or physician may call the office or express concerns to the supervisor or primary caregiver. The supervisory personnel must ensure that the information is communicated and documented. The primary caregiver, who may be a professional or paraprofessional, has the most information about the case. This person should be required to report things that need to be communicated to other members of the care team in writing. Office personnel need to follow up on cases when little information about the client is communicated to encourage the two-way flow of information for all clients.

In addition to supporting decision making in scheduling, communication is a tool for reassuring clients and employees. It is most important to understand that excellent communication between all parties is essential to reduce fear. Under current reimbursement systems, seriously ill Medicare clients are being discharged from the hospital, causing anxiety. Close communication reassures the client and family that the client's condition is being closely monitored and quality of care ensured. In addition, clients are most concerned about the person who will be coming into their home. Describing the employee and answering the client's questions about this person will be helpful in establishing a successful relationship. Similarly, the employee newly assigned to a case will be approaching the situation with some trepidation. A detailed explanation of what is expected is, therefore, very important. Communication is a method of reassuring employees and ensuring good work performance.

Communication can also be a specific task in a care plan, that is, reporting the condition of a client to the supervising nurse and, ultimately, to the physician. A case study is useful to demonstrate the important function communication plays in home care. The case of a chronically ill child with brain damage and hydrocephalus is illustrative. Bobby Gray (a fictitious name) was authorized by a local center for developmentally disabled children and adults to receive 4 hours of licensed practical nurse service per week. The service was to provide support for Bobby's family in caring for him at home. Among the nursing interventions required were the tasks of assessing and reporting changes in Bobby's seizure disorder, observing Bobby to determine the effectiveness and side effects of the medication administered to him, assessing and reporting changes in fluid tolerance status, assessing and reporting changes in Bobby's respiratory status, and assessing for shunt failure and increased intracranial pressure and infection. In this particular case, communication of changes in Bobby's condition was at the core of the care plan.

The specific uses of communication by scheduling staff can be summarized as follows:

1. Discussing the delivery of services with the professional developing the care plan.

2. Explaining assignments to professionals and paraprofessionals providing care.

3. Introducing an agency's services and individual schedules to new clients.

4. Discussing clients' reactions to the care provided and addressing any concerns they have regarding the schedule.

5. Ensuring that the members of the care team closely monitor, and communicate verbally and in writing, the status of their schedules (that is, whether they are going to be late or require vacation time) and the condition of their clients.

TYPES OF COMMUNICATION

The types of communication used in scheduling home care are no different from those most people use daily. The types used in scheduling include verbal communication, which is used frequently in all aspects of home care; written communication, or documentation; and visual or other nonverbal communication, through which subjective impressions are perceived. As described below, the type of communication that one chooses to use will depend on its purpose.

Verbal Communication

Verbal communication is used frequently in home care. It is a very important method of conveying and receiving information in scheduling. In the provision of home care services, as in any situation requiring consistent communication between parties, verbal communication takes place face-to-face and by telephone. Although it seems self-evident, the importance of these methods of communication cannot be overstated.

There are several prominent advantages of communicating verbally in scheduling home care. First, verbal communication is the quickest way to exchange information between two people. The continual scheduling changes that occur in home care require systems for covering cases rapidly or notifying clients of a schedule change immediately.

Another advantage of verbal communication is that it facilitates an immediate two-way flow of information, as compared to a letter, which allows only the transmission of information. Verbal communication allows the receiver of the information to ask questions and clarify any confusing issues. Ensuring that information is understood is a key part of good communication and is especially significant in the scheduling of home care services.

Face-to-face and telephone contact are also the most personal communication methods. Personal communication is most reassuring to clients and families, who, while happy to be at home, have concerns about being quite ill outside an institution. The intonation of the voice can help to convey the message and should be considered a tool of verbal communication. Similarly, employees assigned to difficult or unfamiliar cases frequently require some extra reassurance from the scheduling staff when the case assignment is given. Face-to-face communication is the best way to exchange information.

While supervisors and employees, clients and employees, or supervisors and clients and family communicate face-to-face, most of the schedule information is conveyed by telephone. Good telephone skills are essential. The caller must be courteous, clear, precise, and responsive to questions. Time should be allowed for the person to repeat the information or write it down.

Situations in scheduling where verbal communication is used most frequently include receiving referrals, covering cases, keeping informed of changes, notifying parties of changes, evaluating employees, monitoring schedules, and resolving complaints. These examples are described below.

Receipt of Referrals

In home care, referrals of new clients usually occur as soon as the referral source knows that a client will need service, but with little advance notice for the agency. It is not uncommon for the scheduling staff to receive a phone call from a hospital discharge planner requesting service within 24 hours. Agencies that can take referrals by telephone, simply requesting written physician's orders to confirm the referral within a set time period (and checking to make sure that they are received), have an advantage over those that do not begin scheduling until written orders are received.

Some referral sources may give several referrals at once. Care must be taken to get sufficient information to determine if and how the case can be handled. The speed with which the referral is received requires that the information be organized into a readily usable form.

Case Coverage

The short time frames in which referrals are received require a quick response in locating a caregiver to cover the case. The only feasible method is to phone caregivers not already assigned to see if they can be placed in the schedule. Once an available caregiver is identified, the scheduling staff can immediately inform this person of the requirements of the case, where the client is located, and directions to the client's home if necessary. A confirmation is then required to the referral source, client, and family, where appropriate. As described in the following section on written communication, the assignment must then be documented as necessary for personnel, payroll, billing, case, and other records according to agency policy.

Tracking Changes
Keeping informed of changes in a schedule is an integral component of day-to-day scheduling activities. Each day the staff receives calls from employees who will be late to their assignments or who are unable to go to a case, or from clients who must be hospitalized or who choose that week to change the day of service. Calls are also frequently received from clients whose caregiver did not report as scheduled. Again, the written documentation recording these changes is absolutely essential. Verbal communication allows these changes to be conveyed and acted upon with minimum delay. Complete information must be collected the first time so that additional calls are not needed to generate necessary data.

Communicating Changes
Much of the communication initiated by the scheduling staff involves notifying clients, families, or caregivers who are affected by the changes in the schedule. Upon determining that a substitute must cover a scheduled case, for example, the staff must inform the client as soon as possible. Verbal communication is critical for this task, as clients may be anxious about having a substitute caregiver or fear that their service will not be delivered. A reassuring tone of voice is important in this situation.

Evaluating
Person-to-person communication is necessary for evaluating a schedule once implemented. It is also necessary for evaluating the performance of individual employees to ensure that the services provided meet the standards of the agency. Home visits are generally used as the method of supervision to evaluate the schedule, as they provide the staff the opportunity to speak directly with clients and employees. Frequently, there will be calls from the client or employee. If the call is a complaint, direct and timely handling of all concerns is important. Here again, the telephone is frequently the best way to follow up quickly.

Monitoring Schedules

Although most information related to client care is documented in writing for recordkeeping purposes (as discussed below), ongoing verbal communication between members of a care team is useful. Home care workers serve as schedulers' eyes and ears in their clients' homes, reporting their observations of the clients' condition. Verbal reporting through staff meetings, for example, and communication between all members of the care team allow maximum interaction for discussion, feedback, and decision making.

Sometimes, when there is a specific concern, it is appropriate to have a case meeting attended by all the parties, including the client or family and the caregiver. Such a face-to-face meeting facilitates communication and is particularly useful in the resolution of conflicts.

Complaint Resolution

Verbal communication is necessary for resolving complaints about a schedule or the care provided. For example, when a client complains that a home care worker is late for an assignment, but asks the agency not tell the worker about the complaint, the agency needs to explain to the client that it must inform the worker. The agency then needs to talk with the home care worker. It may be most useful to arrange a meeting between the client and the worker to resolve the problem.

Written Communication

A most important purpose of communication in scheduling is documentation. Documentation is extremely important for conveying information officially and establishing a record of the communication. If it is not recorded, the assumption must be that it did not happen. In scheduling, documentation for recordkeeping and reference purposes is maintained for clients and employees, describing what, how much, and when care is provided. This constitutes the audit record, sometimes referred to as an *audit trail*, which is necessary to support payroll and billing. Record keeping which is accurate and current is necessary if an agency is to provide good-quality care and to operate efficiently. It is also critical for compliance with all applicable federal and state laws and regulations. Documentation which is referred to in this section as written may also include computerized records.

Written communication is particularly useful for clarifying information provided verbally or confirming information for the record. Written communication is also most effective for transmitting a lot of information at one time, to provide the receiver with a written document that can be referred to later as a reminder or clarifier. In addition, written communication is useful for reaching many people. Clearly, written communication cannot be used to ask caregivers to cover cases; however, a change in agency policy regarding vacation time, for example, could be communicated through a letter placed in each paycheck. This would save a great deal of time compared to giving this information to each caregiver by telephone and would avoid confusion or misunderstanding.

Many forms of written communication are used in scheduling. Tools specific to scheduling can be quite simple, such as a note pad or a scheduling book. For additional written records, the scheduling staff can use note pads that have carbon sheets similar to those in phone message pads.

More complex written tools for communication in scheduling include a host of forms used to document each aspect of scheduling, ranging from sheets that list every activity to be performed for a client, to evaluation forms for noting impressions of agency employees, to time sheets. Other more generic tools, such as memoranda or newsletters, may also be useful for scheduling. These tools will be described below.

Written documentation from other sources of the home care agency, such as client files, employee files, and accounting files, are significant because information from scheduling must be recorded in these files. However, because confidentiality is a significant issue in health services, care must be taken to ensure that identifying information appears only in the files of that individual.

The forms of written communication discussed in this chapter are limited to those used directly by the scheduling staff. A more detailed discussion of written communication used throughout an agency's operations is presented in Chapter 10.

Schedules

Written schedules are a means of communicating to an employee the specifics of an assignment or series of assignments. For some employees, a telephone call outlining a week of assignments is sufficient. Other employees need more direction and explanation of case requirements. A written schedule can be as detailed as required. The scheduling staff can include directions to a client's home or additional explanation if a client is known to be particularly difficult or requires heavy care.

Care Plans

The scheduling staff depends on the clinical staff to inform them of the client's needs for service. The plan of care is used to communicate to the scheduling staff exactly what activities need to be scheduled for the client. At a glance, the scheduling staff has all the information regarding the client's needs for medical and support services, preferences, concerns, or any changes that may have occurred since service began. The care plan tells the scheduling staff exactly what types of services must be scheduled, as well as how many hours of service and how long the services will be provided. The plan of care is based on the physician's orders. Those orders must be written. The plan of care can be developed based on verbal physician's orders, but the written orders must be received within the regulatory time limit.

Activity Sheets

Activity sheets are an important written tool in scheduling. Many agencies use them to list the tasks that must be completed on each home care visit. For home health and personal care aides, who usually have numerous tasks that must be completed in one visit, it is suggested that these activity sheets be posted in the client's home, for example, on the refrigerator.

These activity sheets can also be designed for two-way communication. The scheduling staff can use them as a method of control by not only informing employees of what activities are required, but also including space for employees to check off each activity as it is completed each day. Additional space can be left for employees to add comments. In this way, the scheduling staff and supervisors can know exactly what activities have been completed.

Time Cards

Written tools generally used for record-keeping purposes can be amended or expanded to allow communication from employees to agency staff. For example, a time sheet or card used by employees to log hours worked would be an excellent place for employees to record any observations regarding their clients' condition. Space could be provided on the time cards and employees encouraged to use it to pass on information to the agency staff. However, when an employee provides care to more than one client, the record must be separated for filing. If information is put into a client's file, care should be taken to remove references to other clients. Either the clinical staff or the scheduling staff could review the time cards for information regarding the client's condition or problems encountered while the caregiver was in the client's home, and ensure that confidentiality is protected.

Preemployment Documents

Employees are interviewed and records made prior to employment. Preemployment documents such as employment applications, references, and evaluations compiled by interviewers, training faculty, and other agency staff can provide information useful for scheduling. A Trainer's Evaluation Report, for example, can be used by the training faculty to evaluate potential in new employees. Information about the employee's technical abilities, enthusiasm, motivation, and flexibility can give schedulers an idea of what cases the employee might handle. In addition, these documents may indicate the types of work an employee prefers or the type of work for which a reference believes the employee would be best suited.

Memoranda

Written memoranda are an excellent way for the scheduling staff to communicate information to a large number of employees or clients or to ensure that the information provided is documented for record-keeping purposes. Memoranda are usually used to communicate information officially. For example, the scheduling staff might use a memorandum to inform all employees of a change in a company policy, such as procedures for calling in sick. Memoranda might also be requested from employees when they are providing information that will become part of their employee file.

For example, schedulers might require that employees submit memoranda to inform the scheduling staff that vacation leave is requested.

Since home care workers do not have desks and an office, important memoranda should be sent to their homes or included in their paychecks. However, important information should be mailed separately, so that it is not overlooked by an employee focusing on the amount of the paycheck. Distributing memos at inservice classes, staff meetings, or whenever employees come into the agency's offices will not ensure that all employees receive a copy, but it does allow emphasis of key points.

Company Policies and Procedures
Brochures or booklets describing policies and procedures are a most important tool for communicating agency standards and procedures to a large number of employees. The brochure can be brief, summarizing policies such as those on vacation leave or work standards. Another one could present a list of do's and don'ts, describing rules for employees when they are in their clients' homes. Written materials should be kept as simple as possible. Where legal issues are involved, the best approach is to summarize the policy and then indicate where the full information is available.

Newsletters
An employee newsletter or leaflet produced and distributed on a regular basis can be an excellent means of communicating information from the scheduling staff or agency management to the agency's employees. A newsletter can be distributed to a large number of people, so it is useful in education, recruitment, and marketing, for example. While employees might ignore a lengthy typewritten memorandum about a new company policy, a newsletter with bright colors and an easy-to-read format can be eye catching and persuasive.

Information that can be communicated in a newsletter includes news briefs, advisement of new company policies, and advertisement of social events. It can also be used to provide incentives for employees to improve their performance by featuring an employee of the month or listing employees with perfect attendance. Since a newsletter changes with every issue, the scheduling staff can address issues of concern or simply remind employees of good communication practices, such as calling the office if they are going to be late.

The secret of a successful newsletter is simplicity. Only a few concepts should be included in each issue. To test readership, one might want to insert a line in an article indicating that anyone who sees it and calls will receive a prize or cash reward.

A newsletter is also useful for communicating with clients. It can be used to inform them of company programs, changes in managerial staff that might occur, new agency services offered, or recognition that the agency may have received for community service. The scheduling staff could include information on procedures for canceling a scheduled assignment or providing feedback regarding an employee's performance. This type of newsletter could be printed regularly and distributed to clients and their families and referral sources, including local hospitals, religious organizations, and physicians.

Suggestion Surveys

Surveys can be used to encourage clients to communicate their impressions and concerns to the agency. Instruments can be developed to solicit feedback from clients regarding the quality of services received and, in particular, their level of satisfaction with the personnel assigned to their cases. This information can assist the scheduling staff in making future decisions in assigning employees.

Employees can also be surveyed to determine factors such as their preferences for case types and hours. Employees should be encouraged to tell what they like about their job or ideas they have on how to make the job better.

Visual Communication

A significant type of communication involved in providing health and supportive services to clients in their homes is visual, or nonverbal, communication. Caseworkers in the social services emphasize visual cues, particularly when they are dealing with possible cases of neglect or families in need of support services. Nonverbal cues can be louder than anything said verbally, as anyone who has experienced the "cold shoulder" knows.

Information or emotions communicated visually are most evident in body language, eye contact, tone of voice, facial expressions, and behavioral cues. In all meetings with employees and clients, the agency staff should be sensitive to the unspoken as well as the spoken message.

QUALITY AND ACCURACY IN COMMUNICATION

Good communication is measured by the quality and accuracy of the information conveyed. Improvement in communication should be an ongoing process. Good-quality communication is two-way communication whereby the communicator receives information rather than just transmitting it. This two-way flow ensures that the message is understood and provides feedback. Quality of communication also depends on the use of proper communication channels to ensure that the information is received by the appropriate person.

Accuracy is affected by the method or methods of communication. This is why verbal communication is confirmed in writing. The spoken word and the written word are two forms of the language, so reinforcement is needed when the information to be conveyed is of great significance. A verbal schedule is confirmed by written time cards, and a phoned-in referral is confirmed by written physician's orders or service orders. Accuracy often requires increasing the frequency of communication, when necessary, to ensure that information is communicated in a timely fashion or is retained. For example, key information regarding agency standards must be repeated as often as possible.

Establishing a strategy for effective communication requires the development of proper channels for organizing the smooth and timely flow of information; instructing employees in what types of communication to use and who should use them; and moderating the frequency of communication.

Communication Channels

The scheduling staff supplies and receives information through interaction with all the members of the care team, including employees, medical professionals, and clients. The complexity of communication between these parties requires an organizational system to ensure that information is conveyed appropriately. It is inappropriate, for example, for an employee to notify a client that he or she cannot report to an assignment; the employee must tell the scheduling staff, who will inform the client and act on the change. Similarly, an employee should not contact a physician directly to report a slight change in a client's condition, but should alert a supervisor so that the agency can contact the physician if necessary.

Establishing and using proper channels ensures that information is relayed to the proper person in the agency and that no potential problem remains undetected. It also ensures the fewest mistakes and results in improved record keeping.

In a home care agency, as in any business, channels of communication may be thought of as downward, from management staff to all employees, or upward, from employees to their supervisors. Downward communication might be used to transmit company policy and practices to the staff; in a home care agency, written care plans, activity sheets, and employee newsletters are forms of downward communication. Upward communication might be initiated by employees to notify the staff of an unexpected delay in their schedule or a change in a client's condition. Upward communication can also be elicited by managers as a feedback mechanism to ensure that employees have received and understood their messages. Downward and upward communication must both be effective, as they are needed for a two-way flow of information.

A second, more comprehensive way to look at communication in home care is to consider it as conveying information across many channels, between individuals who work together to organize and deliver services. For example, a change in a client's condition sets off a chain of events, including a nursing assessment, notification of the physician, a change in the plan of care, and modification of the schedule. This chain of events is completely dependent upon communication across the care team, between the supervisor, service provider, scheduler, client, and family.

In the literature, interaction among multiple parties is known as an *all-channel communication network.* As shown in Figure 3.1, five members of a care team may form a network with 20 possibilities for communication (or, possibly, miscommunication). This type of communication is called an *all-channel system,* in which each member of the team communicates with any other member to initiate the dispatch of information.

Within a home care agency, the care team uses a modified all-channel system that incorporates additional channels for executive managers and supervisors (see Figure 3.2). Executive managers communicate with supervisory and administrative staff (including schedulers and accounting staff); supervisors and schedulers interact with the clients and their families; the clients communicate with the service providers; and the service providers communicate with supervisory or scheduling staff. Communication also takes place outside the core channel. Supervisors communicate with physicians and executive managers communicate with outside agencies, including fiscal intermediaries, referral sources, and state and local governments.

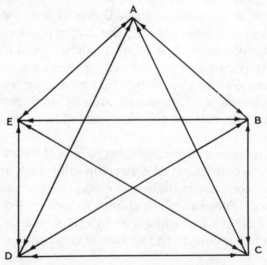

Figure 3.1. All-channel communication.

To demonstrate the flow of information through communication channels, an example of the change in a client's condition is useful. This information is likely to be conveyed by the service provider, who noted the change, to the supervisor; by the supervisor to the physician for a decision as to a course of action, and then to the scheduler; then back through the chain of command, through the scheduler to the service provider and the client.

This all-channel system illustrates the importance of structuring communication in home care to alleviate possible confusion. Case management is often used for this purpose. In an agency's policies and procedures, it is also useful to include a description of proper communication channels, as well as appropriate responsibilities for reporting and documenting information and communicating with members of the care team.

Proper Forms of Communication

The use of a particular form of communication depends on its purpose. A written schedule is the most important tool for communicating task assignments, while one-to-one interviews may be the best method of assessing personalities for staff assignments. Most scheduling operations depend on verbal communication

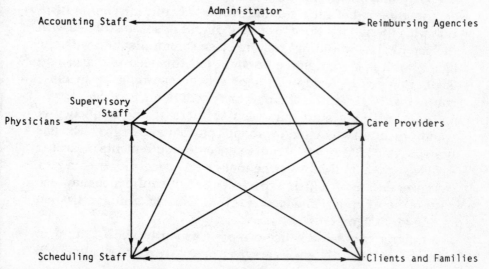

Figure 3.2. Communication channels for the home care agency.

first, such as when a caregiver informs the office if a problem occurs or when a referral comes in for a case requiring coverage on short notice. However, for accuracy and for documentation purposes, it is advisable that most verbal communications be confirmed in writing. Today electronic records are also used, so data entry could replace writing.

In some situations, however, the most effective form of communication is not clear, and the staff must decide which method or methods are most appropriate and in what sequence they should be used. For example, a change in personnel for a client can generally be communicated to the client by telephone, but for a client who is very ill and anxious about his or her care, it might be preferable for the staff person making the schedule change to ask the supervisor to inform the client in person.

Frequency of Communication

Frequency of communication is an important aspect of quality, accuracy, and comprehension. Like monitoring of services, the frequency of communication required between members of the scheduling staff, members of a care team, and a client depends on the case. A client who has been receiving home care services for several years, or who has had the same home health aide for an extended period of time, would require only routine communication with the agency office to ensure that he or she is satisfied with the service, but would not require close communication with the agency unless the employee or client felt the need to discuss an issue. Conversely, a supervisor or scheduler would be in close contact with the family of a new or very ill home care client.

The scheduling staff may wish to increase the frequency of communication when unsure about a particular caregiver who has been assigned. There are, of course, specific requirements regarding supervisory visits that must be met or exceeded. However, a new caregiver or one with little experience or self-confidence may also require more support and feedback from the scheduling staff when taking an assignment.

Similarly, contact may occur more frequently when a problem has occurred with a client, a caregiver, or a particular assignment to ensure that the problem has been resolved and services are running smoothly. Such procedures would be specified in the agency's manual of operations.

Communication may also be required more frequently between members of a care team when more than one employee serves a client or when employees form care teams to serve groups of clients (see Chapter 11). As a member of a care team, an employee who covers different shifts for a client needs to make the employee on the next shift aware of any problems that arose, of tasks that might not have been completed, and of the client's condition on that day. This would have to be done verbally and documented. While it is clear that documentation may not be as detailed as discussion, every effort should be made to document records completely.

COMMON COMMUNICATION PROBLEMS

A breakdown in any of the aspects of good communication can result in misunderstandings and mistakes. Returning to the analogy of television transmission, it is easy to see how verbal and nonverbal interference, such as lack of concentration or incomplete information, can get in the way.

Unfortunately, even with systematic channels and methods of communication, mistakes can arise through misinterpretation or misunderstanding. Not clearly telling a client or staff person who or what to expect is of most concern to all parties in health care. A scheduler can ask an employee to cover a shift at 8:00 a.m., only to discover, when the employee doesn't report to the assignment, that the employee thought the shift began at 8:00 p.m.

Some of the ways poor comprehension of messages can occur are described below.

Vague or Incomplete Information

Poor directions to a client's home, for example, can create confusion and may cause a caregiver to be unable to report to an assignment. A similar error is for a scheduler to tell an employee to report at 8:00, not 8:00 a.m. Carelessness on the part of the person providing the information, and failure of the recipient to clarify the information, lead to mistakes. Questions should be encouraged to reduce the number of mistakes or misunderstandings.

The Trickle-Down Effect

Communication between multiple members of the care team can impede comprehension. The children's game "Telephone," in which children sit in a circle and a message, whispered to the first child, is passed around the circle, illustrates simply how communication can break down when information is passed through multiple parties. The meaning of a message that trickles down from one staff member to another is easily changed.

Mistakes occur in this way when information is not provided through proper channels. For example, a client told his personal care aide that he did not want service the following week because he was going on vacation with his family. The aide reported that the client did not want service at all that week, while in fact the client meant that he did not need service on Monday. The aide did not know the proper questions to ask to clarify the information, and the scheduling staff averted a problem only because they had called the client to confirm the scheduling change and then went back to clarify the problem with all other parties, including the employee and the family. Had the client called the agency to report the change, the miscommunication would not have occurred.

Hurried Reaction to Emergency Situations

Misunderstandings are particularly likely in emergency situations, when a concerned person hears a portion of a hurriedly delivered message and can easily misinterpret its meaning. In a recent event at a high-rise apartment building, an employee phoned the building's security office to report smoke on the second floor, where her client lived. The employee identified herself with her name and the client's apartment number, and explained that the smoke was coming from the laundry room. Minutes later, as the employee prepared to evacuate the client if necessary, the fire fighters knocked on the apartment door, ready to combat a fire inside the apartment. The resident explained that she had called in the report, but that the problem was in the laundry room, not in the apartment. In the security office, the receiver had heard the words "apartment 208" and "smoke" and stopped listening, assuming that the problem was in the resident's apartment. Once the mistake was corrected, the problem (an overheated dryer) was solved, but had this been a real fire, precious time would have been wasted.

Lack of Understanding of the Language or Vocabulary

In a home care environment in particular, comprehension can fail when both clinical staff and laypersons participate on a care team. Communication using clinical terminology with nonclinical staff, clients, and families can create an immediate barrier to comprehension. Similarly, many older Americans who immigrated from other countries do not have a strong command of the English language and may need additional assistance in comprehending information from a home care agency. This factor is an important consideration in selecting caregivers, as well as in alerting all staff that special care is needed in repeating and clarifying information.

Distance and Mobility

Workers delivering home support services have to communicate with their supervisors or schedulers from clients' homes or between assignments, which creates time constraints and physical barriers to communication. For example, scheduling staff members often have to contact employees in their clients' homes in order to inform them of a schedule change for their next assignment. The use of a client's telephone, however, assumes that the client is not speaking on the phone. The need to wait to use a phone can create a lag time in reaching an employee with important information. In addition, employee telephone numbers must be kept current, as must contact points for family members who are part of the support system that may be needed in a case.

Attitude Barriers

The attitudes, biases, and misconceptions of staff members at different levels, from paraprofessional service providers to medical staff, can create barriers that filter information until its meaning is distorted. These barriers include individual attitudes, biases, values, and moods, as well as the receiver's opinion of the message source.

IMPROVING COMMUNICATION

Some of these disruptive factors that distort communication seem obvious. In a people-oriented service business like home care, however, these subjective factors must be addressed to schedule and deliver services smoothly. Implementation of the following suggestions will ease the task of schedulers by strengthening communication between providers of service, supervisors, administrators, regulatory and referral agencies, clients, and families.

Establish Lines of Communication

Whenever new staff members are hired or new clients come in, or when relationships are instituted with new physicians, referral sources, or government officials, the agency should immediately establish methods to open communication. To initiate communication with a new employee, an administrator should meet privately with the person to discuss communication practices. An interview should not be used for this purpose. Time should be specifically set aside to orient caregivers to methods of communication as one of the basics of the agency's operations and procedures. The administrator should emphasize the necessity for close, careful, and direct communication. Acceptable forms of communication, channels of communication, and times at which each is appropriate should be described. The employee should be encouraged to use written communication and to write comments on activity sheets, time cards, and other documents. It may be helpful to ensure the employee that written notes can communicate. Employees should be told not to worry if they do not think they can write well; the idea is simply to convey an idea or concern.

It should also be explained that direct telephone contact is always appropriate. It is quick and can initiate any necessary written communication. As the main form of communication, telephone contact ensures that information is transmitted and provides time to evaluate the appropriateness of other forms. The administrator should also stress that the employee must not hesitate to ask questions or admit to mistakes, and that it is better to catch errors in their early stages, before they turn into serious problems.

The initial home visit can also provide a good opportunity for the agency staff to establish lines of communication with new clients and their families. A face-to-face meeting should be designed to reassure clients that the agency is there to serve them. The staff should explain the importance of close communication between the agency and the client and encourage the client and family to phone in with any schedule changes or concerns or with feedback on an employee. While services are being provided, the supervising nurse performing monitoring visits should encourage the client to communicate openly about his or her concerns or needs.

Agency administrators can also request a start-up meeting for new referral sources and reimbursement and regulatory officials. In this type of meeting, they can discuss the agency's dedication to quality care and efficiency and emphasize close communication as a means of avoiding potential difficulties. Such a meeting allows the parties to develop better impressions of one another and facilitates the working relationship.

Finally, the agency can bring together members of the care team, including the scheduling staff, in brief regular staff meetings. The staff will then be able to expect a regular time at which open discussion is encouraged. Special case meetings can be called as needed.

Gear Communication to the Audience

The perspectives of each member of a communication channel differ based on their level of background and experience, their expertise, and their interests. Families are concerned about the care of their loved ones; clients may be uncomfortable having a service provider in their home or may be emotionally attached to a particular employee; physicians and clinicians are concerned with medical issues; and the staff of regulatory and reimbursement agencies may have legal or fiscal concerns. To ensure that messages are effectively understood by the receiver, the communicator should keep these perspectives in mind and select the best form, tone, and language accordingly. Repetition of information is also important, regardless of who will receive it.

In a recent instance, for example, a supervisor had to communicate with a client regarding an upgrade in his plan of care and schedule from personal care services to home health services. The community health nurse began by evaluating what the client's concerns were likely to be. In this case, the client had had the same personal care aide for several years and had developed a deep trust in him. The nurse anticipated that the client would resist the change in service providers. The nurse then determined that a visit to the client's home, while his regular personal care aide was there, would be the best way to notify him of the change. The nurse then described the changes to the client in simple language, explaining exactly what type of paraprofessional would be coming in, how often, what activities would be accomplished, and, most important, why the changes had been made. The personal care aide, to whom the nurse had spoken previously, reassured the client that the new service provider would be just as qualified and caring as he was. The client was comforted, and the nurse achieved her objective.

Develop Listening Skills

Confusion or mistakes often arise simply because the receiver does not listen carefully to information being communicated and the sender does not listen to his or her audience to see how the information is being received. In home care, where great reliance is placed on the telephone, the staff must be trained to listen closely to all communications, from beginning to end, and to make sure that they understand the information they are hearing. This technique eliminates minor misunderstandings created by a lack of attention.

On a larger scale, careful listening will strengthen scheduling practices by allowing the staff to determine which assignments work and which do not. Often, if an employee or client is uncomfortable with an assignment, he or she will indicate discomfort indirectly to the schedulers or other staff. They may contact a supervisor or scheduler under the pretense of discussing another topic but may hint indirectly at a greater concern. For example, an employee with a client who supervises her work carefully may indicate to the agency that the client is not very friendly. The home care worker means to say that she is not able to perform the care successfully in accordance with the treatment plan because the client is watching intently. Careful listening will also ensure that employees are not becoming lax in their care and that clients are not changing plans of care or activities. In general, careful listening by the staff is an essential part of the effectiveness of the scheduling system.

Similarly, at the close of a conversation or meeting, staff members who are receiving information from a colleague, client, or service provider should pause for a moment to make sure that the communicator has nothing further to say. Just listening for a few extra moments will ensure that the information provided is accurate and complete.

Use Feedback and Follow-Up

Good communication during the scheduling process requires one to ensure that the receiver of the communication fully understands its meaning. The scheduling staff can safeguard against misunderstandings by having employees and clients repeat the information that was provided.

For example, a staff member can simply ask a client, "Do you understand that your aide cannot take you shopping on the way home from the doctor's office?" or can ask an employee, "Now, where are you going to go?". Feedback not only reassures the scheduler that the employee understands but allows the employee to clarify ambiguous information: "I need to be at Mrs. McMahon's house at 8:00. Oh, was that morning or evening?" Similarly, the scheduler can confirm what he has heard by repeating to a supervisor, "Okay, then we need to upgrade the level of Mr. Johnson's home care worker from a personal care aide to a home health aide, effective immediately." It may also be useful for the scheduler to ask for an extra moment to write the information down and then ask permission to repeat what has been written.

Continued follow-up on communication guards against instances in which a person says, "Yes, I understand the changes," but actually misses the point. Following the communication, the sender can follow up with the employee or client to make sure that an assignment or change was carried out as requested. As explained more fully in Chapter 10, monitoring by a supervising nurse or scheduler provides early warning of misunderstanding or confusion.

Neutralize Attitudes and Biases

In a people-oriented business, the biases and attitudes of clients and personnel can disrupt services. A scheduler can complete an entire schedule of clients, carefully matching clients with service providers, only to discover that the theoretical solution is not workable.

One home care agency, for example, was referred a client whom no other agency would serve, a client with a reputation for unpleasantness. The agency placed a service provider in the home, and the verbally abusive client made it virtually impossible for the aide to work. After the supervisor and physician got no response in attempting to coax the client to be more cooperative, the top administrator of the agency visited the client. She advised the client that his cooperation was a prerequisite to his receiving service. She told him that she would send back his personal care aide the next day and warned him that unless he reversed his attitude, he would no longer receive service, nor would any of the other agencies that had already turned him down be likely to help him. The client then told the administrator that he did not like anyone to take care of him or his home since the death of his wife. The administrator discussed these feelings and reassured him that the aide would only assist him, not take over his home. The client eventually agreed to cooperate with his aide, and although it took some time, the situation was resolved. It would have been better, of course, had this solution been worked out at a lower level in the agency.

When an agency is faced with biases or attitudes that impede communication or affect scheduling of services, a supervisor or administrator should discuss the problem directly with the client or employee. The administrator should employ the techniques described above, including indicating the outcome, gearing the discussion to the audience, listening carefully, soliciting feedback, and following up to eliminate problems before they grow deeper and more difficult to resolve. Facing difficulties through honest communication and ensuring that the channels are open will ease the tasks of the scheduling staff and the service providers.

Spend Adequate Time in Communication

In communication and facilitating the flow of information, the adage "haste makes waste" is true. Many of the problems of miscommunication or lack of communication arise because not enough time is spent communicating important information to the appropriate persons and following through. Because of the daily demands on the scheduling staff, from handling emergencies to answering ringing telephones, it is easy to let the listening, follow-up, feedback, or documentation slip by.

However, taking a few extra minutes to ensure that a message was received, understood, and recorded can prevent many time-consuming problems later on. It can also ensure that employees feel a little more confident that they know where to go or what to do at all times, and clients feel more secure that their concerns have been addressed.

ROUND-THE-CLOCK COMMUNICATION

All of the communication systems and practices discussed in this chapter are effective only when they are used routinely and consistently. If a home care agency is delivering services round-the-clock, then it must have backup systems for breakdowns in communication and methods of handling both ordinary and emergency communication outside regular office hours.

Clearly, the most effective method of reaching members of the care team after office hours is by telephone. A number of systems can be implemented using on-call staff, who can call into an answering machine or service at regular intervals during the weekend or at night to receive messages. Some agencies prefer using a beeper system or an answering service.

Each off-hours system has its advantages and disadvantages. The use of an answering machine is usually least expensive and can provide the agency with a complete record of the message. However, the length of the message can be a problem on a tape machine, and the tape could run out or the machine malfunction.

An answering service could be used to ensure that the message would always be received. However, it would be more difficult to arrange to get a copy of the message for the record. This type of system could also be expensive.

In case of emergencies, an agency must also have a network through which care team members can be reached by the staff member on call. In addition, the agency must have a system in place for covering last-minute or emergency cases during off hours. One method is to have stand-by service providers each night and weekend who have agreed to cover cases.

The techniques described above for handling the constant flow of information generated in scheduling should ensure that agency operations are handled smoothly and efficiently. Once an agency's communication systems are in place, agency administrators and scheduling staff can send service providers into the field confident that they will appear where scheduled and deliver high-quality, individualized care. They can also be assured that changes in the schedules will be handled smoothly and efficiently.

4

Determining Times of Service

The schedule for delivering home health services is determined by time and by factors in the plan of care. The times of service are generally determined first on the basis of requested hours and activities required in the treatment plan. If necessary, the times of service can be changed to assign a special caregiver.

The referrals received by the agency are the basis for establishing times of service. A service order may specify total hours or visits authorized, services required, or exact days and times of service. Under many subcontracting arrangements, treatment plans are provided to the agency with a referral, and case management is done by the contracting agency, which may be a certified home health agency. In other cases, the agency is responsible for evaluating the client and formalizing a plan of care which is needed to help a client recover or maintain a client most comfortably in the home.

The supervisor's assessment of the client's condition and need for services and the development of the plan of care are not specifically scheduling issues. However, the schedule is part of the treatment strategy. The information gathered in formalizing the plan of care is a prerequisite for establishing times and days of service. A brief review of those aspects of the nurse's or other professional's assessment and treatment plan most relevant for scheduling is therefore useful. The elements of the treatment plan not related to scheduling, however, are not discussed.

When a service order specifies the total number of hours or visits to be provided, a variety of decisions must be made. The staff must determine on what days, at what times, and for how long service will be provided. These decisions are based on the client's requirements. When a client's service needs are time specific, the times at which those activities must be provided determine the schedule. When a client's needs are not time specific, more flexibility can be used in designing a schedule. Factors other than service requirements that influence quality and continuity of care, such as client preferences and the availability of family or outside support, can then be considered. The steps in establishing times of service consist of evaluating the client's service requirements, analyzing the activities to be performed, and considering additional factors.

EVALUATING THE NEED FOR SERVICE

In determining the days and times for service, the scheduling staff must consider the exact requirements of each case, including the condition of the client (diagnosis and functional capabilities and limitations), the services to be performed for the client, the types of support provided by family members or other agencies and the times of such support, and the client's preferences for service.

Depending on the licenses of the agency and the types of referral and funding sources, the agency may or may not conduct its own assessments and develop a plan of care. Sometimes the physician or hospital discharge planner conducts a thorough evaluation and gives the findings, along with a plan of care, to the agency. In other cases the agency is responsible, in conjunction with the physician, community health nurse, or other professionals, for formulating the treatment strategy, which requires an assessment of the client.

When an agency's clinical staff does perform needs assessment and develop care plans, they must be aware of what information is most relevant for scheduling. As described in the following chapters, the assessment and treatment plans provide information that is relevant for personnel assignments, as well as for determining when service will be provided. The following discussion will be limited to those elements of information most relevant to establishing times for service.

The most useful element of the needs assessment for scheduling purposes is the initial home visit. During this visit, information is obtained regarding the condition and prognosis of the client, service requirements, treatment goals (indicating the anticipated duration of services), and a description of the home environment.

The supervisory visit generally takes place in the client's home or, prior to discharge from a hospital, the hospital room. It is during this initial visit that most of the information on the client's needs is gathered and home care services are explained. Although this is a clinical function of the agency, and not a scheduling function, it may be useful if a scheduling supervisor accompanies the registered nurse or professional assigned. This will ensure that scheduling staff understands all the components of the case when scheduling services.

Medical and Therapeutic Needs

The scheduling staff must understand the medical and supportive service needs of the client. Through the diagnosis provided by the client's physician and an examination of the client, the supervising nurse conducting the home visit assesses the needs of the client and establishes goals for treatment. The client's physical and mental health, mobility, level of pain experienced, and continence are among the items evaluated.

The first element of the assessment useful for scheduling is the establishment of the treatment goals by the nurse or therapist in conjunction with the physician, the client, and family members. The scheduling staff needs to be aware of the expected duration of services. Indications of anticipated recovery or deterioration in a client's condition are useful. A client with Alzheimer's disease, for example, might be expected to deteriorate, while a stroke victim might have an excellent prognosis for becoming stronger and requiring less overall care. This information helps the scheduling staff plan accordingly for an increase or decrease in services.

Most important for scheduling are the service requirements of the client. At the time of the home visit, the nurse will already be aware of the treatments prescribed by the client's physician. For example, the dosage, route, and times when medication is to be administered, special dietary requirements (such as for diabetic clients or those with intestinal ailments, who require special foods at specific times), special procedures (intravenous therapy, parenteral nutrition), physical or other therapy, and exercise would be noted.

The scheduling staff must also be aware of the client's functional capabilities and limitations. The client's ability to perform the activities of daily living, and the level of assistance required for ambulation, personal care, toileting, eating, and other daily tasks, would be noted. The level of assistance required by the client is frequently categorized as independence, supervision, assistance, and dependence or total help.

An assessment of functional capability also includes the client's activity level and endurance. All clients should be encouraged to act as independently as possible. Information on endurance and activity level ensures that the treatment plan adequately reflects the degree to which a home care worker can help the client help himself.

Once the needs of the client have been evaluated by the nurse, a checklist or activity sheet summarizing the client's service requirements is most helpful for scheduling. This list can be appended to the treatment plan and a copy provided to the scheduling staff for establishing times and days of service. It can also indicate if all the tasks can be performed by one type of caregiver or if a team will be needed. A sample activity sheet is shown in Table 4.1.

Services checked on the activity sheet must be allowable under the funding source or service order. If the activity sheet for a Medicare client, for example, specifies aide functions that are custodial in nature, the reimbursable skilled services (nursing, physical therapy, or speech therapy) and acute care tasks must also be indicated on the activity sheet.

The agency should also ensure that physician's orders are on file for all activities that must be prescribed by a physician. For example, the nurse must have physician's orders for respiratory therapy, medication, home chemotherapy, and other medical procedures before they appear on the activity sheet.

Psychosocial Evaluation

An assessment of a client's psychosocial condition is not reimbursable under the major federal funding sources unless it is performed as psychiatric nursing or is incidental to a skilled evaluation. Nevertheless, information of this type, however it fits into the assessment, is necessary to set up a good plan of care. The client's orientation status (alert vs. confused) is vital to determining how much assistance and supervision a client will need. Similarly, a client's emotional state directly affects his or her motivation to remain at home, as well as how safe the client may be when left unsupervised. Other factors such as the ability to employ good judgment, social skills, and motivation, are also important. This information indicates to the scheduling staff the level of care required and affects the frequency with which visits can be scheduled.

Table 4.1 Activity Sheet

Category of Services Required:
Skilled Nursing _____ |___
Physical, Speech or Occupational Therapy _____ |___
Home Health Aide _____ |___
Personal Care Aide _____ |___
Homemaking _____ |___
Chore Service _____ |___

Other Services:
Laboratory Tests/X-rays _____ |___
Supervision _____ |___
Medical Social Work Services _____ |___
Meal Service _____ |___
Transportation Services _____ |___
Other _____ |___

Tasks To Be Performed:
Medical Procedures _____ |___
Administering Medication _____ |___
Bathing _____ |___
Dressing _____ |___
Toileting _____ |___
Feeding _____ |___
Exercise _____ |___
Range of Motion _____ |___
Walking, Exercise Bicycle _____ |___
Transfers _____ |___
Skin Care _____ |___
Meal Preparation _____ |___
Food Shopping _____ |___
Housekeeping _____ |___
Heavy _____ |___
Light _____ |___
Laundry _____ |___
Personal Errands _____ |___
Other _____ |___

Equipment Needs:
Oxygen _____ |___
Hoyer Lift _____ |___
Grab Bars _____ |___
Tub Seat _____ |___
Commode _____ |___
Wheelchair _____ |___
Ambulation Devices _____ |___
Cane _____ |___
Walker _____ |___
Crutches _____ |___
Sterile Dressings _____ |___
Catheter Equipment _____ |___
Other Supplies _____ |___

A few questions are useful for prompting the family to provide information about the emotional and psychosocial status of the client. Family members can determine, for example, whether or not the client responds to their questions, seems interested, or does not seem to care. They can observe the client and answer the following questions: Does the client seem motivated to remain at home? Can he recall the last time he took medication? Does he know the date? Can he recall recent events? Does the client seem to accept the diagnosis of his condition? Does the client appear to be overly dependent on family or friends for tasks he could complete himself? Does the client have good, regular sleep habits? Does the client get agitated? Does he wander? Does the client use alcohol or medication excessively? The answers to all of these questions can help the nurse to determine the level of emotional support, supervision, or simply human contact the client requires. These factors are also incorporated into the activities established in the plan of care.

Other Considerations

A number of additional considerations that affect scheduling can be assessed during the home visit. In particular, the nature of the home environment, the availability of the client, the nature of support provided by family members, friends, or other service agencies, and preferences of the client for service may be used by the scheduling staff in establishing times of service.

The client's home environment can be evaluated during the home visit to determine special requirements for service or equipment. The assessment should include a review of facilities, such as laundry machines, cooking facilities, and shower and tub space. It should also include the neighborhood, determining whether the area is safe at night, whether there are sidewalks or a park nearby for exercise purposes, or perhaps whether there is a grocery store within walking distance and at what hours it is open. These considerations are relevant to determining at what hours service can be provided. If laundry must be done and the facilities are open only for certain hours each day, service must be scheduled accordingly.

It is also important to evaluate the level of family or outside support the client receives, since this factor greatly influences the timing of services. In addition, it is useful for the nurse to record whether or not the family feels capable of providing care (physically and emotionally) and whether they need instruction in treatment procedures. The nurse can ask family members directly about their schedules and the times during which they provide care or supervision. More and more family members will have to be part of the care team, as the population of clients increases and the availability of services is limited by cost, regulation, or shortage of personnel.

Finally, any preferences of the client or family regarding times of service or level of providers should be noted during the intake and assessment processes. As explained in Chapter 3, the nurse or social worker should listen carefully to the comments and questions of the family or client during intake and the home visit, because while many clients are quite vocal, some clients feel uncomfortable expressing their preferences for service. The hours during which family members work or are out of the office for appointments need to be noted, for example.

The purpose of the needs assessment is to refine the plan of care which is presented to the scheduling staff, so that times of service can be assigned. A useful tool is a client summary sheet that describes the client's service needs. The nursing supervisor can complete the sheet after a treatment plan is developed or received from the physician or referral sources.

As shown in Table 4.2, columns can be created for noting the diagnosis, tasks or activities to be provided, the funding source, service authorized (indicating category of worker, total hours or visits, and expected duration of service), support from family or other sources, and equipment needs. Space may also be provided for additional notations.

ANALYZING ACTIVITIES

Some tasks are more time specific than others. While there is time flexibility in some activities, there is none in others. For example, many prescribed exercises can be scheduled somewhat flexibly, but

Table 4.2   Client Summary Sheet

Client	Diagnosis	Tasks	Funding	Service	Support	Equipment	Comments

oxygen therapy must be administered at specific times. Other tasks, particularly nonmedical support services such as housekeeping, can be scheduled with great flexibility. Those tasks which are time specific must be scheduled first. Other tasks that can be provided more flexibly can be scheduled later, considering additional factors such as availability of the client and preferences.

It is useful to evaluate each activity specified in the care plan and assign it a priority, from 1 to 3. This allows the scheduling staff to identify easily those activities to be scheduled first. The more flexible activities can be scheduled around those that have the highest priority.

The priority of different tasks can be categorized as follows:

- Priority 1: Specific, time-dependent services, such as feeding a diabetic client, reminding a client to take medicine, and administering medical treatment or a home test.
- Priority 2: Time-dependent services that must be completed within a given time period, such as meals, exercise, and physical therapy.
- Priority 3: Services, such as changing and washing linens, housekeeping, shopping, or other services designed to maintain a client's physical environment.

As described above, priority 1 tasks must be provided at a set time. Priority 2 tasks are somewhat flexible; there are many choices as to when the services can be provided, but there are also many times that would not be appropriate. For example, personal care services such as dressing a client could be provided at any time in the morning, depending on the client's preferences. However, they certainly could not be provided late in the day or in the evening.

Once the priority of each activity required by the client has been determined, the staff can assess the blocks of time in which services will be scheduled. The first consideration is what units of service are allowable. Before the scheduling staff can begin assigning activities to blocks of time, they must recognize the limitations of the funding source or the agency. The agency may have minimum billing units, such as units of 2 or 4 hours, or a minimum requirement of two visits weekly. In other cases, funding sources restrict the number of times that a nurse can perform a visit and be reimbursed. When assigning blocks of services, the scheduling staff must work within these requirements and the amounts authorized in the service order or by funding regulations.

For illustrative purposes, a minimum billing unit of 2 hours will be assumed. If the staff is designing a schedule for 16 hours of authorized service per week, a number of decisions must be made regarding how the service will be broken down. Four hours of service could be provided four times a week or 8 hours of service twice a week. Similarly, if the amount authorized is 10 hours between Monday and Friday, an employee could go in every day between Monday and Friday for 2 hours or twice a week for 5 hours. The decision depends on the tasks required, the availability of appropriate personnel, and the cost structure. The ratio of professional and paraprofessional visits or hours must be balanced in some instances.

If medical treatments, listed as priority 1 tasks, are required Monday through Friday, service would have to be provided on all of these days for 2 hours in the above example of a request for 10 hours of service. Because of this factor, care is required in more frequent, although smaller, units. Alternatively, tasks such as grocery shopping, errands, housekeeping, meal preparation, and supervision could be provided two times a week in 8-hour units if these are the activities requested in the 16-hour service order.

If a client is receiving no priority 1 services, visits can be scheduled more flexibly. The staff might consider the advantages that shorter, more frequent visits offer. Albeit more costly, more frequent services allow additional supervision and emotional support to a client without family or other caregivers. Because of cost and factors such as availability of personnel, the schedule will usually be designed as the optimum plan, rather than the ideal.

Once units of service and frequency are determined, the staff can look at the tasks and determine the best times for scheduling the services. First, the staff may wish to consult appropriate professionals when determining times of service for highly time-specific tasks. A schedule involving tasks such as giving medication or testing blood sugar levels can be set by a physician. Special types of therapy might need to be timed in accordance with meal schedules, for example.

Common sense also dictates when certain activities can be scheduled. There are some restrictions even on lower-priority tasks. For example, scheduling exercise before breakfast and vacuuming at 10 p.m. are not appropriate.

In scheduling most priority 2 and 3 tasks, which have some flexibility, the scheduling staff can consider the three additional factors described fully in Chapter 2: the availability of the client and family, the availability of outside support, and client preferences for service. The significance of these factors in determining times of service is reiterated below.

Availability of the Client or Family

In determining times of service for tasks which can be scheduled with some flexibility, the scheduling staff can begin by blocking out times during which the client is not available. As discussed previously, many home care clients who receive services are able to leave their homes to attend day care programs, receive outpatient treatments, attend church, or engage in social activities. (As homebound status is required for Medicare reimbursement, some of these clients may be paying for the services themselves; others are receiving service under various home support or adult protective programs.)

Times of service may also depend on the family's availability when the care plan calls for instruction of the family in treatment, such as colostomy care or insulin injections, or for the family to provide partial care. Services must be scheduled when family members are available to learn the appropriate techniques and consult when necessary with the nurse. As more and more family caregivers work, the need to schedule service in conjunction with family members is critical. It should be recalled that the advantage of home care is that it is demand based, responsive to the needs of the client. Every effort should be made to resist trying to set up schedules with institutional patterns.

When determining times of service, it is useful to use a calendar that indicates the availability of the client and family. A simple calendar format with times listed down the side is sufficient (see Table 4.3). Time can be blocked out to indicate periods of availability or nonavailability. It is useful to note the name of the client and name(s) of the family member(s) and their relationship to the client at the top of the calendar.

Preferences of the Client and Family

When scheduling services involving priority 2 and 3 tasks, the agency should consider as much as possible the preferences of the client and family. Individualized service that can be provided according to the wishes of the client is a primary advantage of home care and should be promoted.

In determining times for service, the preferences of clients can be balanced against treatment issues and cost. Although client preferences should be accommodated whenever possible, the scheduling staff should consult with the appropriate professional (nurse, therapist, physician) if there is a question on how to proceed. For example, the client may prefer to have therapy late in the day, remaining in bed most of the day, while the treatment plan indicates that an increase in activity level is a goal for the client. In this case, the therapist might recommend that therapy be provided

Table 4.3   Availability Calendar

Client: _____ Date: _____

Calendar refers to:
  Client _____

  Family members _____

  If checked, specify name of family member _____

  Relationship to client _____

	Mon	Tues	Wed	Thurs	Fri	Sat	Sun
7:00– 8:00							
8:00– 9:00							
9:00–10:00							
10:00–11:00							
11:00–12:00							

in the morning so that the client will be out of bed and moving for a greater part of the day.

Availability of Outside Support

Since many home health clients receive services from other community-based agencies or family members, such as for home-delivered meals, transportation services, or adult day care, the scheduling staff must consider the level, type, and regularity of this additional support. These factors affect the timing and frequency of service.

The significance of the level of outside support is the amount of supervision and stimulation being received by the client and the timing of those additional services. If a client receives no outside support and has no family, the agency should take into account concerns regarding isolation and schedule services over several days to maximize the intervention. Suggestions could also be made regarding the need for other services. The more outside support received by the client, assuming the care plan allows it, the larger the blocks of time in which services can be scheduled.

In determining times of service, schedulers should also consider the effects of outside activities or treatments on the client. Outpatient medical services can greatly affect how the client feels and his or her preferences for service. Even social activities or day care can tire a client and result in a preference for more or less services on those days.

Documenting the times and types of support provided by family members and other service agencies is useful as an easy reference for the scheduling staff. A calendar like that shown in Table 4.3 can be modified to indicate when the client is cared for by family, friends, or even neighbors. Special care should be taken to note the type of service received. For example, if a client receives home-delivered meals, the times, days, and type of service should be indicated on the chart.

Psychosocial Needs of the Client

Creative home care scheduling can address the psychosocial needs of the clients incidental to their service requirements. The timing and frequency of services or a schedule affects the frequency and duration of human contact a client receives, which can be critical to clients requiring greater emotional support or supervision. For example, a client who has been recently discharged from a hospital following an acute illness may be anxious about his or her health and the care being provided. Scheduling shorter but more frequent units of service will not only increase supervision and quality of care but will also reassure the client.

In addition, in carefully establishing times of service, a scheduler may address some of the psychosocial needs of the family. Some family members become overwhelmed physically and emotionally when they become the primary caregiver of an elderly or disabled person. Services provided on a weekend, for example, would not only enable family members to leave their home for a while, but also offer a better chance to get together with friends than services provided during the week. Services provided at night would allow them to get some rest or watch a favorite television show.

ASSIGNING DAYS AND TIMES

When assigning days and times of service, it should be remembered that as long as the activities scheduled are not time specific, the schedule may be changed if the right caregiver is not available. The scheduling staff can then assign days and times of service solely on the basis of the services required.

A generic scheduling chart for each client is helpful for blocking off times of service. When determining the best times for service, the scheduling staff can work directly from the activity sheet, assigning activities to blocks of time and checking off tasks as they go along. As they analyze the different possibilities, the staff can pencil in the schedule on the chart. A sample scheduling chart is presented in Table 4.4.

When blocking out times, the staff may occasionally conclude that scheduling the activities within the authorized number of hours or visits is not feasible. When this is the case, the staff can go back to the family members or client to find out if the times of their contribution to the client's care can be adjusted. For example, if the client receives two insulin injections per day but can only pay for

Table 4.4   Scheduling Chart

	MON	TUES	WED	THURS	FRI	SAT	SUN
7:00 - 7:30							
7:30 - 8:00							
8:00 - 8:30							
8:30 - 9:00							
9:00 - 9:30							

one nursing visit, the scheduling staff must determine when a family member could give one of the injections. If a family member could stop by the house on the way home from work, a licensed practical nurse could be scheduled in the morning so that the needs of the client can be met.

The staff should also recognize, when blocking out times, that some tasks go together. For example, if a licensed practical nurse is being assigned to perform a bowel regimen, it should be assumed that related tasks, such as the bed bath, will be performed at the same time. Grouping tasks together in this manner will help in determining whether service will be provided in larger or more frequent units of time. Grouping is important even when some tasks could be performed by several levels of personnel. Caregivers should be told why they have been assigned activities that they think should be performed by another member of the team.

To illustrate how times of service can be determined, an example will be used based on a real case requiring home health aide services. Mrs. Murray (fictitious name) requires home care due to myocardial infarction. This condition requires a prolonged period of convalescence. Mrs. Murray is paying privately for the home care services. Her children and their families live nearby but work full time, so they can only assist with her care on weekends.

The physician's orders received by the agency stated that she would receive 4 hours of service per day for 5 days per week (Monday through Friday). The physician's orders specified the following medications for Mrs. Murray:

1. Corgard, 40 mg, every morning.
2. Pro-Banthine, 15 mg, every evening.

3. Leucrityroid, 0.12 mg, Monday, Wednesday, and Friday.
4. Lanoxicaps, 0.2 mg, every day.
5. Coumadin, 2.5 mg by mouth, every other day.
6. Nitrodur II, 5 mg; apply patch in morning and remove at night.

When the referral was received, a supervising nurse performed a needs assessment through a home visit. Mrs. Murray was evaluated as alert and oriented and was able to give her medication regimen to the nurse. A nursing care plan was developed to reflect the following assistance required:

1. Assistance with bathing as necessary.
2. Minor assistance with dressing as necessary.
3. Independent ambulation and transfer.
4. Intermittent rest.
5. Assistance with housekeeping and laundry.
6. Assistance with prescribed exercises.

The supervising nurse determined that the medications ordered for Mrs. Murray would be self-administered. The care plan developed by the supervisor thus specified care at the level of a home health aide. The activity sheet specifying the tasks to be performed by the aide reads as follows:

1. Bath. Assist with bed, tub, or sponge bath as required.
2. Check exercises. Aide to ambulate stairs. Aide to help with exercises as reviewed with nurses.
3. Low-sodium diet. Prepare and serve breakfast and lunch.
4. Make and change the bed.
5. Vacuum and dust kitchen, living room, and bedroom.
6. Check before cleaning bathroom floor, sink, tub, and toilet.
7. Clean kitchen, dishes, and stove top.
8. Empty trash.
9. Wash laundry.

For scheduling, all of the information provided above in the physician's orders, nursing assessment, and care plan could be recorded on the client summary sheet for easy reference.

An examination of the activities required by Mrs. Murray reveals that since Mrs. Murray's medication is self-administered, none of the tasks to be performed by the home health aide are priority 1 tasks. They include several priority 2 tasks, including meals, exercises, and bath. The other supportive tasks can be scheduled with flexibility around those that are more time specific.

It would appear that, since a bath and preparation of breakfast and lunch are required activities, service might be most effective if scheduled in the morning hours, from 8:00 to 12:00 or 9:00 to 1:00. The aide could arrive at the home, assist with bathing and dressing, and prepare Mrs. Murray's breakfast. The aide could then perform the homemaking tasks and prepare and serve lunch before leaving.

Since there is some flexibility in the schedule, the preferences of the client can be accommodated when selecting times of service. Mrs. Murray had trouble sleeping at night and preferred to sleep in the morning until about 9:00 a.m. After taking her medication, she preferred to remain in bed, drinking some juice and reading or watching television, until later in the morning, when she wanted to have breakfast and get dressed. To accommodate Mrs. Murray's preferences, an aide was scheduled from 11:00 to 3:00, instead of earlier in the morning. To ensure that Mrs. Murray didn't wait too long after taking her medication to eat her breakfast, the tasks were simply performed in a different order. The aide came in at 11:00, prepared and served Mrs. Murray's breakfast, and then assisted with Mrs. Murray's bath and helped her to get dressed. Lunch was prepared and served at about 2:00. Housekeeping tasks filled in the time in between.

This example is rather simple in that the total amount of service was specified in the physician's orders. When the agency is determining the amount of service required in addition to the times of service, it must ensure that the total does not exceed the number of hours authorized by the funding source or insurance agency. For clients paying privately for services, the agency must ensure that the appropriate amount of care is discussed and agreed to by the agency's supervisor and the client or family. A service authorization form is then signed by the client authorizing the amount of service scheduled. From that point on, any modification in the total amount of service scheduled has to be confirmed with the client.

5

Evaluating Personnel

The quality control mechanism in all aspects of scheduling is the balance between case management, or client care, and personnel management, the evaluation and assignment of caregivers. Intake staff members specify the requirements for each case. Supervising professionals update care plans as client conditions change. From the service order, the staff determines the skill level and other qualities required for the person or persons to be assigned as caregivers. The personnel or services staff then determines the employee who would be best suited to provide the care. Cases are matched against the personnel available to work.

Scheduling home care services is similar to other complex systems of personnel management in that staff members are evaluated and assigned to jobs. However, evaluation is complicated in home care because of the wide variety of work settings and the subjective as well as objective factors that must be considered. In addition, the fact that people who receive the services may also participate in assignment decisions makes scheduling home care much more complex.

The treatment plans developed from the physician's orders are the basis for evaluating clients and establishing requirements for each home care assignment. In order to assign caregivers to cases, the scheduling staff must know what type of assignment is most successfully handled by each employee. Schedulers can obtain this information by thoroughly evaluating each caregiver.

The personal evaluation process involves everyone in the home care partnership: the referral source, the client, the office, and the field supervisor. Staff members who officially evaluate employees should gather performance data from all agency workers who come into contact with the employees. Staff members who interview new employees, training instructors who observe caregivers during orientation and training, and professionals who supervise employees can provide important information about each worker. Referral sources, especially physicians, can also provide facts regarding the care given by home health employees. Clients are a key source and provide feedback on performance that is invaluable. The broad input resulting from several opinions and perspectives on the skills, personal qualities, and performance of the caregiver allows the scheduling staff to make a balanced and accurate evaluation.

EVALUATING SKILL LEVEL

Anyone assigned a job must, of course, meet at least the minimum state standards for that position. The scheduling staff cannot put employees into a schedule unless they know their technical qualifications or skill level. The staff must also know which employees are qualified to perform advanced or specialized duties and should establish their level of proficiency at each job task. For example, many home care workers can use a hoyer lift, but not all of them can use the lift equally well with a very heavy person. Use of the hoyer lift with a heavy person requires an excellent working knowledge of both body dynamics and the equipment, as well as the ability to instruct the client who will be transferred, if appropriate. Because of the expertise and interpersonal skills required in this instance, an experienced worker and one who had the confidence to undertake the job would be required.

The evaluation of professional and paraprofessional skill level is fairly straightforward, since it can be tested or observed. Evaluation of skills is done on the following basis:

1. Credentials.
2. Years and type of experience.
3. Recommendations from previous employers.
4. Personal interviews.
5. Observation by agency staff during training or orientation.
6. Feedback concerning on-the-job performance.
7. Specialized abilities, such as speaking a foreign language.

Credentials

Before any new home care worker is assigned to a case, the agency must have evidence that the person is qualified, with proper licensure and registration, in the case of a nurse or therapist, and proof of completion of training for paraprofessional workers. The agency should obtain copies of all credentials, including licenses or certificates, health forms, or other documents such as references, for personnel files and verify them where appropriate.

The scheduling staff must also ensure that all certifications required for work, such as visas or work permits, are received and posted to the files. This documentation will ensure that personnel being evaluated are eligible for assignment.

The ramifications for a home health agency of employees without proper credentials are serious. In addition to being unethical and engaging in poor business practices, the agency could be subject to civil and criminal penalties. The agency would have to assume liability and damages for any clients at risk. In addition, if knowledge or intent is indicated, criminal prosecution for fraud from the resulting billing errors could occur.

Requirements for training, in-service training, continuing education credits, or credentials for health personnel vary from state to state. Agencies must ensure that their employees have the credentials required by their state laws. The staff must not assume that credentials from other states are valid or assign a new paraprofessional worker without verifying that the person has undergone the required training and, where necessary, certification. Employers of any kind should verify the credentials and check professional references of their employees, but for a health organization, careless checking of credentials and references could have particularly serious consequences.

In addition, the agency must have a system of tracking credentials to ensure that they are current and valid. An employee's credentials may be valid at the time that he or she applies to the agency, but they may expire. Many states require renewal of professional registration or licensure. Logs or lists keyed by month can be used to monitor the expiration dates of these credentials.

In addition to being certified or having a college degree (for occupational therapy or nursing, for example), a new employee may have received continuing education units or certificates. For example, annual meetings of professional organizations, including associations of home care agencies or nursing associations, include credit for workshops and programs relevant to the individual's area of expertise.

There are in-service or continuing education requirements in many states for paraprofessionals and professionals. The agency must determine whether these requirements have been met and have a system for ensuring that they are updated annually or as required. It is especially important to document in-service hours for employees who worked for another agency in the same year, accruing valid in-service hours with their previous employer. Here again, a log or list showing due dates or expiration dates by month is useful. This can be either a paper or computer system and need not be complex. Logs or lists, files of 3 × 5 index cards, or computer programs such as Lotus 1-2-3 (a product of the Lotus Development Corporation) could be used.

Other professionals may have undergone supplementary training in their field or received credit for training in particular clinical techniques. For example, some nurses have been trained in high-technology procedures now being performed in the home, such as infusion therapies (hydration, chemotherapy, or total parenteral nutrition). When cases require specialized tasks, schedulers must know which caregivers have the necessary training, education, or expertise to fulfill the assignment. Individuals who make an effort to increase their knowledge and skill level should be recognized as persons who will usually be the top performers as well.

Another reason why all educational and professional credentials should be evaluated is that the organizations with which a home health agency contracts may have special training requirements for the workers who deliver services. This is common when services call for workers trained in developmental disabilities, child protection, or psychiatric work. Contracts with such agencies often provide not only for special training but also for added orientation or meetings with family members.

Years and Type of Experience

Often, cases involving clients who are demanding or who need a caregiver with special expertise require personnel with considerable experience. An evaluation of a new employee's skill level must consider the length and type of the employee's experience, which may be indicators of maturity or ability to work successfully with many diverse cases.

The amount of experience a worker has is important, as is the relevance of the experience to home care. For example, a person with noninstitutional experience is less likely to require heavy supervision than a person with 10 years of experience in a nursing home, because that workplace allows employees to rely as needed on extra equipment or supplies or on-site assistance from supervisors or colleagues.

The quality of the experience should also be evaluated. Ten years of experience in an organization which has lower standards or lesser requirements would not be equivalent to experience of the same length in an organization with an excellent reputation. The place where the experience is gained should be weighed. For example, someone with excellent experience of shorter duration would be preferable to a person who has a lot of experience which is mediocre or poor.

In addition, knowing the pattern of an individual's career growth can be useful to the scheduling staff. One person may have 10 years of experience but may have remained at the same professional level, while another person may have advanced each year. From this information, schedulers can perhaps determine a person's potential for growth and advancement, and whether or not the person would function best in highly challenging or more routine assignments.

Some cases require skills in a specific area of expertise. Schedulers must know which employees have developed specialized skills through years of experience. For example, an employee may have had extensive experience working with a particular population, such as children of neglectful parents. Alternatively, an employee may have worked with people who have a particular diagnosis (e.g., cancer or other terminal illnesses). Finally, an employee may have practical experience with technical equipment or specialized procedures such as intravenous therapy or postnatal care.

When considering previous experience, the scheduling staff should also consider the experience the person may have in addition to formal work experience. They should evaluate the employee's work with volunteer organizations, including religious groups or hospitals, as well as time devoted to caring for sick or disabled family members at home. For example, an employee may have cared for an elderly person at home for years before entering the health care work force, which may add years of experience to that obtained professionally.

Recommendations

No worker should be hired without a check of references. All employers should review the recommendations of new employees before making assignments to jobs or clients. The recommendations of other agencies, private duty clients, or faculty of an educational institution or training facility (e.g., the Red Cross) can tell a new employer an individual's technical strengths and, in many cases, weaknesses. The most helpful recommendations for home health workers are written by clinical personnel, who have the most expertise in evaluating job skills. For paraprofessional workers, though, such as personal care aides and homemakers, previous clients, as well as supervisors, are the best judges. Even if the person has worked in health care before, references must be obtained. Personal references from a minister or school teacher can be helpful when the applicant does not have work experience.

The staff should remember that the employees sent into clients' homes are the only people the clients may meet, and therefore represent the agency. All references and recommendations should be checked carefully so that the scheduling staff feels completely confident about the professionalism and ability of every employee. No agency can risk its reputation by assigning someone whose competence or proficiency has not been verified through references. This applies in particular to skilled employees, who can simply show credentials and be scheduled for cases without a review of technical proficiency.

Business references are the most useful to the agency. As a general rule, the staff should be sure to check employment references, especially when a previous employer is not given as a reference. When the business reference is checked, the staff should attempt to contact the employee's supervisor rather than a colleague.

Many work references will only verify the dates of a person's employment. However, when speaking to a work reference, the staff member can inquire about the eligibility of the employee for rehiring. The reason the employee left the last job may also provide useful insights if the previous employer is willing to reveal this information.

If the previous employer is willing to provide more information, the staff should inquire about the way the individual demonstrated motivation and the ability to work with little supervision. Both of these qualities affect a person's technical capabilities. Obviously, a person with good technical abilities who does not work without being closely supervised at all times will not be very successful in home care. If this person were to be selected, the importance of these issues would have to be covered during orientation and supervision increased until confidence could be established in the person's independent work skills. In addition, information regarding the employee's ability to follow instructions, punctuality, and communication skills may tell the scheduling staff whether he or she can be assigned to more complex or serious cases.

Once again, the staff should keep in mind that they must focus on key information provided by references and use that information to put together a profile of the employee in a home health environment. Someone who did not work well in a nursing home might be an excellent home care worker if he or she prefers to work independently, has good communication skills, is motivated, and follows instructions well. Qualified applicants should not be eliminated simply because of unsuccessful employment in an institutional environment. However, any negative aspects of a reference must be carefully investigated. In general, a potentially good employee will always leave a job on good terms and with eligibility for rehiring.

Recommendations or references from the staff of other agencies are an excellent source of information. These people know the employee well and also know the requirements of the job. They can address specific questions concerning how the person would work in a variety of situations.

Personal Interviews

Interviews with new employees are an easy way to obtain background information about a worker's technical skills and abilities. Employees can tell the agency details about their experience and skills that credentials cannot indicate. For example, a home health aide may have limited experience in the industry but may have spent a number of years caring for an elderly relative at home, practicing the skills later learned through formal training. This person's amount of formal work experience would not have indicated the full extent of his or her commitment or motivation and experience with the job skills.

Interviews can also be used to gather information from applicants that is needed for scheduling purposes, such as the times and days the candidate would be available and the location and types of cases preferred. For initial screening of prospective employees, group interviews can be used. The staff should carefully observe the discussion between the applicants, and should note their familiarity with technical terms and current advances in the field (such as technological therapies) and how their experience relates to that of the others. After a group interview, however, a second interview should be conducted on a one-to-one basis.

It is important that time and care be taken to make the interview process as useful as possible. This is particularly true where skilled personnel are concerned, as they may be assigned to a case relatively quickly, leaving little time for evaluation. It is also true for agencies whose training is done by persons other than agency staff, which eliminates the training session as an evaluation setting. It is ideal for a member of the scheduling team to conduct interviews.

Interviews should be used not only to gather information but to describe job and agency standards so that employees will know what is expected. Some people may decide at the interview stage that the job does not interest them. This is useful, as it is expensive and frustrating to put someone on the payroll who leaves quickly.

Training and Orientation

Another excellent opportunity for the agency staff to observe technical skills (and the personal qualities the individual possesses) is during training and orientation. Any skilled or paraprofessional person hired will at least require orientation. Of course, each individual who has a professional license or who successfully completes a training program for home health aides or personal care aides must have achieved minimum proficiency in required skills.

If an agency does its own training, the staff can also evaluate an individual's level of skill by how quickly the individual masters new tasks or procedures during training. Frequently, some employees demonstrate greater proficiency in certain tasks, or personal qualities, such as patience, that will influence the quality of their performance on the job.

Again, in training, the life experiences of employees can affect their level of skill. A person who has raised several children may be more proficient in child or infant care than another person without children who completes the same training course. This additional expertise will be evident to the training faculty and orientation supervisors.

In order for the scheduling staff to use all of the available information about a potential employee, it is important to have the training faculty complete a written evaluation at the end of each training course and provide this information to the scheduling staff.

When an agency does not do its own training, orientation sessions become the most important opportunity to observe new employees, and credentials must be relied on more heavily in evaluating levels of skill. Orientation sessions are most important for conveying to new employees the performance standards and expectations of the agency (such as timeliness or quality of care). It is sometimes possible, by assessing employees during the orientation session (particularly by listening to their comments and questions), to gauge their self-confidence and commitment. These qualities affect how an employee applies his or her skills.

Feedback Concerning Performance

The best method of evaluating technical skill is to observe the employee on his or her first assignment. In fact, such a supervisory visit may be required by a state-administered funding source, depending on the level of worker. The supervisor on the case observes the employee in the client's home and reports his or her observations to the scheduling staff. This technique is useful for professional and paraprofessional workers. It can be most revealing for employees performing the more skilled procedures.

Supervisors evaluating skills through performance should look at two factors. First, they should evaluate the skills learned through training. Second, they should evaluate any additional proficiency that the worker may have developed through experience. For example, a worker experienced in providing personal care to a spastic child may exhibit great skill in handling a person with poor motor control. This skill may not be shown in the training or orientation, but it would certainly be evident once the person was on assignment, providing care to this type of client. Supervisory visits or the supervisory component of a visit should focus on the level of performance of the employee in observed skill areas. It is important to keep this perspective and not shift to concerns regarding the client. (Observations about the client's condition should be reported separately.)

In addition, if a client requires a particularly well-developed skill, the supervisor, who will go on the first visit and instruct the worker, should evaluate how the worker performs the tasks or procedures. For example, a client with sensory loss, such as a blind or deaf person, would require a home health aide or nurse adept at communicating to that type of client, whether describing things in great detail for a blind person or, for a hard-of-hearing client who lip-reads, articulating clearly, speaking slowly, and facing the client when speaking. The supervisor would evaluate the worker's ability to pick up the necessary skills and report to the scheduling staff the employee's newfound expertise.

The supervisor should also evaluate the employee's interpersonal skills and how the employee interacts with the client. An employee's sensitivity to the needs and concerns of clients is an important part of his or her ability to provide services to clients with special needs.

Specialized Abilities

In home care, where employees may deal with people from many different ethnic, cultural, and socioeconomic backgrounds, specialized skills beyond those taught in training or nursing school are significant. Linguistic skills, in particular, can be very important. Assuming the proper level of skill, a Spanish-speaking aide would, of course, be the best match for a client whose primary language is

Spanish rather than English. Similarly, an aide with knowledge of sign language would be an excellent match for a deaf client.

Other skills are also important. Being able to prepare meals that are appetizing is not something everyone can do for another person. Ethnic dishes may not be familiar to everyone. A worker with experience and skill in preparing kosher meals, for example, might be the best match for a client who eats kosher meals. Although certainly not essential, even certain conversational skills can be important to scheduling, as in matching an employee with a highly educated client who needs added companionship.

EVALUATING PERSONAL QUALITIES

The personal qualities of an employee that can affect the success of home care scheduling include the following:

1. Maturity.
2. Motivation and commitment.
3. Interpersonal and communication skills.
4. Appearance and manners.
5. Flexibility.
6. Preferences.
7. Professional goals.
8. Honesty.
9. Time management skills.

Evaluating the personal qualities of employees is more difficult than evaluating technical skills, not only because it is more subjective but also because there are fewer ways to obtain information. The scheduling staff has to observe and examine home care workers at every opportunity to obtain an accurate profile of each employee. They must also consider input from clients, who have the most contact with the employees, and by listening closely to employees themselves, who often indicate a lot about themselves without realizing it.

In an agency's regular operations, there are good opportunities for evaluating personal qualities. In particular, the initial interview of the prospective employee, the process of checking references or verifying credentials and experience, the orientation and training sessions, and an employee's first assignments provide excellent opportunities for evaluation. During these activities, the staff should try to learn as much as possible about employees: their personalities, interests, preferences, hobbies, and goals.

Personal Interviews

Prospective employees often reveal much about their personalities, interpersonal skills, and ability to communicate when first interviewed by the agency. If interviewers are aware of the information that could be useful to the scheduling staff, they can not only collect information on background and experience but also observe personality characteristics (e.g., does the applicant talk a lot, seem self-confident, or appear insecure?), as well as strong likes and dislikes (such as smoking or pets) that could affect the employee in the home environment. These pieces of information will be useful to the scheduling staff in deciding how to match the potential employee with clients.

The interview is also a good way to assess personal characteristics, such as the worker's level of motivation, emotional maturity, and quality of caring. An interviewer can easily engage an applicant in a discussion that may reveal the applicant's motivation to apply for a job in home health care. An applicant who simply states that "I like old people" or "I hope someone takes care of me when I'm old" is very eloquently demonstrating a level of caring that may indicate a good match between the applicant and an older client and may alert the staff not to place that person with a young home health client. The interviewer can also discuss with the applicant the demands placed on a home health worker for dependability and understanding, which can reveal much about an applicant's dedication and commitment to home health care and willingness to handle last-minute or difficult-to-cover cases.

In addition, the interview is an important time for describing agency standards for personnel and the quality of service provided.

Through the interview, the staff can evaluate whether applicants understand the importance of quality of care, being on time, and having good attendance, issues the agency must ensure that they know. They can also evaluate whether the applicants understand the importance of the service they will provide.

In particular, the interviewer should ask questions that reveal the applicant's motivations and personal interest in home care. He or she should look for a show of personal commitment to caring and, since money cannot be the biggest motivator for the home care worker, consider the question "Why will this person enjoy this work?" The interviewer should ask the applicant the following questions:

1. Why are you interested in home care?
2. Why did you leave your last job?
3. How did you hear about this job and this agency?
4. Why are you [will you be] a good home care worker?

The interviewer should also make an effort to reinforce for employees the fact that the job is most important and directly affects the quality of life of each client. It may also be useful to note that successful aging and quality care are major issues facing our country. Their work is, therefore, most important.

The purpose of the interview is to find people who would be good for home care, but also to make clear the requirements of the position, so that no one is hired who is likely to quit and so that applicants do not start a job they find they dislike. The interviewer must be a careful listener to differentiate between likeable people and those who are truly interested in the job.

Orientation

Although many workers do not undergo training at an agency, either because they are professional personnel whose skills were taught in colleges and universities or paraprofessionals who have been trained elsewhere, all workers need orientation. When new employees do not go through training, orientation is the agency's first opportunity, other than the initial interview, to evaluate and observe their personal characteristics.

Since the agency establishes its standards during orientation, this is an excellent time to evaluate employees' personal qualities by the questions asked, concerns exhibited, or discussion which ensues. The interpersonal and personal characteristics important to home care should be evaluated in a setting where management staff and employees have the opportunity to talk.

Even with employees who have experience, perhaps with another agency, the staff needs to know their personal strengths and weaknesses. In fact, for some people who may have trained some time ago, the staff should ask questions such as "How did you do in school?" to get a better idea of the person's competence, self-confidence, maturity, and motivation.

As in training, it is useful for a member of the scheduling staff to sit in on each new orientation session. The purpose of this is to observe employees firsthand, to begin to recognize them as individuals rather than as names on personnel files, and to gain ideas for scheduling.

The orientation session is also invaluable for scheduling staff members to explain different situations the employees may encounter. They can describe and contrast different clients and cases, including persons with impaired functioning due to aging, children or adults with developmental disabilities, and persons under psychiatric treatment. They can also explain transportation policies and discuss the different geographic areas where clients are located.

Orientation is also a time to stress the benefits of working for the agency. To the extent possible, handouts should be given that describe benefits precisely and simply. The staff should encourage participation in in-service sessions. They should also try to interest new employees in any programs sponsored by the agency, such as newsletters, an employee-of-the-month program, or bonus programs for perfect attendance.

The staff can also get information on employees' interests and their willingness to work. Some employees do not want to take certain cases. Many home health workers have families who do not want them to do certain types of work, work in some locations, or work with some types of clients. This will become increasingly true as more illnesses are cared for at home and as persons are discharged earlier from hospitals. Orientation is a good time to determine the concerns of employees. It should be remembered that the objective of scheduling is to match employees and cases so well that no rescheduling will have to be done.

Training

The training sessions afford another excellent opportunity to become well acquainted with candidates, gauge their level of skill, and note their personality traits. Skills training for paraprofessionals usually occurs in small groups of about 10 persons, and trainees are usually closely supervised, making it easy to observe and evaluate their interpersonal skills, motivation, and enthusiasm for their work, as well as to test their required skills. Skills are tested in accordance with the approved curriculum. In addition to classroom training, many states have requirements for supervised work experience. Employees will, therefore, be observed in both classroom and work situations. The work experience will enable employees to learn more about home care so that they will know what types of cases they prefer.

To evaluate employees' interpersonal abilities, the staff should look for answers to the following questions, while assessing the proficiency of the individual's skills.

1. How does the trainee work with others? Is the trainee supportive of other workers in training?
2. How does the trainee relate to other members of the group? To the trainer?
3. Is the trainee self-confident? Does the trainee appear to have the confidence to work independently?
4. Is the trainee amenable to being shown how to do things, or does he or she always have a "better way"?
5. Does the trainee appear to be a self-starter capable of following an activity sheet?
6. Does the trainee appear to be a stable person? Emotional?

Does the trainee's performance or behavior vary from day to day?

7. Is the trainee reliable? Does the trainee report to the training sessions on time?

8. Does the trainee appear to have high standards of performance? Does he or she care about the work?

9. If substitute staff members instruct trainees in certain modules of the program, how does the trainee relate to the unfamiliar instructors?

When possible, things that can be measured and qualified should be carefully documented. For example, the occasions when a person arrives for class early or on time should be noted. Other factors, such as how a person traveled to the training site, are also useful to know.

Skills training for paraprofessionals is most revealing when administered by the agency's own staff. However, for either in-house or outside training, staff members can be asked to complete a written evaluation of the employee, emphasizing general areas, such as maturity and enthusiasm, and including answers to specific questions such as those listed above. The evaluation should have a section called "Trainer's Perceptions," where trainers can note any additional observations about personal characteristics.

In addition, a member of the scheduling staff can evaluate an employee by observing a training session. When scheduling personnel are directly involved in training, this offers an opportunity to gain some ideas for future scheduling. For example, a staff member may note that an employee is like another well-known employee as a quick way of deciding how to assign that person.

It should be emphasized that for fairness and accuracy, if scheduling staff members are going to evaluate employees during training, they should attend at least two training sessions. Observing trainees at the beginning of the training period and again at the end ensures a balanced evaluation.

Training sessions can also be used to have employees evaluate their peers. Sometimes employees perceive things about their peers that management staff will not encounter, such as their attitude toward working with other aides as part of a team. Incorporating peer cooperation and evaluation into the records of training not only improves the training but also helps generate information of use to the scheduling staff. In addition, employees can witness firsthand in training their peers' efforts and their enthusiasm for their position.

Recommendations

In verifying a job applicant's references and recommendations, the agency staff has an excellent opportunity to learn more about new employees. Previous employers or supervisors, personal friends, clients, and others who may write letters of recommendation may have great insight into the applicant's personal qualities.

Clearly, the person providing a reference for an applicant is not being interviewed and should not be pressured. However, people recommending a job candidate for work expect to be asked for information, particularly since home care is such a personal business. The staff should not hesitate to ask questions about new employees that will help match them with clients.

Questions that should be asked while verifying references include the following:

1. How does the person know the applicant?
2. How long has the person known the applicant?
3. Has the person observed the applicant as an employer or supervisor? Alternatively, what was the relationship between the person and the applicant?
4. Is the applicant eligible for reemployment?
5. Has the person witnessed the applicant caring for a sick or elderly person?
6. How would the person describe the applicant's personality? What are some of the applicant's hobbies (e.g., smoking, pets, or cooking)?
7. What are the applicant's professional weaknesses (e.g., absenteeism, tardiness, or dishonesty)?

8. Does the person think the applicant is well suited for home care? Why? If not, why not?

Although some of these questions seem broad, staff members can learn much from people's subjective comments. For example, a person who says that an applicant was previously a responsible, caring babysitter for her children, who took extra steps to keep the children happy and comfortable, gives schedulers a good idea of what the applicant will be like in the clients' homes.

EVALUATING ON A CONTINUING BASIS

Evaluating home care workers is an ongoing process. The longer an employee is with an agency, the more opportunities the staff has to evaluate the employee and determine, based on the individual's experiences, the cases for which he or she is a good match. The fact that people change must be remembered. Someone who likes one type of case may decide to change. The ongoing evaluation should help the scheduling staff stay current on the interest, energy, and skill level of employees. Because worker burnout is a problem in home care, it is important to be sure that the employee continues to enjoy the work.

Evaluating on a continuing basis also allows the scheduling staff to follow the development of the professional and paraprofessional staff. The skills and qualities of a home care worker may develop over time, and, with greater experience, people can be upgraded both in the minds of the scheduling staff (and given more sophisticated assignments) and, to the extent possible, in salary or standing.

Although many agencies evaluate the performance of personnel on an annual basis, employees can be evaluated during early assignments, which can be very revealing, and throughout the course of their experience. Scheduling staff members who identify certain employees with the motivation to perform well and the desire to improve and succeed can test employees by scheduling them for increasingly challenging assignments. Supervisors can then evaluate the way the employees handle increased responsibility and different clients or cases.

By looking at supervisory reports on an employee's first few assignments, the staff can assess the way the employee interacts with clients and their families. It is in this environment, when the employees are on cases, that the scheduling staff can best get to know them. They can determine whether a home care worker might be a better match for a depressed client, who needs a lot of emotional support; a client who likes privacy, who might prefer a more subdued worker; or a client who needs a great deal of social stimulation, for whom a very outgoing employee would be the best match.

Useful information can be obtained through monitoring of cases by supervising nurses and other agency staff. Staff members conducting supervisory visits can be asked to look for both successful job performance and subjective, sometimes subtle, indications of the success of the match of client and worker: Is there evidence of rapport between the worker and the client? Does the worker seem bored? Is the worker enthusiastic about his or her work?

As discussed later in Chapter 9, monitoring employees through regular supervisory visits provides a great deal of information to schedulers. The information covered in ongoing supervision includes an employee's:

1. Attendance record.
2. Punctuality.
3. Completion of assigned tasks.
4. Communication with the office.
5. Appearance and manners.
6. Quality of caregiving.
7. Caring qualities.

Supervisory visits also allow the agency to observe the progress of professional and paraprofessional employees new to home care. Few nurses and therapists with institutional experience have had much background in community health. Through supervisory visits, the agency can follow up to see how well these professionals are able to deliver skilled care in the home, without the benefits of staff support, supervision, and equipment available in an institution.

In addition, supervisors can respond to concerns that nurses with primarily institutional backgrounds may have. Sometimes nurses with institutional experience may not fully understand that they have more responsibility than in an institution or that quality care can be delivered in nontraditional settings. For example, nurses in home care may voice concerns regarding the sanitary conditions of the home environment. The supervisor can evaluate the way the nurse attempts to overcome or cope with these conditions.

The information gathered through supervisory visits can be used by schedulers to get to know employees in depth. Staff members can also learn by asking employees questions after the first few days of an assignment. They should ask the employee what he or she thought about the case. The worker may indicate that a case was very rewarding by saying that "Mrs. Johnson seemed to really need me." Or the worker may indicate feeling uncomfortable in a particular situation by saying something like "I didn't like working with Mr. Smith because he is very young and so am I." These comments can be used by the scheduling staff in making future assignments.

The scheduling staff should also pay attention to the feelings employees express from day to day regarding their cases. Employees' comments about their perceived successes or the problems they may have encountered can reveal much about their personal qualities, including their level of understanding, patience, and motivation. One employee may complain about a client who is particularly demanding—"Mr. Jones drove me crazy today. I can't take it anymore"—while another may say, "I wish I could get Mr. Jones to calm down; maybe I'll try singing softly while I work." These employees are clearly two very different people. Comments about what cases employees like and do not like can help the staff understand the employees they are scheduling.

It is also useful for schedulers to elicit information from clients and families about an employee, to guide them in making future assignments. Feedback from clients helps the scheduling staff create a mental profile of a worker on a case. Creative or notable solutions to problems should be recorded for reference. Letters or phone calls to an agency from a client or family should be encouraged; they are excellent ways to assess a worker's performance. Sometimes clients or their families will write notes about workers. If a family writes or says that an aide was "so warm and caring" or that "she listened to all my husband's stories," or tells the agency that the client received a card from an aide while the client was hospitalized, schedulers can learn more about their employees. This information helps the scheduling staff to know whether the assignment is successful, to rematch the employee if the client needs care at a future date, or, if not, what type of case would be better for the employee. The compliments as well as the complaints should, of course, be communicated to the employee.

The most important thing to remember about evaluating employees is that information about them is useless for matching unless it is communicated to the scheduling staff. It is critical that information from supervisory visits, interviews, training sessions, and client and family feedback be provided to the scheduling staff quickly and followed up. (A sample form used for documenting supervisory visits is presented in Chapter 7.)

It is also important that comments from employees regarding their peers be conveyed to the scheduling staff. It is useful to create opportunities for employees to get to know one another, such as through social get-togethers or in-service sessions. Although employees can be asked to evaluate their peers formally after a training program, they can also provide valuable information about their peers in an offhand way during their day-to-day communication with nurses or schedulers. For example, when the scheduling staff is trying to cover a case involving a patient with Alzheimer's disease, an employee may say, "I can't take a case that day, but you might try Mrs. Long. She has the patience of a saint and might be great with an Alzheimer's client." This type of peer evaluation can provide some useful clues for scheduling.

It is also important that the information provided by trainers, supervisors, and clients be pieced together to form a portrait of the employee useful for scheduling. Consider an example of evaluating an employee for a specific type of case. If an agency has a requirement for a nurse or home health aide to cover a multiclient assignment, for example, the scheduling staff knows that an employee who serves a group of clients, or several clients in one home, has to manage time, tasks, and functions and have greater responsibility for monitoring clients' needs. Since service delivery is more complicated, the staff knows that it must assign a worker who can handle increased responsibilities. That worker must have excellent time management skills, flexibility, communication skills, ability to handle increased responsibility, and a lot of enthusiasm and dedication. How does the scheduling staff evaluate these characteristics?

1. *Time management skills.* The scheduler could first examine the individual's background for clues regarding time management skills. Persons who successfully manage large families and work, for example, are generally used to planning their activities carefully. The scheduler can also look at the worker's previous assignments and ask: Does the employee complete tasks on time or ahead of schedule? Does he or she then complete additional tasks for the client? Are all tasks for the client completed on days when the client requires more care than usual? Is the employee attentive to his or her environment and able to identify and assess new developments that could affect the timely completion of tasks? Is he or she energetic, inclined to go the extra length to accomplish a task?

2. *Flexibility.* The scheduler can look at previous assignments to see how the employee has reacted to schedule changes in the past and to covering last-minute assignments. Does the employee find an alternative way to get to an assignment if it snows? Has the employee ever said, "I like to have only one or two cases at one time" or "I don't like surprises"? These comments tell the scheduling staff that the employee would perform best when task and responsibilities vary little from day to day, not in a multiclient assignment.

3. *Ability to handle responsibility.* Indicated by the employee's maturity, dependability, and conscientiousness, this characteristic can be determined through the interviewing process. An interviewer can note whether an applicant asks questions regarding training, experience requirements, and agency expectations, questions that indicate that the applicant is thinking in terms of responsibilities. An employee's training instructor can note how the worker follows directions. By looking at a current assignment, the scheduling staff can answer these questions: Does the employee submit time sheets on or before the deadline? Is the attendance record good? If the employee finishes the tasks early in

a shift, does he or she complete additional tasks for the client? Is the employee's documentation of cases clear and complete? Does the employee enjoy functioning independently?

4. *Enthusiasm and dedication.* A dedicated, caring individual who takes pride in his or her work lets people know. These individuals exude self-confidence, energy, and concern, and obviously feel that they are making a difference in the life of a sick or elderly person or a family. For this type of characteristic, the staff should listen carefully to the things that the worker and the clients and families say. On a recent visit to a client who is diabetic, wheelchair bound, incontinent, and semialert, a family member told a supervising nurse, "All you've got to do is find more people like her [the home health aide] to do this job, people who have a genuine concern or even some pride about themselves." The message to the agency couldn't be clearer.

Similarly, by evaluating employees, the scheduling staff should be able to distinguish the exceptional employee from the average. For example, people who are best suited for home care often include those who:

1. Like to work independently.
2. Like to be creative in the application of their skills.
3. Are able to emphasize the human, interpersonal aspects of health care.
4. Are self-motivated.
5. Are self-confident.
6. Have good telephone and communication skills.

How are some of these characteristics indicated?

1. *Motivation.* The commitment of highly motivated people is shown in all aspects of their work. An employee's desire to succeed and perhaps advance in the agency is evident in the extra steps taken to cover last-minute cases, substitute for other caregivers who have to cancel cases, and go to the hard-to-cover cases, those scheduled at night or on weekends. Excellent attendance is another sign of a motivated employee, as well as the extra effort to provide plenty of notice if he or she cannot go to a scheduled case. The most

likely people to recognize a highly motivated employee are the services staff, who speak with the employees regularly and assign them to cases. A highly motivated person may also set limits on what he or she is able to do, so careful listening is required to differentiate between motivated people who have limits and less motivated workers.

Supervisors can evaluate motivation easily through an employee's eagerness to perform well. For example: Does the employee seek feedback from the supervising nurses or physician regarding performance? Does the employee ask how he or she can improve? Does the employee make the effort to improve?

2. *Interpersonal and communication skills.* An employee's contact with the agency is the best indicator of his or her communication and interpersonal skills. Whether the person followed up with the agency after the initial interview is the first sign of a good communicator. The scheduling staff should look at a person's ease in interacting with peers and faculty during training, with clients and their families while covering cases, and with supervising nurses and management staff. The scheduler can also ask: Does the employee call the office as frequently as necessary? Does the employee communicate a change in a client's condition or a client's concern right away? Does the employee let the office know immediately if there is a problem or a delay? A good communicator will stand out to schedulers and the clinical staff.

3. *Caring.* The willingness of some workers to go beyond what is expected or required indicates to the scheduling staff that they are especially dedicated and caring. One very caring home health aide stayed with her 86-year-old client, as a volunteer, the night the woman's pet died. She also helped the client the following day to bury the pet in the client's yard. This willingness to do something extra for the client, on the worker's own time, told the schedulers immediately that this worker was a very special person.

Here again, there may be limits to what an employee can do. Another way an employee might approach the above situation would be to notify the family, follow up with a call, or send a note.

The people who work in the client's home are the most important component of home health care. It is critical that the staff evaluate them carefully in terms of both skill level and qualifications and personal qualities. These characteristics are important to the scheduling staff in making assignments of home health aides and clients that will be lasting and successful. By evaluating personnel, the scheduling staff can select them carefully for different types of assignments, matching caregivers to the requirements of a case or client. The agency which has the best people and makes the best matches will have the most satisfied clients and workers and the most business.

6

Selecting and Assigning Personnel

Setting up a home care schedule requires assigning caregivers to individual cases. The selection of caregivers is based on objective considerations, such as the type of service, employee availability, and the location of the case, and subjective concerns, such as personalities and the home environment. For each case, schedulers must look for a caregiver who can perform the job tasks required and meet the psychosocial needs of the client while ensuring that the schedule remains efficient.

Matching personnel and clients requires that each worker and client be considered individually. Through the evaluation of employees, the scheduling staff knows what type of assignment is best for each individual. Once the level of care, time of day, days of service, and expected duration of care have been established for a particular case, the available home care worker who best matches the requirements of the client and case can be selected and assigned.

SELECTING PERSONNEL

Matching of personnel to clients and cases must be careful and calculated. All agencies sometimes have an urgent need to cover a case, particularly when one requiring heavy care comes in with little advance notice. In general, however, assigning staff to cases should never be casual. Assignments made carelessly cause problems and then create work for the scheduler who has to rectify the bad matches.

The repercussions of schedules that are not well thought out can be costly and detrimental to quality care. Some home care clients have a difficult time adjusting to the presence of a stranger in their homes. No client wants to have to go through three or four workers before finding a match that is successful. And a good employee can experience unnecessary frustration or become disillusioned if too many assignments prove unsuccessful. The frustration on both sides negatively affects quality, and repeated beginnings slow progress on the learning curve and, therefore, productivity. When an agency plans its schedules carefully, following a system for deliberately assigning personnel, errors or mismatches will be much less likely to occur.

The approach used to assign cases varies with the agency. Assignments depend on the skill requirements of the case, but within a skill category (such as licensed practical nurse or home health aide), the scheduling staff might assign difficult cases to workers as test cases when additional supervision is possible or when other members of the care team are frequently in the home, to help them determine the capabilities of people about whom they are unsure. On the other hand, an agency may feel that assigning difficult cases prematurely could deter a good person from home care. Similarly, an agency's policy may be to assign new people to the type of schedule they want right away, even if it involves changing personnel or cases. Other agencies may emphasize continuity above any other factor.

The most important element of a successful approach to selecting and assigning personnel is that the scheduling staff work systematically, considering the requirements of the case, the availability of the caregiver, the location of the client, and special factors such as the home environment and the preferences and interests of the client and caregiver. This way, schedulers are looking at manageable pieces of information when scheduling cases, not profiles of an entire staff of employees or pending referrals which may be coming in rapidly.

Matching Personnel

In selecting and assigning personnel, the scheduling staff must consider the service needs of the client, the availability of qualified caregivers, the location of the client, employee preferences, and special factors.

Service Needs

All scheduling must consider the requirements of the case first. The physician's orders specify the level of worker needed to provide care. The scheduling staff must select personnel who have the appropriate skill level, such as a registered nurse, licensed practical nurse, medical social worker, therapist, home health aide, personal care aide, or homemaker.

Among qualified personnel, the scheduling staff must look for employees who have the expertise to meet any special requirements of the case. For example, a treatment plan may call for a technical procedure, such as administering home dialysis, that requires equipment as well as specific skills. Other cases may require someone who has significant experience with a particular type of client, such as a terminally ill child or a person with Alzheimer's disease. Selecting from among personnel who have specific experience and thus a special understanding of the client's needs will ensure a good match.

The scheduling staff should also consider what is required of the caregiver as a member of a care team. If a case requires round-the-clock care involving nurses, therapists, and home health aides, the employees assigned to the case must have the skills to interact closely with the other members of a complex care team. The caregiver must have exceptional verbal communication skills because this person, in addition to documenting regularly in writing as required, will have to communicate with the other members of the care team during his or her shift and between shifts. Reporting changes in a client's condition is vital to continuity and quality of care.

It is also important that the scheduling staff consider the prognosis of the client when matching client and caregiver. Since scheduling should usually be done with a permanent match in mind, the requirements of the case in 2 weeks, 1 month, or 3 months should be considered when making an assignment. Specifically, staffing concerns include the following:

1. Are the requirements of the case expected to change over time, so that it may have to be reassigned to a lower level of personnel as the client's condition improves (e.g., from a home health aide to a personal care aide)? This would mean that the case might be, for the home health aide, a short-term assignment.

2. Is the client's condition expected to worsen, so that heavier care will be required? This could mean that the home health aide assigned should be able to continue to handle the case even as it becomes more difficult, but that additional skilled services might be added.

3. Is the case a short-term assignment that is not expected to be

renewed? Changing a sterile bandage must be done until the wound is healed. If the case is funded by Medicare, authorization by the physician might be for only 2 weeks of service; however, the client might be expected to continue receiving some services through an alternative funding source, or by paying privately. This would determine whether or not the assignment will be short term or possibly longer term.

Availability

In assigning personnel, the scheduling staff is limited by the availability of qualified workers to cover the cases. There are always many more clients than workers, so that a client's schedule depends on when the worker is available. Schedulers, therefore, have less flexibility in making assignments when staff is limited. The scheduling staff can only assign employees who are available at the time required by the case.

Frequently, the scheduling staff may find that all qualified employees are assigned during a particular time slot. They may also find that some employees do not work at all during the particular hours required. Home care workers, who range from career professionals to suburban homemakers and college students, may have set hours in which they are able or willing to work. Homemakers may be willing to work when their children are at school. College students may be able to take cases in the mornings, afternoons, or weekends, depending on their class schedules.

Most agencies have difficulty balancing available personnel against the number of clients. Since continuity of care is extremely important, schedules must not be changed arbitrarily. However, when there is an immediate need for service by a client, an existing schedule may have to be changed. Agencies frequently receive referrals from hospital discharge planners that require immediate or emergency service. In these cases, changes can be made to the schedule of the most appropriate caregiver.

If existing schedules are shifted, other clients to whom the caregiver was assigned for that period must be rescheduled as soon as possible. It is critical that this process occur with minimum disruption to the client and that the new assignment be in keeping with the client's service order and plan of care. The new schedule must be negotiated with the client and approved by the funding or referral agency and the physician.

As another alternative, the agency can temporarily assign an employee with a different skill level to cover the case. A substitution to a higher skill level would not require approval if the lower rate was billed. For example, if the care plan calls for a personal care aide and no one is available, schedulers can assign a home health aide. If a home health aide is required and no one is available, the staff may assign a nurse or a personal care aide (with approval of the supervisor) to cover the case.

For cost reasons, the agency should not go to a higher category of personnel than necessary. For example, if the agency does not have a personal care aide available, schedulers should try to assign a home health aide before a licensed practical nurse. The agency will be reimbursed only at the personal care aide level. Obviously, downward substitutions (e.g., assigning a home health aide to cover a visit by a licensed practical nurse) can never occur without prior approval.

Because of the costs and requirements for approval when a substitution is made, a lack of available skilled personnel (such as a nurse, therapist, or medical social worker) is best resolved either by modifying the times or days of service, if they are not time specific or by changing an existing schedule. It is also possible that an agency may not be able to provide the needed services and may have to refer the client elsewhere. Because of the shortage of home care personnel, agencies should be aware that a considerable amount of negotiation on service orders is possible.

Geography
Once the staff has identified qualified caregivers available to cover a case, they should look to see who is geographically closest to the assignment. Location is a practical and necessary consideration. Sending caregivers across town to cover cases is inefficient and raises costs, as it is generally required that travel time and transportation between cases be paid by the agency. However, employees pay for their travel to and from their homes. High travel expenses and a long commute discourage workers from covering cases. In home care there are also many obvious advantages to

working in a geographic area with which one is familiar. Therefore, schedules are most successful when cases are close to the employee's home and when travel time in between, should more than one case be scheduled for an employee in a day, is kept to a minimum.

If the case to be covered is in a remote part of town or a neighborhood not on a bus line, the scheduling staff should look for any caregivers who are already covering other cases in the neighborhood. Employees who have a long drive to a case may be willing to see more than one client while they are in the area, although they may exceed the number of hours they are willing to work.

Geographic preferences should be carefully considered, as they influence continuity of care and the ability of workers to carry out their assignments reliably and on the days scheduled. Many employees are quite vocal regarding their geographic preferences and where they will go or how far they will travel. Some employees, such as part-time homemakers or students, might have to be scheduled for cases near their home or school.

Sometimes, through incentives, employees can be convinced to cover cases outside their preferred geographic location. Most often, financial incentives, such as supplementing transportation costs, are used. This works as a short-term strategy to cover a difficult case until an acceptable permanent schedule can be reached. Because of the cost to the agency, however, and the negative signals given to employees, this approach should be used rarely. Economic incentives, when used to excess, reduce the creativity of scheduling personnel and create the impression among employees that transportation expenses to the job will be paid.

Geography greatly influences employee satisfaction and quality of care. However, staff must not base scheduling decisions solely on proximity. Sometimes simple geographic proximity may not be the way to assess ease of access, since public transportation routes and schedules can vary. Workers and clients who reside on main transportation routes may be closer together than seemingly nearer employees and clients when a walk is required.

The use of geography as a criterion for organizing requires that schedulers thoroughly know the agency's service area. An important reference tool for determining the best geographic matches for scheduling is a current and detailed map of a service area, as described fully in Chapter 7. The map can be posted and cases and employees identified by pins placed in the map. Bus or other public transportation routes can then be drawn on the map.

When an agency uses a computer in scheduling, routes for public transportation, the location of employees' homes and neighborhood boundaries can be input. Codes can be assigned to represent the geographic location of clients' homes when the referral is received, so that schedulers have immediate access to the information.

Schedulers must use their judgment when selecting caregivers by location. Sometimes clients need caregivers with special qualities, such as extraordinary patience or supportiveness. Judgment must determine when schedulers should select personnel on the basis of special factors, such as personal qualities, ignoring geographic considerations. This situation might occur when there is more likelihood, because of the characteristics of the client, that the schedule can be more stable with a caregiver who has the special personality to fit the client's needs, even though transportation becomes more difficult. In this example, a premium for special transportation might also be charged.

Employee Preferences

Ongoing, day-to-day contact between agency staff and employees can reveal much about an employee's preferences. Whether or not some of these preferences are met can greatly influence the quality of care provided, as they affect job satisfaction. Only careful attempts by the scheduling staff to listen to employees' preferences and accommodate them wherever possible will ensure that employees continue to enjoy their work and that continuity of care is maintained.

The preferences and goals of employees may vary. Workers may prefer long- or short-term cases, stability or variety in their work, busy days or a slower-paced plan of care. A home care professional may also prefer to keep up on current technological procedures and therapies, while other workers may not want to handle cases requiring these specialized or new technical treatments.

Workers who prefer serving clients in particular age groups are common. Personnel often express interest in caring for special clients, such as children or elderly persons, or feel most useful with certain types of clients, such as clients with dementia. Accommodating these preferences not only enhances an employee's self-confidence and job satisfaction but also ensures that employees become highly experienced with clients suffering from certain disorders. This specialization may prove valuable to the agency in making future assignments.

Because each of these preferences is important, the scheduling staff should take the time to listen to employees' comments about their work and the persons to whom they give care. As home care workers are contacted about assignments, the scheduling staff should listen for indications of how satisfied they are. While some assignments must always be made that may not fully suit a worker, anticipating preferences may prevent burnout or dissatisfaction. Some employees will need new assignments and challenges with greater frequency than others. If the scheduling staff listens and recognizes this personality trait, successful matches can be made.

Although many employees state their preferences clearly, many others do not. The supervisory staff can, however, pick up additional information through an employee's questions, requests, and other interactions with agency staff. If an employee requests training in a particular therapy, it is clear that he or she is interested in performing the procedure. If an employee's attendance drops considerably after being assigned to a particular client, the schedulers should investigate the possibility of a poor match between client and worker and reevaluate the assignment.

Special Factors

Attention to special personal factors can also improve the quality of care. It is easiest to do a good job when you like what you are doing. This is true for the home care worker who provides the care and also for the client who is supposed to benefit from the care.

In assigning personnel, the scheduling staff should carefully consider the evaluations of each employee. It is here that all the comments gathered from recommendations, faculty, supervising nurses, and services staff are useful, and where attention to small things such as a love for pets or an interest in music can make an assignment particularly good.

When assigning workers to clients, it is very important to

consider the personalities of each. Some workers, however, gain great personal satisfaction from covering the more difficult cases, while others experience stress and frustration that can lead to burnout. Placements must be made on an individual basis.

Employees may wish to specialize in the care of certain types of clients, based on their special capabilities. One person may be particularly good with children. Another person may feel most fulfilled serving patients who are terminally ill, who are difficult to serve. Others prefer to work with patients who are less seriously ill and more participatory in their own care. The interests and skills of staff should be strongly considered as part of the scheduling process. It is worth noting again that stress is caused by frustration, not by specific elements of the case. One employee can be energized in the same situation where another person becomes depressed.

Other special abilities should be considered when assigning personnel, such as linguistic or cultural skills. A worker who understands the dietary restrictions of an orthodox Jew, is experienced in wrapping a sari for an Indian client, or speaks a foreign language can be assigned to cover special cases.

Client–staff placements can be particularly rewarding when attention to the special interests of each are considered. Many clients and employees share common interests, such as cooking, sports, or reading. Inquiring about both the clients' and the workers' interests can help the scheduling staff to ensure not only that the client–employee match is acceptable but that it is particularly rewarding for both parties.

Another essential component of the scheduling process is the home environment of the client. Whether or not the client smokes or keeps pets can influence how satisfied an employee feels and, ultimately, the continuity of care. Some clients are very attached to their pets; an employee who is allergic or is not a cat or dog lover is certainly a less than ideal match. While these factors are secondary considerations, they are significant. Services can be scheduled in shifts of up to 8 hours, 7 days a week, and there is room for these factors in designing a schedule. In any case, special features of a client should be given as background to the employee.

The preferences clients express about employees who deliver services can also help schedulers to select and assign caregivers. Some clients develop favorite workers, or articulate a preference for a particular type of person, such as a talkative, friendly person or someone who is more quiet. While an agency cannot always accommodate staffing requests, it can often respond when a request is made for a specific employee. As long as an agency has a large enough pool of workers from which to choose, the scheduler can consider these preferences. When certain employees are requested frequently, quality of their work should be recognized by the agency.

The scheduling staff should also be sensitive to the concerns of employees who are being assigned. Particular types of cases require an employee with a certain self-confidence. To cover a series of short-term cases, for example, a worker is needed who is comfortable with new situations. One of the most difficult tasks for many home care workers is to enter a client's home and start the services. Because of the difficulty and importance of this step, an agency may not want to assign a new worker with little confidence or experience to several clients who need service for short periods.

When selecting caregivers for assignment, the scheduling staff should look first for obvious matches and mismatches. If a worker served a client on a previous occasion and the assignment was successful, the scheduler can rematch the client and worker and be relatively assured of a good match. On the other hand, if a match would clearly be against the stated preference of the worker or client, the scheduler should automatically look for another match. Similarly, if the employee being considered is small and the client is overweight and requires transfers and lifts, the scheduler could also anticipate a poor match and assign accordingly.

Other Considerations

Other elements of a successful approach to selecting personnel are enumerated below.

1. The scheduling staff must think out each assignment carefully. Scheduling is assigning people to people, with their personalities, their fears, their concerns, and, sometimes their eccentricities. Regardless of the requirements of the case, the scheduling staff must take the time to think through each match carefully. It is understood that arranging coverage on Saturday night for a Sunday morning case may leave the on-call scheduler

short of time and creativity. In most cases, though, assignment should occur as deliberately and carefully as possible.

2. The scheduling staff should use all information available to them when assigning. They must consider what they know about each employee, the success of previous matches, and what employees and clients have said about previous assignments.

3. The scheduling staff should also be creative wherever possible to identify successful matches. It is sometimes possible to predict how a match will work out by analyzing how another employee, similar in personality or preferences, may have worked out in a similar situation. Conversely, the staff can often predict when an assignment might fail. Even though the staff should not limit their options by being too conservative and eliminating someone who might be a good match, they can learn much from mistakes made with other matches.

4. After matching a caregiver to a case, the scheduling staff must note what works and what doesn't. Sometimes the best matches are made accidentally, such as when a new client enters the schedule or a new employee comes on board. That is why careful attention to the suitability of client and employee matches is important; when a client and employee appear well matched, the schedule should continue to hold for the duration of the treatments or services.

The scheduling staff should also listen to their employees and their clients. The people being matched can provide valuable insight about their cases that can be useful in making future assignments. If a client found a particular employee unsatisfactory, it should be noted in the employee's record or computer file so that the staff will not make the mistake of matching these two people again.

Most importantly, the scheduling staff should try to determine why a match did or didn't work. If a client has been unsuccessfully matched with two or three young aides, perhaps the scheduling staff should try someone older. If an employee has had unsuccessful assignments with male clients, an assignment with a female client can be considered. Sometimes these changes can help.

ASSIGNING PERSONNEL

Staff members must match personnel to cases with the idea in mind that, in most instances, each case is one of several to which the caregiver will be assigned. In considering the employee's other assignments as well as the present case, the scheduling staff can anticipate when one more case might cause a good person to quit or when it might appear to other employees that a few caregivers are receiving the best cases. These considerations are necessary for the retention of home health personnel, particularly paraprofessionals, and as training and orientation costs are high and exceptional employees are sometimes hard to identify, it is important for agencies to retain their employees.

The scheduling staff should attempt to achieve a *balance* in making assignments so that the heaviest cases are not all given to one person. A particular caregiver may be good at cases that challenge his or her skills, such as those that are physically or emotionally demanding. However, to ensure that the person does not burn out, schedulers must ensure that the total caseload is not overwhelming.

For example, some clients are more pleasant to work for than others. The scheduling staff should ensure that the same caregivers are not always assigned to the most difficult clients. Since some caregivers are more willing to accept such assignments than others, it is easy for the scheduling staff to call on them first. The danger is that the difficult cases will eventually burn out the employee.

The staff should also pay special attention to assignments for new employees. It is sometimes useful to schedule cases that will allow a new employee to develop confidence and gain experience. Some new caregivers need to become accustomed gradually to different clients and tasks. The scheduling staff should consider more seasoned employees for the most difficult cases.

Attention should also be given to cases requiring nighttime and weekend coverage. Again, the scheduling staff naturally wants to assign people who are most willing to take these cases. However, the same employees should not be assigned the last-minute sub-stitutions or off-hours cases all the time. As discussed above, if a case requires 7 nights of off-hours coverage, the staff may want to alternate the people assigned, perhaps spreading the assignment among two caregivers, rather than scheduling one person every night for the duration of the assignment.

One useful approach is to assign employees to clients as teams.

This method allows regular persons to serve as substitutes and facilitates continuity. An alternative might be to have a regular substitute or stand-by who is ready to be called on short notice to go to any case assigned.

Precautions should also be taken against developing favorite employees who receive the best cases, however those may be defined. Favoritism, whether real or imagined, can create resentment among employees.

In general, employees are assigned to three types of cases: permanent assignments, temporary assignments, and substitutions. These assignments are described below.

Permanent Assignments

The best way to proceed is to start with the assumption that assignments should be permanent. That is, the first consideration should be given to assigning caregivers who would be expected to provide the specified care for the duration of the care plan. In developing a permanent schedule, the agency personnel may realize that an alternative to the service order is the best way the situation can be handled. When this is the case, the rationale and plan should be presented to the supervisor and the referral source. Although some matches last for the duration of the service order, not all matches thought to be permanent will last indefinitely. Even when it is thought that such an assignment has been made, it needs to be followed up. The scheduling staff must track the cases for quality and ensure that the client and caregiver remain satisfied.

The scheduling staff should not let routine cause a decrease in the quality or continuity of care once progress along the learning curve has enabled an employee to complete the required activities quickly and easily. They should also be aware of possible indications that a change in the assignment may be needed. For example, poor attendance by a generally reliable home care worker could indicate that a reassignment is required.

Temporary Assignments

Temporary assignments occur when no ideal match of an employee with a client is currently available. The concept of temporary assignment fits the home care agency's belief that no one should be forced to stay in an institution who can be cared for at home.

A temporary assignment is made with the understanding by both the caregiver and client that the plan is indeed temporary. Notification of the temporary assignment must also be conveyed to the referral source, the physician and, as necessary, the client's family. When scheduling a caregiver on a temporary basis, the staff should have some idea of the duration of the assignment. In cases where no permanent caregiver may be available in the immediate future, a time frame for a permanent assignment may be left undefined.

When a case is extremely difficult to cover, such as one involving only 2 hours of service, a client with a difficult personality, and inordinate travel time, the agency may have to restructure it temporarily to make it more desirable, such as by providing the service over more units (e.g., 4 hours) to make the case more attractive to caregivers. Depending on why no permanent placement can be found, the temporary alternative may even end up as a revised care plan.

Substitutions

Substitute assignments are one-time matches that can occur for a variety of reasons. A client may request a change in the time of service on a particular day, a change that the caregiver cannot accommodate in his or her schedule. In this event, the scheduling staff would assign a substitute caregiver to cover the case for that one day.

The caregiver may also request a substitute for an assignment. Illness, unexpected car trouble, and vacation time are all things that may prevent a caregiver from maintaining his or her regular schedule.

When a substitution is made in a permanent schedule, the client must be notified in advance. In addition, the physician and/or referral source must be notified if the change contradicts specific days or times specified in the physician's orders. It is useful for the scheduling staff to have a replacement in mind when contacting the client so that they can describe the new caregiver and help the client to feel comfortable with the change. In long term cases, regular back-ups or substitutes should be part of the scheduling plan.

The scheduling staff can also make substitutions to provide a short break for a permanent caregiver on a particularly arduous case. A caregiver serving a client who requires heavy care or is difficult to serve may last longer on the case if given short breaks in the schedule from time to time.

When the scheduling staff notes frequent substitutions on particularly hard-to-cover assignments, such as those involving many hours or nights and weekends, they should consider breaking up the case among a team of caregivers. Rather than permanently assigning one caregiver, personnel can be assigned in rotation. The rotation would cover different days or shifts so that a single caregiver does not serve every night or weekend. Part-time employees in particular would be excellent choices for team coverage of cases.

It is useful when substituting to note the success of individuals when covering specific cases. If a match works well, the scheduling staff can try to assign the same caregiver when there is a future need for a substitute. In addition, if the regular assignment must be rescheduled after a period of time, the staff can have someone in mind for a new permanent match.

It should be remembered that personnel are usually assigned after the times of service have been determined. However, the scheduling staff may decide that it is necessary to negotiate an adjustment in the times of service in order to assign the best employee for the case. In addition, the scheduling staff must never find that there is no one to cover a case once it has been accepted. When coverage is difficult, it may be necessary to adjust the times of service so that an available caregiver can be assigned or a difficult case split between two different caregivers at different times.

Selecting and assigning home health personnel to clients is a calculated process. It is important to consider the service needs of the client when selecting the appropriate level of personnel (e.g., a home health aide versus a personal care aide); the availability, geographic location, and preferences of the worker; and the worker's talents and strengths. The scheduling staff must carefully think through each match to make the best assignment possible. When assigning people to people, it is essential to closely match each person's interests, personality, and temperament, and to be creative in trying to find the right match. Careful matching will reduce the frustration of unsuccessful assignments. Correctly matching clients and workers and designating back-up personnel will result in smooth scheduling and satisfied clients and employees.

PART 3

7

Manual Scheduling

The factors of scheduling have been discussed in Chapter 2. The format and procedures of scheduling can be achieved manually or with a computer. This chapter discusses manual methods that can be used for scheduling. Automated scheduling is discussed in Chapter 8.

Manual methods of scheduling are most common in smaller agencies. With large or small caseloads, the scheduling staff can implement simple techniques, with the help of a few materials that are specially prepared or purchased from any office supply store, to ensure that cases are scheduled for efficiency and quality of care. Although a manual process can become cumbersome with an extremely large or complex caseload, services can be scheduled accurately using very simple manual methods. Whether the system is manual or electronic, its success will depend on the ability of the scheduling staff to discipline themselves to record information as it comes in. Trying to remember information to be documented later invariably causes problems in a system.

SCHEDULING TOOLS

Simple materials developed by the agency or purchased at an office supply or stationary store will make scheduling organized and easier. Basic forms and file folders for client and personnel records should be standard for organizing scheduling information. Chapter 10 describes the contents of these records.

Card Index

A card index for all clients receiving service is useful as a reference tool for schedulers. An index card can be used to summarize the information on each client that is relevant to scheduling, so that it will not be necessary to refer to the complete file. The organization of individual records and their use as reference tools can serve as a precursor to computerization.

The index card for each client should abbreviate the information in the patient care record relevant to scheduling. Key information includes the type of service authorized in the service order (skilled nursing, physical therapy, home health aide, personal care aide, homemaker, or other), any specific requirements regarding days and times of service (particularly weekend or nighttime coverage), any special requirements or conditions, location, and personal preferences for service. Notations should also be made on these cards when a match between a client and a caregiver is particularly successful. It is possible, for example, that even when a permanent assignment is stable, a client might find a substitute caregiver especially pleasing. This information is useful when a client's schedule must be changed.

The reference cards for each client should be filed in the card index alphabetically. It is easiest to recognize the clients this way. The scheduling staff know clients by their names, not by their diagnoses or addresses. A number is needed for each client as well for confidential referencing; this number is the same as the one on the client record.

Although the cards can be filed alphabetically, additional steps can make referencing easier. For example, color coding allows easy visual reference. Since clients are frequently sorted for scheduling by geographic area or level of care, color coding allows cards to be pulled at a glance. A combination could be devised using colored cards coded by level of care and colored dots to indicate geographic location. Colored dots could also be used to indicate those clients requiring medical or support services of the greatest urgency.

Maps

Maps are useful for sorting caregivers and clients by geographic location. The scheduling staff could obtain a detailed, current map of the agency's service area. Maps can be purchased from a local chamber of commerce or a city department of transportation. They can also be found at bookstores or through retail companies.

Once a map is obtained, the agency should mark off neighborhoods so that it will have an idea of the type of area indicated by a client's address. It is useful for the staff to recognize areas that might not be safe for a caregiver alone at night, that are residential, or that have easy access for shopping or for errands. The agency should then superimpose bus routes or major routes of access so that the staff can immediately determine which cases will be difficult to reach.

Next, the staff can put markers on the map to represent clients and caregivers. If they choose to use the method of writing and erasing names on the map, a photo, printing, or graphics store could laminate the map. If not, the agency can use pins or flag and pennant markers. Clients and caregivers could be color coded by level of care required and skill level of workers, respectively. Alternatively, colored pins are now available that are numbered, so a master list of clients and caregivers could correspond to numbered pins on the map. These techniques can help the scheduling staff to narrow down the choice of possible caregivers for new clients by level of skill and geographic location.

Matrices

Homemade matrices, or preprinted forms, can be used for scheduling. A *matrix*, loosely defined, is an arrangement of facts, terms, or numbers in rows and columns. For scheduling, names of clients, names of employees, and times of service are organized in a matrix, with time on one axis, the name of the client or caregiver on the other axis, and the name of the other person filled in in the resulting squares. An example is shown in Figure 7.1. Tables 7.1, 7.2, and 7.3 show samples of completed matrices.

Calendars can be used for scheduling matrices, as can other office forms such as general time or attendance records or ledgers,

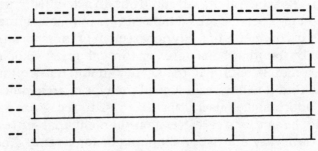

Figure 7.1. Matrix.

Table 7.1 Scheduling Matrix in a Weekly Format

Caregiver	Mon.	Tues.	Wed.	Thurs.	Fri
A	Jones 9-1		Collins 7-10		
(Phone Number)	Smith 2-5				
B	Walke 10-2	Pit 6-10			
(Phone Number)					

Table 7.2 Scheduling Matrix Organized by Client

Client	Mon.	Tues.	Wed.	Thurs.	Fri
A	Cole 9-1		Cole 9-1		Cole 9-1
(Phone Number)					
B	Street 7-3	Street 7-3	Street 7-3	Street 7-3	Street 7-3
(Phone Number)	Hall 3-11	Hall 3-11	Hall 3-11	Hall 3-11	Hall 3-11
C					
(Phone Number)					

Table 7.3 Scheduling Matrix in a List Format

Name	Service Order	Day	Time	Employee	Employee Confirmed	Client Notified
A	8° x 2 PCA	Sat/Sun	9-5	Clark	Yes/init.	Yes/init.

which tend to have more open spaces for changing schedules at the last minute. The best preprinted forms to use for the master schedule are those set up weekly, so that the scheduling staff does not have to refer to separate sheets to see what is scheduled for the following day. The size of the caseload will determine the feasibility of the different tools. It is not recommended that the staff use laminated, erasable matrices for the master schedule, because past schedules are needed for planning continuity of care, for verification, and for record-keeping purposes.

If the scheduling staff chooses to prepare individual schedules for each client or employee in addition to the master schedules, a pad of daily schedule forms, purchased in an office supply store, is sufficient. The agency can also create its own forms for recording assignments. In creating its own form, the staff should include space for the name of the person and the date and list the hours of the day down the side of the page, like a date book. Space could also be included for any notes or special instructions, such as directions to a client's home.

The agency may also want to develop a separate schedule specifically for weekend coverage. Because more family caregivers are available on weekends, there are generally fewer clients to be scheduled than during the week. A simple form can be developed solely for covering Saturday and Sunday cases.

Lists

Lists of an agency's caregivers, clients, or both can be useful, depending on how the agency sets up its schedules. An agency that schedules manually can benefit from maintaining lists on office machines such as memory typewriters or word processors. This facilitates updating and changing the lists without retyping.

A roster of all active employees, listed in alphabetical order, is a useful reference. The telephone number of each employee can be listed underneath the name for easy reference. To save time in searching through the list when scheduling, different colored inks or colored dots can be used to code employees by category of worker (e.g., licensed practical nurse or registered nurse). This list should indicate the availability of each employee to work, so that staff members do not waste time scheduling personnel who cannot meet the assignment.

Any new personnel being added to a schedule should be flagged on that week's list of caregivers. This will remind the staff that their first cases should be carefully assigned and alert the nursing staff that supervisory visits must be performed.

Lists of clients who need service each week can be compiled from the service orders. From these lists, cases can be crossed off as they are scheduled, so that open cases are easy to spot. The clients can also be listed alphabetically if they are going to be listed on the schedule alphabetically. However, it is useful if clients can be listed in the order in which the cases must be scheduled. Those clients with the highest priority or time-specific service needs should be listed first, followed by other hard-to-cover cases. This type of list should be generated daily.

In addition to the clients' names and telephone numbers, the roster of clients should identify their service requirements, including the category of service and the number of days and hours authorized. This information can be abbreviated in terms of type of caregiver (e.g., "HHA" or "LPN" to refer to home health aide and licensed practical nurse, respectively) and days and hours of service (such as "$4° \times 3$" to indicate 4 hours of service provided three times per week). If notation marks used to abbreviate information are specific to the agency, rather than common notations, definitions should be included wherever they are used so that they can be understood by others. Lists can also be maintained to help the scheduling staff monitor personnel information. For example, monthly lists can be used to track employees who are due for performance assessments, physical exams, or in-service training. A notebook that has a page or two with index tabs can be used so that at the start of each month, the scheduling staff can be sure that everyone is eligible for assignments.

Other Tools

Other forms and records are also useful for scheduling. A log can be used to track what has been done so that one can see what needs to be done. Telephone logs, which are lists of telephone calls with room for notations, are useful for recording calls from clients or caregivers so that the staff has a reference when making changes to the schedule. The agency can develop simple forms or call-in sheets for documenting incoming messages concerning the schedule. The log may include space to note the date and time of the call, the name of the caller, the message received, and the initials of the staff person who took the call in case questions arise regarding the message (see Table 7.4). Complaints, in particular, should definitely be logged, whether received verbally or in writing, and a space left to indicate a date by which resolution is required and the results. Again, this log is simply an index to the complete documents in client and employee files.

Attendance records are useful for tracking changes to the schedule that are brought about by the employee. Although the scheduling staff should note on the master schedule any substitutions that were made, the explanation for the substitution (such as a no-show, a late arrival, or calling in sick) should be noted in the employee's attendance record. (Sample attendance records are found in Chapter 10.) Attendance records can be used as documentation, in billing and in payroll, of services provided.

ORGANIZING THE SCHEDULE

With these materials, the staff can prepare the schedule. A schedule is a matrix which matches clients and caregivers in specific time frames. As discussed previously, there are many ways to organize this matrix. While it is useful to have schedules subdivided by geographic area or caregiver type, the agency must have a master

Table 7.4 Telephone Log

DATE	TIME	CALLER	MESSAGE	MESSAGE REC'D BY
1/9	9:10am	Joe Johnson	Mrs. Johnson hospitalized.	LD

schedule so that it can ensure that all clients are covered and that caregivers have assignments.

As described above, the alphabetical approach offers the greatest flexibility for the master schedule. It is the simplest to work with, as it requires the scheduler to recall the least information and remember the person by name rather than by address.

In one method of manual scheduling, the caregivers could be listed alphabetically down a sheet of paper. Because each caregiver will have to be reached, it is also useful to list the phone contact. The days of the week could be shown across the top of the page. This format enables the staff person making the schedule to fill in the client's name and the time the care is to be provided in each day's slot. A sample matrix in a weekly format is shown in Table 7.1.

Once all the caregivers have been listed in alphabetical order, the cases of the highest medical priority should be assigned. Next, the most difficult-to-cover or least flexible cases should be assigned. Difficult-to-cover cases may involve clients who require care at very specific times, live in a hard-to-cover geographic area, have a particularly challenging personality, or have difficult living environments (many pets, an uncooperative family, or other adverse conditions). These cases should be scheduled first because they allow the fewest options or, rather, the fewest caregivers can successfully be assigned. Assigning these cases first ensures the largest pool of staff from whom to choose. In addition, if difficult cases are not handled first, other carefully planned case and caregiver combinations may have to be changed, causing frustration and extra work when assignments must be made later in the scheduling process.

To ensure that the most difficult cases are screened first, a client list as described above can be used, or the staff can work directly from client summary sheets or a card index. Whichever method is used, the names should be sorted into cases by medical priority and by expected difficulty in finding a suitable caregiver. Difficulties can be categorized by either objective or subjective factors, like geography or personality, and clients listed or ranked in descending order of difficulty.

These clients can then be assigned one by one. If staff members are unsure why a person is listed as a high-priority or hard-to-cover case, they can refer back to the card index or, if necessary, to the patient care record.

Once the difficult-to-cover cases are scheduled, it is useful for the scheduling staff to analyze the list of caregivers who still have time available. In fact, it is useful to review the list of available caregivers after each assignment is made. While closest attention to matching clients and caregivers is given in assigning the hard-to-cover cases, assignment to more standard cases must also maximize the positive elements or factors by careful selection of personnel.

An alternative method of organizing the schedule is to list the clients in the left-hand column and fill in the names of the caregivers and times of service on the appropriate day (see Table 7.2). This method allows the scheduling staff to identify at a glance those clients who have not been scheduled.

The disadvantage of this type of matrix is that the priority of cases for scheduling is not obvious. An alphabetical list of clients is not required; the only consideration is that it is sufficiently systematic to ensure that no one is omitted. The matrix could also be organized by client in a list rather than a calendar format (see Table 7.3). While this type of matrix does not allow the staff to view the overall schedule, it is useful when fewer cases are being assigned, such as for weekend coverage.

Regardless of which matrix is used, it is important that the scheduling staff mark every schedule with the dates to which it applies. The staff should also initial the schedule by each case assignment when it is confirmed. If an agency has more than one scheduler, the staff person who prepared the schedule should mark it with his or her name or initials in case questions about the schedule arise.

CREATING THE SCHEDULE

A useful analogy in scheduling is a crossword puzzle. Putting together a schedule is like solving a crossword puzzle. Like a key word in a crossword that will reveal key letters needed for other words, a key combination of assignments to one employee may help the scheduler determine how to break the coverage of clients into workable units.

The analogy may also be useful when the converse is true. Sometimes it is necessary to try to solve a puzzle by skipping over one part of the crossword and working on other parts that can be solved. In that way, a key letter or new thought may be revealed that will enable one to work out other parts of the puzzle that couldn't be handled until additional clues were found or new ideas developed.

Likewise, when a person making assignments becomes frustrated in approaching a scheduling problem, there are usually some cases, or places in the schedule, where an appropriate employee can be easily identified. When one has difficulty scheduling, an easier case may help by opening up additional possibilities.

The crossword puzzle analogy also holds when one thinks about how solving a crossword can be stopped when a wrong word has been used. Similarly, it is sometimes necessary, when resolving difficulties in a plan for the delivery of home care, to change a schedule in order to have this plan work. In general, scheduling changes should be avoided when possible because continuity of care, or using the same plan for the delivery of services for the entire period of the care plan, is desirable when all other factors are satisfactory. However, there may be times when a caregiver will need to be reassigned to allow the scheduler to arrange other assignments. For this reason, open cases should be looked at together, and the matches between caregivers and clients determined, before the scheduling personnel make the calls and confirm the assignments.

It is true that assignments may not be accepted, causing one to replan the schedule. This is similar to trying a word in a crossword and then erasing it. In working crosswords, most people use a pencil because changes are expected. This is equally true of a scheduling plan; it should be approached with some degree of flexibility in mind. However, with careful forethought, the number of false starts should be reduced.

In developing the master schedule, it should be kept in mind that the schedule assignment should be permanent. If an assignment is successful, it is to the advantage of the client, the employee, and the agency to maintain it whenever possible. Continuity of care is important, so once matches have been successfully established, they should not be disturbed.

The stability of the match is also a factor in creating the schedule. As will be discussed in Chapter 9, when an employee is assigned to a case, the scheduler should follow up with both the employee and the client to evaluate the success of the match. In doing so, the scheduler should make clear to both clients and employees that they should be as satisfied with their assignments as possible, and that schedules can be changed until stable matches are achieved. Stable matches thought to be permanent should be placed automatically into a new week's schedule and continued for as long as possible, until the end of the service period, unless the condition of the client changes.

When an ideal match cannot be found, the scheduling staff can assign the case on a temporary basis. However, the client and caregiver must be informed that the assignment is temporary, and the scheduling staff must continue to search for an employee to fill it permanently. Scheduling records should reflect any temporary assignments so that the scheduling staff knows that these cases need to be permanently scheduled.

In addition to permanent and temporary assignments, the scheduling staff may have one-time assignments to fill. Some skilled nursing services, for example, are scheduled for the purpose of teaching the client or family to perform a particular procedure, such as administering an insulin injection. This type of visit should be marked or coded on the schedule so that the staff can recognize that it should not automatically be scheduled again the following week.

One of the most difficult aspects of scheduling home health care is balancing the number of available caregivers with the cases to be assigned. The number of clients and caregivers never seems to come out even. With proper planning, the number of caregivers increases together with the number of new clients, but sometimes new employees cannot, because of skill level, geography, or other factors, be matched with new clients as they come in.

In other instances, employees outnumber cases. This is a difficult situation, because it is very important to give new employees assignments in order to attract and retain them, especially given current shortages in home health workers. Some new employees need the reinforcement of a full, successful schedule.

Existing schedules should not be changed unless the imbalance between available personnel and clients to be scheduled is critical. The agency should first develop new clients through its referral sources to generate assignments for available caregivers, telling hospital discharge planners, for example, that the agency has an excellent new employee who is available to take a case. When there is a shortage of caregivers, the agency must recruit additional employees. This planning problem is discussed in Chapter 6.

These efforts take time, however, and cannot always be successful by the time a case must be covered. Therefore, even though the rule is not to disturb successful assignments, the reality is that schedules must sometimes be changed. The best way to do this, if possible, is to alter time schedules rather than shift people.

Available options to the times of service requested by the client can be considered. For example, the staff may be able to schedule service requested for the morning at a different time or on a different day. The scheduling person can try to cover the case for a limited time until a permanent schedule with a suitable caregiver at the preferred time can be arranged. Alternatively, to allow a special caregiver or team of caregivers to be used, the staff can try to reach agreement on a suitable schedule on a different day or time than the one requested.

When unexpected, short-term shortages of personnel occur (due to illness, for example), the scheduling staff can cover open cases with part-time workers who prefer to be substitutes rather than have permanent case assignments. The staff can also use individuals identified early in the scheduling plan as willing to help out when short-term assistance is needed. Conversely, the staff should not waste time trying to cover cases with workers whose schedule of available time is inflexible or who have been unwilling to help out in the past.

CHECKING THE SCHEDULE

Cross-checks are an essential part of the scheduling process. Since the most common matrix used is that listing the employees' names, the agency must ensure that every client is included. One way to do this is to cross-check the complete list of service orders, or index cards that summarize the orders, against the schedule for the week. The need for confidential treatment of service orders and other patient records should be kept in mind.

If an individual who has service orders does not appear in the schedule, the staff should check to see if the client is supposed to receive service that week (the client may receive service less frequently than every week). If it is found that someone has been omitted from the schedule, this person should be contacted immediately, as should the source of the referral.

Another way of cross-checking is to keep a list of cases to be covered by week. This list, prepared from the service orders as described above, is a working list of clients' names and service requirements. A scheduling staff person could cross names off the list as the assignments are made. In addition, a clean copy of a checklist for each day could be cross-checked with the daily schedule to ensure that all clients have a caregiver scheduled for the days service is required.

Use of the telephone log described above is another method of ensuring that changes are posted to the schedule. At the end of each day, the messages recorded on the call-in sheets can be compared to the schedule to ensure that each was followed up appropriately and changes made to the schedule as needed.

CHANGING THE SCHEDULE

The schedule is the most dynamic part of the home care business and changes frequently. Clients' needs and preferences may change, as may the availability and work preferences of employees. New cases are referred, and coverage of other cases is terminated. In other instances, the staff may anticipate a change in personnel.

In setting up a schedule, it is important to let the caregiver and client know if changes are expected. Both clients and caregivers usually expect that there will be some adjustments to a plan of care. However, last-minute changes with little notice to clients and caregivers should be avoided when possible, and when they must be made, it is important for everyone to know why a change is necessary.

When an agency is advised that a caregiver cannot handle a case as assigned, a decision must be made on how to revise the schedule. Sometimes an alternative caregiver can be assigned temporarily if the change is occurring because of illness, for example. In this case, a staff member could call the client and advise him or her of the substitution. Each change must then be posted to the client and employee files, and whenever a substitution is made, the referring physician or any third party monitoring the case must be so advised. As mentioned previously, the staff should note the substitution on the schedule but should never erase the permanent caregiver's name, so that it can be transferred to the schedule the following week.

In addition to recording the substitution on a schedule, it is useful to maintain a log for recording all substitutions that have occurred on the schedule. The names of each substitute, client, and regular employee involved should be listed as substitutions occur. The substitutions on the list can then be compared to employee time cards, when submitted, to ensure that the correct employee is paid for the case.

When a substitution is to be made on a more permanent basis, there are several ways to handle it. First, an alternative caregiver can be asked to go to the assignment at the regular time. Second, a new time can be decided upon that will be agreeable to the client and the caregiver.

An agency may be advised that a client must be removed from a schedule temporarily. For example, a client might be hospitalized for a medical procedure. In this case, the agency staff must decide how to proceed. The employee assigned to this case could be reassigned as a temporary caregiver for another client. The employee could also be used as a substitute until the client returns home.

Other changes may occur in a case that is permanent. If the time of service must be changed, the existing personnel assignment can be kept if the caregiver is available at the new time. If not, another available caregiver must be assigned. When this occurs, it is important to reassure the client that the new caregiver is an excellent, hard-working employee.

When the level of care changes, the agency must usually assign a new caregiver. Although an employee can continue to cover a case that has been downgraded (i.e., a home health aide can continue to cover a case that has been downgraded to service at the level of a personal care aide), this is not cost-effective for the agency. However, the agency can allow this service to continue until a suitable employee can be found to take the case. Of course, when the level of care is upgraded, such as from home health aide to skilled nursing service, a caregiver at the appropriate level must be assigned immediately.

Because home care schedules change often, the staff should review the schedule each morning, and again each afternoon, to see that all cases have been covered.

When a case has not been covered for a day, the scheduling person must decide, in cooperation with the patient, how the case should be handled. Sometimes a missed visit causes more difficulty than others, depending on the rapport that the agency has with the client and the referral source. If the agency schedules high-priority, time-specific, and difficult-to-cover cases first at all times, a missed case should never be one in which the mistake threatens the well-being of the client. Nevertheless, because the agency is paid on the basis of services or care provided, it is to the agency's benefit to reinstate the requested service as soon as possible.

SCHEDULING SUPERVISORY VISITS

Visits by nurses, therapists, and other professionals are performed to supervise assigned paraprofessional personnel, monitor the condition of the client to update the care plan as needed, and follow up on patient complaints. The specifics of conducting supervising visits are discussed in Chapter 9. The mechanics of tracking and scheduling these visits are discussed below.

The frequency of supervisory visits is often determined by outside regulatory agencies. Participation in Medicare, for example, requires that registered nurses visit the client's home at least once every 2 weeks to provide general supervision of home health aides. The frequency of supervisory visits under other funding arrangements differs under the laws of each state. Regulations governing Medicaid cases, for example, vary widely. The regulations usually specify when the first supervisory visit must occur for each new assignment and when follow-up visits must be performed, but the specific time frames for conducting the visits differ.

Some state laws govern the frequency of supervisory visits for all paraprofessional personnel, regardless of the client's funding source. In New York, for example, it is required that home health aides be supervised by home visits a minimum of once every 2 weeks and personal care aides once every 6 months. Similarly, visits conducted to follow up complaints may be required by the states; in New York, a visit must be made within 12 days of a complaint.

Even clients paying privately for services must be visited by a supervisor as necessary for updating the care plan. Many agencies find a visit no less frequently than every 6 months to be appropriate.

Since there are many different requirements, depending on the type of case, funding source, and reason for the visit, the agency must have a system to track and schedule the visits in accordance with the requirements for each case.

Charting and Logging Visits

A log is useful for tracking nursing visits. The log should be consulted regularly to ensure that the regulatory requirements for supervision are met.

The log should contain a list of every visit required. Each entry should be color coded to indicate the period of time in which the visit must be conducted (e.g., 12 days, 2 weeks, 6 months). Under this system, one color would be used for visits to supervise new employees, another for routine home health aide supervision, another for complaints, and so on. Every new employee added to a personnel roster at the beginning of a week, or every new case referred and added to a schedule, must be entered into the visit log and color coded.

The supervisory visit log should include space for recording the dates on which every visit is performed and when the next visit for a case or employee is required. The log could also be used to record additional information, such as who conducted the visit and whether a visit report was filed. A sample visit log is shown in Table 7.5.

To track visits, the staff may wish to cross off visits as they are completed, as a visual aid. Alternatively, they can use a colored highlighting pen to indicate which of the entries on the list require immediate attention.

Visits can also be charted on a calendar matrix rather than a log. Cases would be charted in color on a calendar section indicating the time period in which the visit must be made. All supervisory visits are important. However, special attention should be given to visits that must occur as part of a complaint investigation. These visits should be flagged in the visit log at the time the complaint occurs, as well as charted by color. There is usually a much shorter time frame for performing visits as follow-up to complaints. The agency must ensure that the visits are performed as required.

Assigning Supervisory Visits

Supervisory visits can be scheduled by a supervisor or by the scheduling staff. If a supervisor schedules these visits, he or she must work closely with scheduling staff.

It is important that efficiency and time be considered when scheduling supervisory visits to minimize lost time. In addition to considering the deadlines required by various regulations, the staff must consider the times that the employee is scheduled to be in the client's home and the location of the client's home.

First, the staff must consider the employees' schedules. There are generally two types of supervisory visits: one to supervise employee performance and one to obtain feedback from the client and/or family concerning the employee and the care provided. The former

Table 7.5 Supervisory Visit Log

CASE (NAME OF CLIENT OR EMPLOYEE)	DATE VISITED	VISIT PERFORMED BY	REPORT FILED	DATE NEXT VISIT REQ'D
Ada Jones	7/10/87	LDJ	YES	7/24/87

would be scheduled during a visit by the employee; the latter would be made when the employee was not on the premises, to encourage the client and family to speak freely. In either case, the staff must know when the workers to be supervised are in the clients' homes. When a case is due for a supervisory visit, the staff must check with the current schedule to determine when the caregiver will be in the client's home.

The second item to be considered is geography. As in scheduling cases, the location of the client's home is an important consideration. Reducing travel time between clients is the simplest way to lessen the time demands on the supervisory staff. It would be highly inefficient if two different supervisors monitored paraprofessionals who were assigned next door to each other. Thus, case management could be determined geographically as well as individual assignments.

Ideally, the scheduling of visits should allow for the maximum number of visits to be done by one professional on a given day. It is inefficient and inconvenient to have all of an agency's supervisors performing one visit per day. Rather, one professional should be scheduled to perform as many of a day's visits as possible, or cases should be divided geographically between two supervisors.

A problem in scheduling nursing visits is that most agencies have a limited number of professionals who can perform supervisory visits, particularly compared to the number of paraprofessional employees. In addition, nurses and other professionals usually have other demands on their time besides case management, such as performing skilled nursing visits of their own. Therefore, the agency could train nurses to perform thorough visits that take no more time than necessary. The agency might also consider incentive payments for greater productivity.

The scheduling staff may also consider making supervisory visits to aides incidental to reimbursable skilled visits, thereby rendering the visits billable. Scheduling administrative or nonreimbursable functions at the same time as billable visits is one method of minimizing costs. Although many regulations specify minimum requirements for supervision, these visits are frequently allowed at any time prior to the due date, facilitating the scheduling of these visits concurrent with skilled visits. On the morning of a scheduled supervisory visit, the nurse should check the master schedule to ensure that no changes were made—for example, that a substitute was scheduled for the day or that the client was hospitalized.

ANTICIPATING PROBLEMS

Some of the frantic scrambling to cover missed cases or last-minute changes can be avoided by anticipating difficulties and problems. One way is to look at changes in the past. The best indicator of whether a schedule is good or bad is the number of changes that have had to be made on a daily, weekly, or monthly basis to the schedule of each client and each employee.

The scheduling staff should also listen carefully to what clients and caregivers say about the schedule. Although it is not always true, employees who do not have good attendance records may be unhappy with their schedule or may not understand their responsibility as a home care worker. This may be a staffing problem or a training problem. The staff must analyze these changes and be aware of future indications in order to head off problems before they occur.

The staff can also avoid problems by paying attention to the indications of which employees will serve as troubleshooters and which ones should be kept in as constant a schedule as possible. The staff should observe employees for their willingness to take other assignments; they will then know that they can expect good outcomes when asking these workers to fill in.

The scheduling staff may want to maintain a list of permanent substitutes. Some part-time workers may prefer to work on a substitute basis. Some agencies pay a few employees each day to be available to cover a case. Alternatively, the agency could have a rotation of employees on call each day to cover cases as substitutes.

The scheduling staff may find that some employees resist changes in a schedule because they have become attached to a particular client they are currently serving. There is usually a mutual sense of bonding, meaning that the client would also prefer to retain this worker. If this is recognized, the staff can use the opportunity to change the time of service, if necessary, rather than the client–caregiver match.

To help the scheduling staff recognize patterns that indicate problems with the schedule, comprehensive records should be kept and made available (see Chapter 10 for a detailed discussion of documentation). These records should be reviewed periodically for patterns in order to help the staff evaluate the success of various assignments. Noting absenteeism and tardiness from attendance records is helpful in ensuring smooth schedules. For example, if an employee is routinely late, possibly because of a bus schedule, the problem should be discussed with the employee to determine if an earlier bus can be used or if the scheduled time should be made later. The employee needs to understand that the client is awaiting his or her arrival at a designated time and that dependability and timeliness are critical to quality of care.

It is also useful for the scheduling staff to flag on the personnel roster those employees with a history of attendance problems. The staff can then avoid scheduling these employees for high-priority cases. The staff may also institute policies to deter employees from being tardy or missing an assignment without calling to notify the office. Disciplinary measures are usually the last resort of personnel managers. However, they may be the most effective method for consistently poor performers.

Accurate and effective scheduling can be achieved manually. Careful consideration of every aspect of the schedule and an effort to follow through with questions and changes will ensure a smooth scheduling process.

8

Computer-Assisted Scheduling

In home health care trade publications and journals, computer software companies place advertisements for electronic scheduling systems and software. Many computer programs have been written to reduce cumbersome manual practices by automating the assignment of personnel and the production of supporting documentation and cost reports.

In the last several years, the cost of computer equipment and software has decreased, while computer capability for scheduling home care has increased. Cost-effective systems are available to organize the detailed information handled by schedulers and to provide an instant resource for recalling and manipulating information.

Most management information systems are designed to improve operational efficiency. Automation in scheduling can expedite tasks that are most time-consuming and tedious, such as searching through rosters of employees to find a good match for a client. This can offer many advantages in home care. Decreasing the administrative and clerical workload of the home care staff increases job satisfaction. Automation provides a mechanism for tracking cases, to eliminate common scheduling errors and serve as a control. In addition, since many home care agencies use the nursing staff to schedule cases, automating the process allows nurses to spend less time scheduling and more time performing other tasks.

Many of the tasks just described could be accomplished with currently available commercial software packages, many of which have the capability to generate and manipulate lists of names. A scheduling manager with knowledge of basic software packages could set up a system to satisfy many of the agency's information needs. Some of the computer needs of a home health agency, such as payroll and billing, could be subcontracted to an outside computer company.

In this chapter, all aspects of a fully automated scheduling system are described. Depending on the agency's plans for growth, it may or may not be necessary to incorporate all of them in order to develop a workable system. However, growth-oriented agencies should consider the points in this chapter as they automate their scheduling systems.

CHOOSING TO SCHEDULE ELECTRONICALLY

Scheduling home health care, like any business, requires data for recording the details of daily transactions and for providing managers with information necessary for making decisions. Computer systems for home health care scheduling have been designed to perform these functions. In contrast to manual scheduling, computer-assisted scheduling has certain advantages and disadvantages which have an impact on the functioning of the home health care agency. For example, the transition to a new computer system may at first seem more disruptive than helpful, while a few months later, the staff may not believe that they were able to work without it.

The advantages of electronic scheduling are as follows:

1. Automation improves efficiency and productivity. The scheduling staff is freed of time-consuming clerical tasks which can be performed by the computer. More hours of home care for more people can be scheduled more quickly.

2. Computer-generated scheduling systems can be integrated with other automated systems in the agency such as payroll, accounting, and personnel. This raises productivity and reduces personnel requirements. The agency's operations are more efficient and speedier.

3. Many systems have built-in quality controls that help the staff to ensure that all cases are covered.

There are also disadvantages in converting to automated scheduling:

1. The transition from a manual to a computer-assisted scheduling system is disruptive. Sometimes it takes months for a new system to be fully functional.

2. While software has been developed for scheduling home care, an agency-specific requirements analysis must be performed when this software is designed. Because of the special problems and requirements of home health care scheduling (as

opposed to database and spreadsheet requirements), home health care agencies are less likely to benefit from off-the-shelf software packages. The need for customized software obviously raises the cost.

3. Staff members using computers for any operation are dependent on the computer to perform their tasks. Systems can malfunction. It can be frustrating to experience down time on a computer and to accomplish the work when the computer is not functioning.

4. There can be hidden costs in implementing a new computer system. In addition to the cost of the software and hardware, an agency may need to pay for training, technical assistance, and supplies. Further, physical system preparations may require electrical and floor plan work in the office.

DEVELOPING A COMPUTER-BASED SYSTEM

Home care schedulers considering the development of a computer-based scheduling system should carefully review the agency's requirements for automation so that a system can be selected that is suitable for the agency's purposes. Schedulers will have more confidence in a system that they believe fits their needs. The system must work well technically to ensure that schedulers use it, it must be developed in the most cost-effective and efficient manner, and it must be flexible. Accurate information makes the system worthwhile. Flexibility ensures that more than one person can use the system at one time.

Feasibility

The home care schedulers must first assess the feasibility of the potential system. This assessment should cover the system's technical, operational, and economic aspects.

Technical feasibility refers to the existence of technical capabilities, such as programs, hardware, and software, for performing the specific tasks required by the scheduler. *Operational feasibility* refers to the impact that the new system will have on the home health care agency as a whole and the behavior of the schedulers who will use it. The implementation of the new system requires that the schedulers do not undermine the automation process by physically abusing the system, avoiding it, or blaming it for their own errors. Lastly, the *economic feasibility* of the system should be assessed to ensure that the benefits derived from its development and use outweigh the costs.

Anticipated Growth

Once the feasibility of automating has been established, the next step is to analyze the structure, type, and growth pattern of the agency. The size of the agency and its expected growth pattern will determine the size of the investment that can be made in the electronic system. If the clients of the agency are sponsored by government institutions, so that government regulations may require greater tracking of cases than private paying citizens, this will have an impact on system design. Some systems can expand with an agency's caseload; others are designed to handle a fixed volume of information.

Reporting

An agency must determine what the computer should produce. Reports or other output from the system should tell the schedulers what they need to know regarding a particular item without providing superfluous information. Reports need to be easily understood for the information to be useful. Content, therefore, is the key to scheduling decisions. Form and layout, or the way reports are presented to users, should also be considered when designing a computer-based scheduling system. Reports can be summarized or detailed expressions of the information, and can be represented either numerically, graphically, or in words. The layout affects the value of the report to the scheduler. Crowded, confusing data on a report will only make information management more cumbersome. Report titles and dates, for example, should be listed on every page of the report. The most important information should be easily found. The report should read from left to right and from top to bottom for ease of reading. Full spellings of words should be used whenever possible.

A computer system can organize data to generate many types of reports, records, and other materials. An agency must decide what it needs from a computer system, whether it be cost reports, schedules, productivity analyses, or blank matrices. The funding sources of clients served by the agency, or those with whom the agency contracts, may therefore be important in selecting software. Information should be organized according to the formats specified in the regulations of the various funding sources.

Tasks to Be Performed

The tasks that the schedulers perform have a strong impact on the development of the computer system. The nature of these tasks influences the design of the input of data. By analyzing these tasks, the home care agency can ensure that a computer system does what it is supposed to do.

For example, do the schedulers assign employees to work on weekends? If so, the computer system screen should have a field in which this information can be recorded. Do the schedulers track employee attendance at seminars on various health-related issues? If so, the system must be developed to monitor this activity. Do schedulers work after hours at home on an on-call basis? If access to the computer is desired by these schedulers, the system should be designed to accommodate modern communication modems.

It is useful to list in a matrix each of the agency's scheduling needs by scheduler's task and corresponding computer system requirements. The agency's management staff must then prioritize the items on the list. Applying the principles of cost-benefit analysis, management must determine at which point the benefit of the additional scheduling capability no longer justifies the additional cost. This technique will encourage the schedulers to prioritize their needs in a computer system and maximize the resources of the agency.

As has been stated, the computer is a labor-saving tool to be employed by the scheduling staff. Therefore, it is important that the agency identify specific scheduling problems under the current system so that the new system can address these issues. For example, if the agency provides home support services, such as homemaker and chore services, and has many cases that entail biweekly care, the staff may be creating a new schedule every week, instead of transferring previous assignments to a new schedule. In this case, the agency would need a system that can generate a primary schedule for the first week and an alternate schedule for the second week, representing a 2-week series of assignments.

Purchase

Once an agency is fully aware of its own needs for scheduling software, it can begin to evaluate the products that computer vendors offer. In this assessment, the agency should compare the features of the system offered by each vendor to its own recently completed needs analysis. It should also consider the ease of use and the postinstallation training and service provided.

Some software companies do provide unique features, however, or offer to tailor their software to the particular needs of the agency. Features unique to a software package might be the number of users who can access the software at one time; the type of hardware on which the system would run; and the types of hardware and software with which it would be compatible. An example of a unique feature that might meet an agency's needs is the ability to run the system from two different offices. One software company offers the ability to process financial applications in one location and operational functions such as scheduling in another.

Vendors that offer customized software should be evaluated carefully. The agency must know exactly what it needs for scheduling and other operations. Some vendors specialize in software for scheduling, but not necessarily in scheduling home care services, where numerous variables must be considered. Unfortunately, not all computer programmers understand the complexity and intricacy of home care. The better and more completely a home health care scheduler understands the tasks to be performed and the other requirements of the agency, the better the evaluation of competing software and computer systems.

In comparing the types of software available, an agency may

consider how easy a software product is to use. The term *user friendly* implies that a system is easy to use for people not trained in computer technology. However, user-friendly programs are not always the best programs. The scheduler should take into account the computer experience and aptitude of the scheduling staff before selecting a software or system design simply because it is user friendly. An agency should look for on-screen prompts, help menus, or simple written guides that will assist the scheduler to become an adept operator. Extensive technical documentation and work manuals should be avoided.

The agency should also evaluate the computer vendor. Will the company work with the agency to solve problems after the system is installed? Some companies offer training, technical assistance, and consulting services, along with installation. These services may be quite important to an agency.

Integration

The agency should examine the ability of the computer-based scheduling system to be integrated with existing computer systems in the agency. The functions likely to be automated include payroll, accounting, personnel administration, and tax records. While the agency may choose to keep its financial and operational functions separate, it is prudent to select software compatible with existing hardware and to ensure that the data input during the scheduling phase can be transferred for use in accounting and billing.

Security

Since scheduling software is usually joined with other automated functions of a home care agency, a well-designed computer system should include security controls. The agency should be able to designate which staff members can access which portions of an agency's operations. If accounting and scheduling functions are automated on the same computer, it is necessary to have a system that limits access to scheduling functions and restricts other operations. In addition to being good business practice, this safeguard protects the database from an error by an untrained operator who inadvertently accesses the wrong computer function. The computer system should have backup procedures that guard against physical or electrical damage to the system. The schedulers should copy all the information in the system to floppy diskettes or magnetic tape for off-site storage.

Implementation

Once the computer system has been designed or selected, the agency must consider its implementation strategy as it prepares to use the system. The users of the new system will need to be trained to operate the system and briefed on interpreting the output. Users are not limited to the schedulers who actually sit at the terminal and schedule the patients. They also include individuals in the agency who use the data in the system, such as the nursing or personnel staff, who may maintain data in permanent master files. These individuals must know how their interaction with the system affects its other functions. This will ensure the smooth functioning of the system.

The implementation of the computer-assisted scheduling system should be done with a minimum of disruption to the scheduling operation. Timing of the implementation is crucial. There are several ways that the home health agency can shift to the automated system. Computer-based scheduling can be phased in gradually over time, allowing the scheduling staff the opportunity to spot potential problems and errors before their impact affects the agency. Alternatively, the computer system can be implemented in a pilot program. This entails using the computer to perform some of the scheduling transactions, while the remainder are done manually during the transition period. When it is clear that the electronic system works well, the rest of the scheduling operations can be converted to the computer. As another alternative, the agency can implement a new system immediately. Although this involves the risk of a malfunction, all-at-once implementation does force the scheduling staff to use the new system and adapt quickly to it.

Another necessary step in moving from a manual to a computer-assisted scheduling system is to ensure that the staff does not duplicate its effort by continuing to schedule manually and then repeating the work on the computer system. The staff should ensure that the forms and other paperwork used in scheduling are revised to match the data required for the computer. The information collected in a nursing assessment, for example, should match the prompts given on the computer so that the information doesn't have to be collected again at a later time.

Evaluation

Once a computer-based scheduling system has been installed and seems to be operating effectively, the scheduling manager must monitor the system to ensure that it continues to do so. The manager should watch for improvements and adaptations that could be made to the system, correct errors in the functioning of the system (or alert the technicians to malfunctions), and train new users in its operation.

COMPUTERIZED OPERATIONS

The specific scheduling functions that an electronic system can perform vary, depending on the needs of the agency and the type of system purchased. In general, however, computer systems used for scheduling home care perform three essential functions. First, they automate tedious clerical tasks, such as documenting which employees covered which cases. Second, they provide schedulers with information needed for decision making. For instance, if a scheduler wishes to assign an employee to a 2-hour case at a particular client's home, the computer will provide the information necessary to determine whether that assignment is feasible and efficient. Third, computer systems provide information that serve as controls for the scheduling staff, such as lists that enable the staff to spot cases that have not been covered or see that two cases have been assigned to the same employee at the same time. Ultimately, the success of a computer system for a home care agency depends on the functions the computer is programmed to perform and the ability of the scheduling staff to learn the system and take advantage of its capabilities.

Capabilities

A computer is a tool that schedulers use to facilitate their job of scheduling home health care workers. As a tool, the computer is capable of performing a variety of functions and operations. Those operations and the tasks they help perform for the schedulers will be described here.

Transactions

The act of scheduling a home care worker to work for 8 hours at a client's home can be considered a transaction, similar to a sales order in a warehouse for a manufacturing firm. For each transaction, certain data must be maintained which affect the transaction. For example, the data relevant to scheduling a caregiver include the client's name, address, number of hours of service required, type of service required (homemaker services or skilled nursing), and time when the service is needed. The computer system helps the manufacturing company track this information; computers can perform the same function for home health agencies.

Classifying

The computer can assist schedulers by manipulating data in various ways. For example, the computer can classify data or group it according to some characteristic, such as type of caregiver or clients with uncovered cases.

Another example of the computer's function of classifying data is in distinguishing between different types of assignments. It is essential that the scheduling staff be able to see which assignments are permanent and which are temporary or substitutes. The permanent assignments should remain in the database for each time that assignment must be scheduled (such as every Monday, Wednesday, and Friday morning). The temporarily scheduled assignments should reappear as open or unassigned visits in the following week's schedule. Substitutions should appear only on the appropriate schedule, and the computer should revert to the permanent assignment the following week.

Classification of employees by the times they are available to work is another use of the computer's ability. If an employee's schedule is going to be viewed, the staff available for nighttime or weekend assignments could have a code inserted to indicate this. Staff could then tell at a glance which employees were available when attempting to cover a weekend case.

Sorting

The computer is able not only to classify or group data but also to sort it. During the sorting process, the data are arranged in an order or sequence based on a particular piece of data. For example, when a scheduler is looking for an employee to cover a given case, the computer can sort by zip code to determine which employees live closest to the client. In this way, the sorting function of the computer expedites the scheduling task.

Lists can be generated and printed according to desired criteria which will be helpful to the scheduling manager. For example, after sorting the list of employees by zip code, the computer can tabulate the number of employees living in each area. The scheduling manager can then use this information to manage the agency more efficiently. For example, it will be clear whether the agency has obtained most of its employees from certain zip codes and very few from others.

The computer is a convenient place to store information about clients, employees, and transactions. The computer system can be designed to search the storage areas for particular pieces of information or for entire client or employee files. The storage capability of the computer minimizes space requirements. Data can be stored on tapes or diskettes for reference at a later date. The search capabilities of the computer save the scheduler time that would otherwise be spent looking in file cabinets.

Searching

To improve efficiency through automation, the computer should not only be a record keeper but should also perform the scheduling tasks of a manual system more rapidly. The computer's capacity to search the database is a function that is most important for increasing efficiency. The scheduling staff can use the search function to precisely match clients and caregivers. The system should be able to search for specific employees by skill level, location, or availability, and even by personal factors such as smoking. Depending on the particular software, the computer could then generate a list of employees who would be a good match or could automatically assign the employees to cases.

A feature of a good scheduling system is the ability to view scheduling from either the employee's perspective, the client's perspective, or both, depending on the agency's needs. For an agency with a large caseload involving different categories of home care workers, a system that allows a view of the schedule from the employee's and client's perspectives is most important. This simply means that the computer can organize the data for viewing by employee or by client. A scheduler could then view a client's schedule to see what services must be assigned or an employee's schedule to see how many assignments that employee already has for the week.

To conduct search operations, the agency must determine the factors to be used in matching clients and employees. That is, the agency must determine the criteria for the matching process, both the actual variables to be used (such as geography, type of care needed, and smoking habits) and the restrictiveness of the selection. In addition, an electronic operation for matching can be either client driven or employee driven. This means that the system can be designed to search for employees who match client criteria (client driven) or clients who match employee criteria (employee driven). Given the need for an agency to satisfy the requirements of the client, client-driven matching may provide more flexibility for covering cases. The more variables that can be matched for each client, the better the fit of caregiver to client may be. However, the selection of employees who would match all of these criteria severely restricts the scheduler's options of who can be assigned. A scheduler may prefer to use some variables as mandatory matching criteria and others as optional criteria in narrowing down a large list of possible caregivers.

Files

Scheduling involves maintaining written files on each client and employee. Each file contains information relevant to the scheduling process. As the information in the file changes, the file must be updated to reflect the new information.

Computer-assisted scheduling works in a similar manner. Master files on employees and clients are permanent collections of information which are crucial to successful scheduling. If the data in the master files are not current, the files are of little use to the scheduler. This necessitates constant updating of the master files. Files provide a structured and logical method of accessing and processing the data.

Updating

A most important feature of electronic scheduling is the ability to change information once it has been input. In scheduling, the staff must be able to go back to an employee's schedule, a client's schedule, or a master schedule to indicate a no-show, a substitution, a cancellation, or other changes. Otherwise, the staff would not be able to input the information until the entire schedule had been created and carried out, which would make the computer no more than a file or word processor.

Processing

The computer system's method or mode of processing files and handling transactions is related to the way the scheduler handles transactions. In a home care scheduling environment, the scheduler inputs transactions (scheduling assignments) directly into the computer system through a terminal. Therefore, for home health care scheduling, the computer system must necessarily be on-line. That is, the data input by the scheduler enter the system directly, and the results (output) are sent back to the scheduler. There is no intermediate step of data key punching on cards or preparation of magnetic tape.

Computer-assisted home care scheduling must be on-line because the response time required by the scheduler is very important. The scheduler requires that response time of the computer be virtually instantaneous. The scheduler must know within seconds whether a given employee is free to work on a particular day or hour or whether a client has coverage at a particular time.

In addition to being on-line, a computerized scheduling system must be able to process in real time. That is, it must be capable of receiving input, processing it, and returning the output to the scheduler in time to make decisions based on this output. The results directly affect the scheduling task at hand. For example, suppose the scheduler has queried the computer regarding the schedule of a certain aide and has received the output (the computer screen shows the aide's schedule for that week). The scheduler sees that the aide is free during the time slot under consideration and schedules the aide for the case. This computer-assisted scheduling assignment has taken place in real time.

Flexibility

Another important feature is the ability to use the information in the database for functions other than scheduling. Most electronic scheduling systems are tied to other automated functions, such as accounting or general ledger, payroll, and cost reporting. Any computer system should be able to take its database (i.e., the schedules) and transfer it to the next automated function, so that data do not have to be keyed in at every step of an agency's operations.

Some of the most important features of a good computer system are those that can be used as controls. Schedulers should be able to view the master schedule to see what visits have not been assigned. A system could have a symbol (such as an asterisk or a number) as a flag that is removed from an assignment when it is filled, so that the staff could look at a master schedule and see what symbols remain. In a more sophisticated system, the computer should be able to generate reports that list unassigned or overlapping visits, so that the staff could print a document on a regular schedule throughout the day to see what cases remain to be covered.

Staff Commitment

The most important tenet of electronic scheduling, regardless of the type of system employed, is that the computer will only perform as much as the scheduler asks it to do. A common difficulty experienced by home health agencies implementing computer systems is the resistance of the staff to learning and using the computer. More experienced staff members may not trust the computer, mistakenly believing that it will require a lot of unnecessary work since they may already have excellent assignments in mind. Some staff members worry about making mistakes, fearing that they will ruin the new computer. Others simply are unwilling to take the time to train and learn the new system.

Regardless of the varied features offered by a computer system, the system cannot be effective unless the scheduling staff agrees to use and support it. Using a system halfheartedly not only fails to maximize the advantages of the system but probably makes the process more difficult or time-consuming than manual scheduling would be.

It is important for the staff to realize that the computer will not schedule for them. Electronic scheduling is not computer scheduling, it is computer-assisted scheduling. The time and personnel variables that are considered when scheduling home care preclude the use of the computerized scheduling that is effective for planning school bus routes or airline flights.

The computer system should instead be designed to allow the scheduling staff to access quickly and easily the information they need to make scheduling decisions. The staff should not expect the computer to make scheduling assignments, but rather to provide them with a list of all possible employees who can be matched. The staff decides who should be assigned and when the time of a case should be changed to make the best possible match of employee to client.

The functions that the computer can perform for the scheduling staff vary. The system can be used to print out open scheduling matrices that show every client and visit to be scheduled. The client and times of service are input, the matrix is printed, and the scheduling staff manually fills in the spaces with the names of employees to be assigned. This type of system simply organizes the information regarding visits and provides the tools for the staff to schedule each assignment manually.

A more sophisticated computer system can perform the initial steps of scheduling, that is, narrowing down the pool of employees who can be assigned to cases. Systems that can search the computer and match clients and employees can greatly reduce the work involved in scheduling and can work much more quickly than the scheduling staff. Often a system that simply generates information about clients and staff which must then be put into a matrix manually is not worth the cost of installation. The object of computer-assisted scheduling is to simplify and expedite the work of the scheduling staff.

Daily Use

The mechanics of computer-assisted scheduling depend on the particular type of system and its features. However, it is recognized that the scheduling staff in most agencies is under daily pressure from ringing telephones and the need to cover every case. Some simple guidelines can help the schedulers ensure that they use their computer system effectively and minimize mistakes.

The best way to minimize mistakes and maximize the use and efficiency of the system is to ensure that the staff knows how to use the computer properly. This cannot be overemphasized. Training in the use of the system when it is first installed is obviously necessary, but the training should not end there. When new employees are hired, more training in the system is needed. Sometimes the present users of a system tend to change procedures in using the computer and pass this misinformation along to new schedulers. After a while, no one is really sure how to use the system the way it was intended, or what the implications are of making small changes in the way the computer is used.

To avoid this problem, written procedural documentation should be part of all new training for new staff. This documentation can be in the form of a manual, either written by the vendor that sold the agency the system or written by agency staff. Clear, accurate computer system documentation ensures that everyone is using the system correctly.

Agency managers should ensure that all members of a scheduling staff use the computer. When some staff members do and others do not, the information in the computer becomes incomplete. The computer system is an information resource. Decisions are made by schedulers based on the information retrieved from it. Computer-based scheduling can be successful only when the information in it is up-to-date and accurate. Thus, every assignment and every change must be input into the computer, even when case coverage can be arranged immediately without the computer's assistance.

The scheduling staff often performs mental matching and scheduling. Schedulers know their employees, their clients, and the geography of the community, and can sometimes assign people easily by making personal decisions. However, it is critical that all information be input into the computer. Neglecting to input scheduling information into the computer when on a computer-based system can have serious consequences. Cases can be overlooked or two caregivers can be assigned to the same case because it shows up in the computer as an unassigned visit. Employees can be scheduled for two cases at the same time.

To facilitate daily use of the computer-assisted scheduling system, reports can be produced that summarize key pieces of information for the schedulers. For example, at the beginning of each day, the scheduler can generate a report of workers with available hours, or of clients who want home health care but have not yet been scheduled for service. This report then becomes a reference document from which the schedulers can work. For management analysis at the end of the day, the agency administrator or personnel manager can monitor the number of open cases scheduled.

Reports can also be generated to assist the scheduler with corollary duties not directly related to scheduling, such as tracking workers' compliance with state regulations and training requirements, as well as performance and salary reviews. These reports can be sorted by month so that the scheduler has the list of workers who will need inoculations, physical examinations, performance evaluations, or in-service training.

In addition, computer-based scheduling is frequently the basis of computerized accounting and billing. The schedule becomes the basis of payroll and then billing to clients. Therefore, it is important that the schedule be accurate before payroll and billing functions are initiated in order to avoid perpetuating inaccurate information or making payroll errors and to reduce work in accounting. For example, a 4-hour case that was not updated to reflect a cancellation becomes a mistake in payroll when the aide is paid and a mistake in billing when the client is billed for services.

Information needs to be shared among all the schedulers, as well as among the payroll and bill staff. They cannot know whom to bill or whom to pay unless they know the schedule for the previous pay period. Any computer system is dependent upon sharing of information and the availability of information to all by way of a continuously updated computer system.

A number of steps can be taken to assist the staff in keeping the computer up-to-date. First, client intake should be performed on the computer. Inputting patient information when the referral is received will save an additional step when the patient is first scheduled. Similarly, records for new employees should be placed in the computer immediately. The hours and days they are willing to work would also be entered to show availability.

It is also recommended that the scheduling staff have a computer terminal or keyboard within reach while they are at their desks or on the telephone. When a hospital discharge planner, employee, or client calls in with a scheduling problem, a referral, or a scheduling change, the scheduler can work directly on the computer, pulling up the appropriate record or schedule to make the change or inputting the new referral.

It is also important that each scheduling person be responsible for inputting data on the computer. Instead of assigning support staff to enter information, the staff should be encouraged to work directly on the system. This reduces duplication of effort, as well as lag time between a change and the time when the information is put into the computer.

Lag time cannot be avoided when schedulers are on call in their homes and must wait until the next workday morning to update the computer. In these instances, it is important to make updating of the computer the first priority before any new scheduling takes place. This can be difficult when the phones are ringing and the daily routine of scheduling has begun. However, the staff must ensure that information on the system stays current to avoid serious mistakes.

During the design of the computer system, controls will have been designed such as reports showing clients without aides, clients with two aides at the same time, or aides who have been scheduled for two assignments at once. The staff should consider when to use certain control functions. That is, at which point in the daily routine do these reports work best to ensure smooth operation of the scheduling process?

The staff should decide carefully when to close out the current period's computerized schedule, thereby releasing these data to the accounting staff, and move to scheduling cases for the following period. Once the closeout time has been selected (and it should mark consistently equal periods), the staff should no longer enter that period's file and change any assignments. Ideally, the closeout is at a logical breaking time, such as Friday evening, or whichever day is the end of the agency's scheduling period. However, the staff needs to begin scheduling for the weekend or the following week, so the closeout must be conducted earlier in the day or the previous evening.

It is also important to note that computers are fallible. Although many systems have internal safeguards, in others information can be lost at the touch of the wrong button or with a surge of power in the electrical circuits. For this reason, all records required by law should be backed up by either a hard copy (printed out by the computer) or copies made on computer diskettes.

To support daily operations, it is a good idea for staff members to have a notebook at their side when scheduling with a computer. They should be proficient enough on the computer to handle telephoned changes and requests directly. However, some cases require follow-up or written documentation. A dated notation would serve as a reminder that the case requires additional action.

One additional issue that should be recognized is confidentiality. A client's right to privacy is stated in the laws of many states. The same confidentiality that is afforded written files must apply to computer files. Each computer file should be assigned a number by which it can be referenced. When a routine review of client care files is conducted by the agency, the client's privacy can remain protected.

9

Monitoring and Schedule Adjustment

Home care agencies monitor services to meet requirements for supervision and to obtain needed feedback on quality of care. In scheduling, monitoring provides the opportunity for appraising the success or quality of the schedule. Through monitoring, staff members also oversee problem cases, such as those with high worker turnover, or investigate complaints about the schedule or other aspect of the agency's services.

The monitor, or case supervisor, is the evaluator of the schedule. The indicators by which the quality of a schedule are measured include the condition of the client, client satisfaction with the employee and the services provided, continuity of care, employee's work performance, and level of job satisfaction.

Careful monitoring of each case by nursing and scheduling supervisors is also necessary for providing support and reassurance to clients, families, and the employees who are scheduled. Because of changes in health care financing and early hospital discharge practices, clients cared for at home may be quite ill. This creates anxiety in the client and family and more pressures for the employee assigned to the case. The establishment of effective systems for monitoring ensures that assignments are successful and rewarding and that any problems in the schedule are resolved without disruption to the client or services.

Monitoring a schedule involves clinical and administrative case supervision. Clinical supervision is a function of the agency's nursing staff or other legally designated professionals and is ultimately the responsibility of the director of patient care. This function is critical to the scheduling process, since the schedule must be adjusted if monitoring reveals that an assignment could be improved. The scope of clinical services goes beyond the discussion in this context. Only those aspects of clinical supervision relevant to scheduling are discussed. Specifically, clinical supervision related to scheduling includes:

1. Monitoring the condition of the client.
2. Ensuring that the treatment plan is adequate and appropriate for meeting the client's needs.
3. Evaluating whether the schedule (including times of service and category of home care worker assigned) is suitable.

4. Ensuring that the requirements of the treatment plan are met and that the client progresses toward the treatment goals.

5. Ensuring that the match between client and caregiver is successful, so that there are fewer changes of personnel.

6. Providing general support to the employee assigned, answering questions, or demonstrating techniques.

7. Ensuring that the client adjusts to the transition from hospital to home-based care.

Administrative supervision is an important component of monitoring a schedule. A schedule cannot be effective unless agency standards for personnel and services are upheld. Administrative supervision related to scheduling includes:

1. Ensuring that the agency's work standards are met.

2. Monitoring whether employees arrive on time, perform all required tasks, and stay the full time scheduled.

3. Ensuring that a schedule is as efficient as possible.

4. Ensuring that, whenever possible, the preferences of clients and employees are accommodated.

TYPES OF MONITORING

Most systems for administrative and clinical supervision include on-site supervision through home visits as well as off-site supervision, which includes review of records, telephone communication, and peer review.

On-Site Supervision

The goals of monitoring individual assignments through visits to clients' homes include:

1. Monitoring the condition of the client to ensure that the treatment goals in the plan of care are appropriate.

2. Monitoring the work performance of the employee to ensure

that care is provided as stated in the treatment plan and that the work standards of the agency are met.

3. Monitoring the quality of the match between client and employee to determine whether a permanent assignment that ensures continuity of care has been achieved.

Agencies frequently rotate home supervision among supervisory staff members. To ensure uniformity, written policies and procedures for conducting supervisory visits are useful. Steps in monitoring an assignment in the home include:

1. Examining the client and environment.
2. Checking the client activity sheet to see that all tasks have been completed.
3. Observing how the employee and client interact.
4. Evaluating the work performance of the employee, including adequacy of safety measures observed.
5. Talking to the client about the worker's performance.
6. Discussing the assignment with the worker.
7. Documenting the findings of the visit, using a checklist or other tool, so that information can be communicated from the clinical to the scheduling staff.

In the most productive home visits, supervising staff members assess the condition of the client, the completion of required tasks, the quality of the work, the personal performance of the employee, and the success of the personnel assignment. This additional intervention assures quality and helps the client progress along the treatment plan. In addition, employees like to be measured against agency standards and like the recognition and support provided by a supervisor.

Client Condition
A major aspect of case supervision particularly important for scheduling is evaluating the condition of the client. The nurse or therapist must determine how the medical and support service needs of the client may have changed, ensuring that activities in the treatment plan and the service schedule are appropriate.

A useful method of evaluating changes in the client's condition is to refer to the original assessment when examining the client, comparing the information on the nursing assessment to current observations. For example, a client recuperating at home following surgery for a hip replacement would likely have been assessed as requiring total help with ambulation. However, after a while, the client may be able to walk with continuous support and then with supervision. The nurse or therapist would update the care plan as the client improved or notify the physician if the client failed to progress as anticipated.

In addition to talking with the client and performing an examination, it is useful to discuss the client's condition with the employee. Since the employee has viewed the client regularly over a period of time, he or she may have noted changes in the client's condition not evident to family and friends. For example, the work may have noted a subtle change in the client's physical condition, attitude, or motivation. These observations would be important to bring to the attention of a supervisor. Although a change may only signal a bad day for the client, it may be indicative of something more serious, such as toxicity from medication or an underlying medical complication.

Input from the family about the client's condition and service needs is also beneficial. Many clients are cared for by family members when an agency is not providing service. They can provide feedback about the condition of the client at those times.

A client's condition while receiving home care can decline or improve. This fact should not be overlooked. Home care services are provided to meet the needs of clients while encouraging them to remain as independent as possible. Any improvement may require modifications of treatment plans to encourage the clients to do more things for themselves. For example, clients who require assistance with eating should be encouraged as their condition improves to eat independently. It would be appropriate to update the treatment plan from "assistance with feeding" to "encouragement to feed himself."

As a client improves, supervising nurses may be required to evaluate the client's need for continuing service. Although privately paying clients can receive service indefinitely, as can others under different funding arrangements, Medicare regulations specify that clients require intermittent skilled nursing care to continue with services. This must be appropriately documented and cannot be overlooked when evaluating a client's condition.

Completion of Tasks

The supervisory staff must also determine whether the requirements of the treatment plan and schedule are met by the personnel assigned. The supervisor may check the activity sheet posted in the client's home and inspect the client and environment to see if tasks have been completed.

For example, if the activity sheet specifies personal care tasks like bathing, shaving, and dressing a male client, the supervisor may check to see if the client is dressed properly and completely, appears comfortable, and has been washed and shaven. If the activity sheet specifies homemaker or chore tasks, the supervisor may evaluate the cleanliness of the environment and, if shopping is required, check to see that the client has appropriate and sufficient food in the house.

Supervisors can also check for the completion of tasks while evaluating the condition of the client. If an activity sheet specifies skin care, for example, the supervisor can check the client's skin for areas of breakdown to see if the client has been receiving appropriate care.

Quality of the Work

The quality of the employee's work is evaluated to ensure that the service provided meets the agency's work standards. Most important is whether scheduled tasks are being properly done and recorded. It is fraudulent to bill for services under federal funding mechanisms if hours of service and work accomplished are not properly recorded.

High-quality work means that all procedures are done well and that any required follow-up is performed. For example, if injections are provided by a licensed practical nurse, a supervisor should check the sanitary conditions in the work area and ensure that the employee disposes of used needles and other materials carefully. Similarly, the nurse should check to see that equipment used for physical or occupational therapy is kept clean and stored properly.

For paraprofessional staff, supervisors should pay special attention to the home environment. If the caregiver is responsible for preparing meals for the client, the nurse might check to see if the kitchen is clean and the stove free of spilled foods. Food in the refrigerator might be checked for freshness and proper storage.

In addition to checking the quality of individual tasks, supervisory staff members should ensure that the agency's policies and procedures are being followed. Compliance with policies such as those on eating meals or making personal telephone calls is important, as an agency's employees are its representatives in the clients' homes. Supervisors can gather information regarding the quality of service provided by speaking with the client about work performance.

Personal Performance

The personal performance of the employee is important to note for personnel files, as well as to ensure quality and continuity of care. This factor is particularly important when assigning workers to a schedule. One aspect of personal performance is the appearance and presentation of the employee. Information about the employee's appearance, personality, and attentiveness is useful in making future assignments. Whether an employee is wearing a uniform and is well groomed at the time of the visit should be noted, as well as more subtle factors such as the tone with which the employee addresses the client.

Administrative issues related to the schedule can also be monitored during home visits. The supervising nurse can spot check an employee's reliability or timeliness by arriving at the client's home at exactly the time the employee is scheduled to be there. Conversely, arriving at the end of an assignment might reveal whether an employee stays the full time.

It is also helpful for the supervisor to ask the client his or her opinion of the quality of the service provided. Whether or not the client thinks the employee is reliable, motivated, and dependable should be kept in mind when assigning the employee to future cases.

Personnel Assignment

The home visit allows the supervising nurse to evaluate the relationship between the client and caregiver. The quality of the match is an important aspect of the schedule. The supervisor might consider the following: Do the client and employee appear comfortable with each other? Is there rapport between them? Does the client speak highly of the caregiver? Does the aide seem enthusiastic about the assignment? The client–employee relationship is especially important for continuity of care, as a successful match reduces worker turnover. Problems with a personnel assignment should be identified early to ensure that an assignment can be changed promptly if necessary.

Off-Site Supervision

Much monitoring and supervision takes place in the agency office, rather than in the clients' homes. Important aspects of monitoring are the ongoing review of clinical records, peer review, contact by telephone, and informal contact with clients and employees.

Review of Documentation
The documentation maintained on all aspects of a case reveals many clues regarding the adequacy of the schedule. The routine review of patient care records is a practice required by law in many states. However, this review must occur as part of monitoring a schedule to ensure that all information regarding a client's condition is noted and acted upon. For example, an agency may use time cards and activity sheets for employees to note observations about changes in a client's condition or to document why certain tasks could not be completed. These notations, which become part of the clinical record, should be reviewed regularly by the supervisory staff.

Personnel records are also useful for monitoring. Attendance records, for example, are helpful for determining the reliability of the employee and the continuity of care for the client. Late arrivals, no-shows, and other absences shown on the attendance record can indicate dissatisfaction with an assignment. This information, as well as changes in personnel that indicate high worker turnover, are useful in assessing the success of an assignment.

Peer Review
Another means of monitoring individual assignments is peer review. An employee might unintentionally provide clues to quality

of care that may not be directly communicated to a supervising nurse by a client. For example, when a substitute is sent to cover a case, he or she may report to the scheduling staff that the client thinks the regular caregiver is excellent and is anxious for this person to return from vacation. Alternatively, a client may tell a regular caregiver, "I'm glad you're back; that substitute did not do many of the tasks on the activity sheet." These comments can aid the supervisory staff in ensuring that the work is performed in accordance with agency standards.

Employees may also provide information regarding their peers when a client is served by more than one caregiver. If clients are dissatisfied with one employee or with the times or type of service received, they may express their feelings to one of the home care workers with whom they feel closest. If this information is communicated to the scheduling staff, they can investigate the client's concerns and adjust the schedule accordingly.

Telephone Contact
Ongoing telephone contact between the agency, the employees, and the clients is useful for monitoring the success of an assignment. The scheduler should make a point of following up once assignments have been made. He or she can phone the client or family to check up on the work performance of the aide. In addition, this person can note calls that come in from clients with praise or concerns, or from employees with questions or feedback.

Informal Communication
Feedback through informal contact between the staff and the home care workers provides valuable information regarding the success of a schedule. For example, if employees come to the agency's office to pick up paychecks or drop off time cards, they may casually mention their thoughts on how an assignment is working out, whether their own assignment or one of a peer. An employee may tell the staff how much she enjoys working with a particular client: "Mr. Albert has the most interesting stories to tell about the past. I think he likes having someone to talk to." An employee may also indicate dissatisfaction with an assignment: "I am really having a hard time with Mrs. Cone. Nothing I do seems to be good enough for her." The staff should be alerted immediately to a potential problem in this assignment.

ORGANIZING A SYSTEM OF MONITORING

Regulatory requirements and the importance of monitoring for evaluating the schedule require that the staff plan supervision and evaluation carefully. Particularly important issues are how frequently monitoring will occur, which staff members have monitoring responsibilities, and how supervisory visits will be scheduled.

Frequency

The method and frequency of clinical supervision are determined in part by funding regulations and state laws. In-home supervision occurs during the initial service visit to demonstrate and instruct the home care worker in the treatment and care to be provided. Subsequent visits occur to monitor and evaluate the condition of the client and the quality of care the employee is providing.

Home visits are usually conducted soon after service is initiated. The specific time frame in which the visits must be conducted depends on the payment mechanism and state law. For a Medicaid case in New York, for example, the initial visit must occur within 5 days.

Follow-up supervisory visits occur on an ongoing basis for as long as the case remains active. The frequency of follow-up visits depends on the level of care being provided (e.g., professional, home health aide, personal care aide) in addition to the payment source. The agency must ensure compliance with all applicable legislative requirements in scheduling these visits, determining how the time limits for visits are calculated in its locality.

State and federal regulations for Medicare and Medicaid programs require formal, on-site supervision for paraprofessional and professional home health workers. Agencies delivering services reimbursable by Medicare must, by federal statute, send a nurse once every 2 weeks to the client's home to observe home health aides directly and discuss their work with the client. Although regulations governing Medicaid cases differ under the laws of each state, requirements for on-site supervisory visits range from a visit every 2 weeks to one every 60 to 90 days.

The frequency of clinical supervision for clients paying privately for services may also be regulated by state law. Some state laws simply specify that any home care client must be visited by a supervising nurse as frequently as required for updating the care plan. Many agencies find a visit no less frequently than every 6 months to be appropriate.

In contrast, administrative supervision is ongoing and occurs as frequently as necessary to ensure quality of care and to keep assignments running smoothly and efficiently. Problem cases, such as those involving high worker turnover, are monitored especially closely, and complaint investigations usually require immediate attention.

Within the regulatory requirements for clinical supervision, the frequency and intensity with which an agency monitors its cases are discretionary. An agency might want to supervise and monitor more frequently than required to get a clear, ongoing picture of the success of a schedule, as well as to catch problems early. However, the cost of this monitoring should not be overlooked.

When creating a system for monitoring, it is important to note that home care workers tend to be quite independent. Many of them choose to work in home care because, in comparison to institutional care, home care seems to offer more responsibility and a feeling of being one's own boss. To encourage employees' sense of confidence and worth while ensuring that a schedule is successful, supervisors have to attain a balance between checking too much and not checking enough. Therefore, working within the regulatory requirements, the staff has to identify a frequency of monitoring that works best.

The intensity of monitoring may also depend on the individual assignment. The staff can monitor assignments routinely simply to catch snags in the schedule and ensure smooth operations, quality of service, and maximum satisfaction of clients and employees. In certain circumstances, however, monitoring should be increased, such as when assignments involve new clients, new employees, clients known to be difficult, or workers who have had unsuccessful experiences in the past.

An agency might expect, for example, that any schedules involving a new client or a new caregiver will require especially careful supervision. A new client or family may need extra contact with a supervising nurse to feel comfortable about having home care service. Close monitoring of an employee's performance may prevent difficulties that can arise because of the new client's fear or uneasiness about the service.

As another example, a new staff member might be supervised more closely than other employees. Until the agency knows how the employee will work independently and interact with the client, it may wish to monitor the case closely to ensure that the match between client and caregiver is good. Similarly, a case requiring a procedure new to either the employee or the client (e.g., a high-technology procedure) may be more closely monitored to ensure that the employee performs the procedure correctly. Most people feel frightened when they have to undergo new medical procedures. Clients receiving these procedures feel better if they see the supervising nurse frequently.

Assignments involving clients or caregivers who have had previously unsuccessful experiences might also be supervised carefully. Difficult clients and workers with attendance problems or strong personalities should be carefully monitored and the schedule adjusted if it seems that an assignment will not proceed smoothly.

Although intensive monitoring may be required for certain cases, such as those involving difficult clients or problems, it is true that no one likes to be supervised in a heavy-handed way. An important aspect of monitoring is the attitude with which it is conducted. Rather than approaching monitoring from an adversarial perspective, the scheduling staff should encourage a supportive relationship between supervisors and employees. This way, employees will feel that the staff is not simply checking up on them, but rather working with them to ensure the best quality of care for the clients and assignments for them. This encourages coordination between members of the care team and maximizes the flow of information.

A supportive approach to monitoring encourages feedback from employees regarding their assignments. Feedback better equips the staff to detect potential scheduling problems early. Feedback regarding a client's condition can also be very important to the well-being of the client. Some states, such as New York, require formal, written documentation of the case from all levels of caregivers, including aides as paraprofessionals. Not only open communication but also documentation should be encouraged.

Staff Responsibilities

The most effective monitoring systems are collaborative, employing the expertise of both the scheduling and clinical staff. Administrative case supervision can be performed by the clinical staff, as part of its monitoring duties, or by the scheduling staff. The clinical staff is responsible for monitoring the condition of the client and determining whether a schedule meets the client's needs. Since nursing supervisors must perform home visits to evaluate the client, they can also assess the work performance of the employee and the success of the match of client and caregiver.

In addition, schedulers often have the most frequent contact with clients and employees and are usually responsible for personnel management. Thus, administrative supervision frequently falls within the responsibilities of schedulers.

The benefit of clinical–administrative collaboration is that the information can be looked at broadly and decisions made by the scheduling staff. However, when schedulers and supervising nurses share the responsibilities for monitoring and supervision, close communication between them is critical. Since schedulers are in constant contact with employees and clients by telephone, they must keep nurses apprised of any information that affects nursing supervision or the well-being of the client. Similarly, supervising nurses must understand the importance of communicating any information affecting service delivery to the scheduling staff so that a case can be reassigned or adjusted accordingly.

One method is to use written forms for circulating relevant information between clinical and scheduling staffs. For example, a home visit report could be used for monitoring a paraprofessional worker. This report could include the name of the supervisor, the date, and the purpose of the visit (routine home visit, complaint investigation, response to a change in the client's condition, or other reason). The form should include a checklist for each of the elements of a home visit and space for recording observations.

Space should also be available for writing recommendations for a change in service or a schedule. Alternatively, if paperwork is a problem for the agency, regular staff meetings can also be held for scheduling and clinical staffs to discuss the findings of supervisory visits or necessary personnel changes.

Scheduling Supervisory Visits

Supervisory visits can be scheduled by a supervisor or a scheduler. Alternatively, supervisors from both disciplines can collaborate on scheduling the visits. Scheduling of supervisory visits depends on the times that the employee is scheduled to be in the client's home and on the client's geographic location. The mechanics of scheduling supervisory visits are described in Chapter 7. From the monitoring perspective, a number of issues should be recognized.

A most important consideration is that ample time be scheduled for the goals of monitoring to be achieved. Most agencies seek to maximize the number of visits to be done by one supervisor on a given day, encouraging greater productivity and efficiency. However, one purpose of the home visit is to provide reassurance to the client and family. In scheduling initial home visits, the staff should allot sufficient time for the supervisor to complete an evaluation and for the client to be able to ask questions or voice concerns. For both new and old clients, this is the time when they feel that they are receiving personal attention from the agency. The supervisors should not be so tightly scheduled that the client feels hurried.

Unfortunately, scheduling sufficient time for an unhurried supervisory visit can be difficult, particularly for initial home visits, which take more time than follow-up visits. Most agencies have a limited number of professionals who can perform supervisory visits, particularly compared to the number of paraprofessional staff employed. In addition, most supervising nurses or therapists have other demands on their time. One thing the agency can do is to train supervisors to perform visits efficiently while seeming to be unhurried. Incentive payments or stringent work standards are also used by some agencies to encourage efficiency in performing supervisory visits.

ADJUSTING THE SCHEDULE

When it is discovered through monitoring that a schedule is not right for a client or caregiver, a number of options for adjustment are available. A good rule is that the fewest possible changes be made to an existing schedule. Thus, if a caregiver must be changed, the times of service should, if possible, be held constant. If the day of the service must be altered, the personnel assignment should remain stable as long as the caregiver is available.

Three types of changes are made to existing schedules:

1. An alternative plan, or a change in the care provided.
2. An alternative schedule, or a change in the time or day of service.
3. An alternative assignment, or a change in personnel.

A change in a client's condition may require that different services be provided or that more services be added to the activity sheet. This may or may not require a change in the level of personnel. Sometimes changes are made that do not disturb a personnel category, such as increasing the frequency of administering medication or reducing a client's exercise. If new personnel must be assigned, it is advisable to try to keep the time the same.

A change may also be required in the days or times of service. It may be determined, for example, that the client is much more alert in the afternoon than in the morning and that services would therefore be more effective in the afternoon. This observation would lead to an alternative schedule, or a change in the time or day of service. Again, if the personnel assignment appears satisfactory, it is ideal to change the schedule and have the same employee provide care under the new schedule.

The third option applies when the match between a client and an employee is unsuccessful. Perhaps a client is unhappy with the service or an employee on a difficult case reaches a point of burnout, which becomes evident in his or her attendance and motivation. In this case, an alternative assignment of a different caregiver must occur. Again, it is best if the times and days of service remain the same when a caregiver is changed. However, when no other caregiver is available, a change in the schedule can be considered.

Supervisors must exercise good judgment in monitoring an assignment. They must analyze the cause of problems. If a client seems to be sluggish and not getting enough exercise, the treatment plan can be changed to include more range-of-motion exercises performed by a home health aide. However, the possibility should be considered that the client is not getting sufficient exercise because the aide is not assisting with the exercises already prescribed. Supervisors should check to ensure that the requirements of the treatment plan are being met before changing it.

If a supervisor encounters a potential problem with a personnel assignment, he or she must decide whether or not to reassign the caregiver. Sometimes clients are simply nervous about having strangers come into their homes to provide care. In this instance, the supervisor may want to allow the caregiver and client to get to know each other better before reassigning the case. A useful guide for supervisors when evaluating case problems is that if they feel confident in the match between a caregiver and a client, they should analyze the problem and evaluate the alternatives, such as discussion or careful follow-up, before reassigning the case.

Even an attendance problem should be carefully considered. Switching an unreliable caregiver out of an assignment simply to assign him or her to another case would not solve the problem. If the client agrees, the staff might try other methods to improve the worker's performance, such as providing incentives for good attendance or making the employee feel like an important member of a care team. Schedules should not be changed unnecessarily or rashly; the best interest of the client should be considered first.

Supervisors must decide for each case whether a problem or potential problem warrants changing the client's schedule or whether the problem can be resolved. As an example, a problem may center on the match of a client and a home health aide. If the client feels that the aide is too young, the supervising nurse may be able to smooth over the situation by pointing out all of the characteristics of the aide that make him or her such a good caregiver and by telling the client that the agency chose this aide because he or she provides such good-quality care. The client may agree to try the assignment again on a trial basis.

Each of these measures is an attempt by the scheduling staff to ensure that a schedule maximizes the benefits of home care. Careful monitoring ensures that the schedule of services meets the needs of the client and that all tasks in the plan of care are performed. It also ensures that the work meets the standards of the agency and that any problems that may arise are handled swiftly and with the least disruption to the client and schedule. The result is the best quality and continuity of care, clients who are content, and employees who have the greatest possible job satisfaction.

PART 4

10

Documentation

Documentation in home care scheduling touches every aspect of the business—client care plans, personnel records, payroll, and billing. Documentation, as a task performed by persons who schedule home care services, consists of two types: that used primarily within the scheduling group and that used by other persons and departments in the agency.

Documents in home care are revolving and interactive, affecting all aspects of an agency's operations. For example, employee observations recorded on time cards are sent to the accounting department, but they must be recorded in the client file and brought to the attention of the case manager and the scheduling staff for necessary changes. Procedures must be in place for the times when this documentation is received or changed or when information is added. Procedures must delineate the action required by the department receiving the information, such as keeping all copies, dating and sequencing copies, routing copies to other departments, or only keeping the final referral information.

Careful documentation is an important part of operational procedure, because of the possible repercussions of scheduling errors in terms of quality of care, and because of stringent regulations for licensed and certified home health agencies to document all services provided. It is necessary that comprehensive systems for record keeping and verification exist and that staff are oriented to agency policies and procedures.

The major steps in a system of documentation include record keeping (documentation of services provided) and verification. The purpose of record keeping is to meet operational and legal requirements for documenting what services are provided, by whom, to whom, and when. In addition, the accounting staff uses scheduling documents as the basis for the payroll and the billing for services.

The purpose of verification is to check that services are provided as authorized and scheduled. Cross-checking is important, as it catches errors in care provided and should reduce the potential for billing or paying erroneously. Agencies need checks against fraudulent activities. In addition, cross-checking ensures that errors do not occur in the delivery of services, such as inadvertently leaving a client off the schedule.

RECORD KEEPING

Record-keeping systems for the home care agency can be quite complex. State laws and licensing regulations require that extensive records be maintained for each aspect of an agency's operations, from daily patient care to fiscal administration. For this reason, a distinction will be made between an agency's general records and those related to its scheduling operations. For the purposes of this discussion, record keeping related to scheduling involves records in which scheduling information is recorded. *Scheduling information* refers to any information used by the staff in creating the schedules, such as the client's plan of care, and information recorded by the staff to document services provided, such as activity sheets. The records most relevant to scheduling include the agency's client or patient care records, personnel files, and accounting files.

The patient care records are among the most comprehensive. A client's file generally contains a range of items from documentation of a referral to the client's bill of rights. For scheduling purposes, the relevant portions of the client records are those which document care needs and requirements for service, personnel assignments and visit histories, and, most importantly, all services provided. The client file includes the following.

1. Physician's orders or other service orders, if applicable.
2. A client data sheet, including contact numbers and demographic and descriptive data.
3. A plan of care, revised as necessary to reflect changing care needs.
4. Activity sheets or other documentation of services provided.
5. Changes in the client's condition, adverse reactions, and problems with the home environment.
6. Documentation of any complaints made by the client and their resolution.
7. Problems occurring with particular caregivers and their resolution.

8. Termination or closeout documents.

Some of the tools used by schedulers to gather and document this information are discussed in the next section.

The second major set of records used extensively in scheduling are personnel files. The contents of personnel files may also be regulated by state law, funding regulations, or contracts signed by the home health agency to provide services. The elements of a personnel file most relevant for scheduling include:

1. Preemployment paperwork, such as applications for employment, reference checks, interview reports, and evaluations by training or orientation faculty and other staff (if applicable).

2. Verification of qualifications, including records of professional licences, registrations and proof of training (if applicable).

3. Dates of employment, resignations, dismissals, and other information.

4. Records indicating attendance, absences, and punctuality.

5. Availability calendars.

6. Commendations or complaints made by clients.

7. Termination or resignation information.

The third set of files related to scheduling are the agency's accounting files. Again, the scope of these records goes far beyond that relevant to scheduling. For these purposes, the contents of the records that are useful are:

1. Written authorization of the type, amount, and duration of services scheduled for each client.

2. Client authorization for home support services not funded by a third-party payer.

3. A copy of the service schedule, including where, when, and by whom service is to be provided.

4. Time sheets or other written documentation of the service

provided, completed by the employee and verified by the client's signature.

5. Notification of changes to a schedule, such as substitutions or changes in the times of service.

TOOLS

It is critical that record keeping and documentation be complete, accurate, and thorough. Since many schedules evolve and change, it is important that the scheduling staff record each change as it occurs. For example, a supervisor may change an activity sheet and leave the sheet in the client's home for the employee. Care must be taken that the updated list of activities is added to the client's file so that scheduling personnel will have accurate references. This could be critical if a substitute or change of personnel is needed.

Updating is particularly important when computerized systems are being used and when more than one person is working on the schedule. In addition to the legal ramifications of incorrect or incomplete documentation, the use of scheduling information by the accounting staff for billing and payroll makes it imperative that records of services scheduled and delivered be accurate, since a mistake in the schedule would cause time-consuming follow-up and cross-checking. For example, if a schedule was not updated to show that a 4-hour assignment was canceled by the client, a discrepancy would be found when the employee's time card did not show that the services were provided. Further investigation would be required to determine the cause of the discrepancy.

The more frequent use of computers as primary instruments in scheduling requires that policies be set for the use of computer records by all agency staff. Agency policy on computer documentation should address the issues of when hard copies (printed records) of information must be posted to the files and when the computer record is sufficient. It must also address issues of protecting the documentation from damage due to operator error or computer malfunction, such as preparing backup diskettes of computer information. Damage to computer files can occur from a power surge, a loss of electricity, or operator error. The agency should protect its files in order to maintain its ability to provide written documentation of every service provided.

The use of good tools for written communication within a home care agency is an effective method for ensuring that necessary documentation is kept accurately and thoroughly. Several tools for documenting scheduling information have been discussed in previous chapters, such as availability calendars used for assigning employees. Some tools useful for recording information when planning a schedule are client data sheets, physician's reports, client rosters, and forms for documenting changes. The tools most important for recording and verifying services delivered are time cards and attendance records.

Planning the Schedule

Client Data Sheet

An identifying record of each client served by the agency is useful as a reference for all aspects of scheduling. Client data sheets can be used as master records for each client and can contain as much information as the scheduling staff finds necessary for planning the schedule. Any data sheet should contain the basic identifying information, such as name, address, telephone number, primary diagnosis, and referral source. It is useful to record demographic data on the client, such as age and sex, as well as the type of funding for the services to be provided, such as insurance information. An important item that the sheet should include is the name of one or more contact persons in the event of an emergency or a change in service. The physician, family members, or personal friends who might be contacted by a scheduler can be noted on this form. Finally, any special or personal instructions specified by a client, family member, or referral source might be listed on this data sheet, as well as strong preferences regarding service.

A record-keeping tool like the client data sheet allows the scheduling staff to readily obtain information on any client. The need to reference this tool numerically for reasons of confidentiality must not be overlooked.

Physician Report

Agencies are required by state and federal regulations to have physician's orders for services provided under certain funding mechanisms. An agency should have a system for ensuring that written physician's orders are posted to necessary files prior to the initiation of services or within the time required by law.

To enhance record keeping, a form specifically for tracking physician's orders can be used. A Physician Report can be used to document the receipt of written physician's orders for services. Notations on the report can include dates during which service will be effective and amount of services (hours or visits) authorized. It can specify duties to be performed, particularly skilled services, and types, times, and routes of all medications to be administered. The report should indicate whether the service orders specified are new orders, renewed orders, or orders that have been changed. Most importantly, the report must be signed and dated by the physician and maintained in the client care file.

Frequently, physician's orders for cases are received by phone, usually for quick coverage of clients being discharged from the hospital. When this occurs, the nurse should complete the Physician Report and then send it to the doctor for review and signature. A copy of the Physician Report should be posted to the client's file and a notation made indicating that the orders were received verbally by the nurse and that written confirmation was requested.

The Physician Report must be signed and returned to the agency within the number of days specified by law. The receipt of the written orders should be noted in a written log and the orders placed in the client's file. If the written orders are not received within the prescribed period of time, the supervising nurse must follow up with the physician to ensure prompt action.

The written log can also be used to track the expiration dates of physician's orders. The log should be reviewed regularly (weekly or monthly) to ensure that expired service orders are renewed or terminated as determined by the physician.

Employee Data Record

A data record similar to that described for clients above can be useful for summarizing identifying information about the agency's employees. Basic information about each employee can be kept for easy reference. This tool can be kept very simple, including the employee's name, address, telephone number, and contact person in case of emergency. It can also include additional factors such as level of training, preferences for case assignments, previous experience, and other information gathered in processing employment applications.

Client Roster

A client roster is simply a list of clients being served by the agency. Two types of client rosters are useful. First, a list of all active clients can be compiled from the master client files. This is done to document how many clients an agency is serving at one time so that personnel issues and possible staffing problems can be addressed. The scheduling staff must be kept apprised of the agency's total clientele for planning purposes.

A second client roster used in scheduling is a list of all clients on the schedule each week. This list is the basis for generating the schedule. It includes only those clients who are receiving service in a particular week. Some clients receive service biweekly. Others may receive service for a month at a time and then may not need service until 6 months later. These clients would show up as active on the weekly client roster only during the period they require service.

Changes Forms

A critical part of documentation is the communication of changes that occur in the schedule. Each change to the schedule requires that the relevant information be posted to client and employee files. In many cases, when a mistake is discovered or changes are made to a schedule, the scheduling staff can correct the problem immediately, arranging case coverage and phoning the client to advise him or her of the change, but it is critical that these changes be corrected in the records. In addition, it is extremely important that these corrections occur at the time of the change, not at the end of the day or week. If the accounting staff does not have the right information when it is needed, they may bill for services that were never provided or pay the wrong caregiver.

A variety of tools can be used for this purpose. The telephone log, described in Chapter 7, is an excellent tool for ensuring that changes are acted upon and entered in the record (see Table 7.4). This method ensures that regardless of who takes a message about a change affecting a schedule, whether the information comes from a client or caregiver, the information can be communicated systematically to the scheduling staff.

More complicated are changes in the funding authorization or care required by a client. One method of ensuring that these changes are recorded in the files is to use a standardized form. Each time a call comes in advising of a change, or a mistake is discovered, the staff can note the change on the form. At the end of each day, the changes that have been logged in can be made to the schedule, posted in client or employee files, or written up for accounting use.

A form specifically developed for tracking changes can be used. A sample Change in Service Form (shown in Table 10.1) can be used to

Table 10.1 Change in Service Form

Client Name: _____   Date _____

Notification of change by: _____   Phone _____

Requested change:

    Funding _____
    Level of Service _____
    Amount of Service _____
    Other _____

Comments:
_____
_____
_____

Reason for requested change:
_____
_____
_____

Notify:

    Client _____
    Physician _____
    Family Member or Contact Person _____

document the type of change requested, the reason for the change, and the action taken to implement it. In addition, the name of the person communicating the change to the agency must be noted as a contact person for schedulers who have questions when they adjust the schedule. The person completing the form should list the names of other people that schedulers must notify of the change, such as the client, physician, and family members in the case of a funding change. Space should be included for the scheduler to sign off upon implementing the change. The form should then be posted to the client and accounting files.

Verifying the Schedule

Time Cards

The time card or time sheet is the tool for verifying that service was provided as scheduled. Unless an employee submits a written report signed by the client to verify that the service was provided, an agency must verify every assignment with every client.

A simple time card is shown in Figure 10.1. The sample card is for a period of 1 week, although labor regulations vary in terms of how frequently paraprofessional employees in this category must be paid.

On the sample time card, space is provided for recording the visit date, time arrived, time left, total hours, and, if necessary, mileage or other information. This organizes the information by day, by time, and by client. Note that space is provided at the side and bottom of each day's card for the employee's and client's signatures. This ensures that the information recorded is verified by the client each day.

Other systems can also be used. Depending on state law and the system the agency chooses to use, a time sheet can be used to document the dates and times services are provided throughout a pay period, what activities are provided, and any clinical observations the employee would like to note for entry in the clinical record. Some states require that time sheets be separated from documentation of activities performed. Other states and third-party payers require detailed verification on the time card of each task completed for a client.

NAME _____

PAY PERIOD _____

LAST DATE TO SEND TIME CARD IN _____

PAY DAY _____

CLIENT	FOR OFFICE USE ONLY	MILES	TIME IN	TIME OUT	HOURS	CLIENT SIGNATURE

SIGNATURE _____

Figure 10.1. Simple time card.

The agency may require for other reasons that the employee complete a separate time card for each client taken care of each week. While this is a somewhat cumbersome system, it not only allows accounting to compile the data by employee, by looking at all of an employee's time cards for a pay period, and by client, by collating all the time cards signed by a particular client, but also allows filing in client and personnel records without references to other clients or employees. If separate time cards are to be used for this reason, even clients who live together should be listed on separate documents.

When a more complex time card is used, the employee should verify not only that he or she performed a visit but also that the activities scheduled were completed. The employee should indicate the duties that were performed each day. As shown in Figures 10.2A and 10.2B, a two-sided time card can be used. There is space for the employee to check off activities completed and explain for the record why certain tasks may not have been completed. For example, a client's activity sheet may specify assistance in showering and dressing in preparation for day care, but the client may feel tired and choose not to attend on a particular day. If the client prefers to remain in bed rather than get showered and fully dressed, the employee should note that he or she did not assist the client with dressing and that, instead, the client was assisted into a fresh nightgown and made comfortable in bed.

A time card may also include space for the employee to note any changes in the client's condition. Again, a separate record could be used for this purpose, but combining information may be useful. When observations are noted, the supervisory nurses can be alerted to a possible change in a client's condition. Since the employee has the most contact with the client, he or she is most aware of changes in the client's condition. Any observations noticed can be important, such as loss of appetite, dizziness, confusion, weight gain or loss, or any other circumstances that seem to be unusual for the client.

When client information is recorded along with the hours of service provided, a different time sheet may be needed for each client because of confidentiality. That is, if a time record has other data that would be put in the client's file, that document should

Employee _____

Dates _____

Week Ending (Friday)

Client Name _____ Address _____

	Sat	Sun	Mon	Tue	Wed	Thur	Fri
Visit Date:							
Time Arrived:							
Time Left:							
Total Hours:							
Errands-Miles:							
Office Use:							

Activity*   Enter (X) For Each Activity Performed

Activity	Sat	Sun	Mon	Tue	Wed	Thur	Fri
1. Bath/Weigh Patient							
2. Soaking Patient's Feet							
3. Skin Care/Cast Care Dressings							
4. Clean and File Nails							
5. Mouth Care							
6. Hair/Brush, Comb, Shampoo, Shave							
7. Assist Dressing/Prosthetic Devices							
8. Turning/Positioning of Patient							
9. Assist With Toileting/Ostomy							
10. Measure/Record Output/Test Urine							
11. Assist With Urinal/Commode/Bedpan							
12. Bladder/Bowel Training							
13. TPR							
14. Exercise							
15. Ambulation							
16. Transfer							
17. Reality Orientation Therapy							
18. Medication Reminder							
19. Tube Feeding							
20. Special Diet Prepare/Teach							
21. Breakfast/Lunch/Dinner							
22. Record Intake Fluid/Solid							
23. Grocery Shopping							
24. Make/Change Beds							
25. Vacuum/Mop/Dust							
26. Clean Bathroom							
27. Clean Kitchen							
28. Laundry							
29. Care of Patient's Room							
30. Maintain/Care of Special Equipment							
31. Assist with Oxygen							
32. Other — Specify							
	Sat	Sun	Mon	Tue	Wed	Thur	Fri

Emp/Client Signature Emp/Client Signature Emp/Client Signature Emp/Client Signature Emp/Client Signature Emp/Client Signature Emp/Client Signature

*If any activity that has been ordered has been omitted, please note number(s) and a reason for omission on back.

Figure 10.2A. *Two-sided time card with verification of activities: side 1.*

WEEK DAY	NUMBER OF ACTIVITY AND REASON FOR OMITTING ACTIVITY
SATURDAY	
SUNDAY	
MONDAY	
TUESDAY	
WEDNESDAY	
THURSDAY	
FRIDAY	

Please note any information you feel we should know about the client.

Signature _____

Figure 10.2B. Two-sided time card with verification of activities: side 2.

not have information about services to other clients. An original copy of a time record should be entered in the client's file and a copy passed to the accounting department and processed for payroll.

Attendance Records
Attendance records are most important for personnel and accounting reasons. Facts like tardiness and absenteeism should be

noted in the personnel files. The information should also be sent to the accounting staff, and time cards submitted by employees compared to records kept by the scheduling staff. From an up-to-date schedule that reflects last-minute substitutions or changes in assignments, the scheduling staff should note any changes of caregiver, such as substitutions, or changes in the visit or time care is provided.

An attendance log is useful for recording this information. Figures 10.3 and 10.4 represent simple attendance records. In both yearly attendance records, a calendar is marked for every absence and late arrival, as well as for vacation time and sick leave taken. At a glance, the scheduling staff can evaluate the attendance record of each employee.

VERIFICATION

The most complete record keeping and the best quality of care require that performance of activities be verified, as well as the time care was given or a visit made. In addition, the staff must verify that all necessary documentation is in place before billing for services or paying employees. The best cross-check is done as part of accounting.

Verification includes ensuring that information is documented accurately and completely. It also includes ensuring that adjustments made to a schedule be posted to accounting files in order to account for discrepancies that appear in billing and payroll.

As well as a check across documents, it is important to verify that records are current. Spot checks by calling or visiting should be made to ensure that hours of service are being delivered in accordance with the schedule. Sometimes a client and an employee implement changes without consulting the office. Every effort has to be made to minimize such changes, as they can cause problems, particularly in supervision. No agency wants to be in the position of trying to prove that services were performed at a different time than that specified on the plan when a supervisor or auditor checks and finds that the employee is not in the home as scheduled.

Documents are interrelated and must also be cross-checked against departments. Internal audits are useful, and samples of

EMPLOYEE: _____

N – No Show
R – Requested Time Off Without Pay
S – Sick
V – Earned Vacation
L – Late

1985
YEARLY ATTENDANCE RECORD

JANUARY

		1	2	3	4	5
6	7	8	9	10	11	12
13	14	15	16	17	18	19
20	21	22	23	24	25	26
27	28	29	30	31		

FEBRUARY

					1	2
3	4	5	6	7	8	9
10	11	12	13	14	15	16
17	18	19	20	21	22	23
24	25	26	27	28		

MARCH

					1	2
3	4	5	6	7	8	9
10	11	12	13	14	15	16
17	18	19	20	21	22	23
24	25	26	27	28	29	30
31						

Figure 10.3. Attendance record in calendar format.

ATTENDANCE RECORD

CODE

Employee Name: _____

A Excused Absence in Advance
B ½ Day Excused Absence in Advance
C Unexcused Absence (Called in)
D ½ Day Unexcused Absence (Called in)
E No Show
F ½ Day No-Show
V Vacation
L Late

January

| 1 | 2 | 3 | 4 | 5 | 6 | 7 | 8 | 9 | 10 | 11 | 12 | 13 | 14 | 15 | 16 | 17 |
| 18 | 19 | 20 | 21 | 22 | 23 | 24 | 25 | 26 | 27 | 28 | 29 | 30 | 31 |

February

| 1 | 2 | 3 | 4 | 5 | 6 | 7 | 8 | 9 | 10 | 11 | 12 | 13 | 14 | 15 | 16 | 17 |
| 18 | 19 | 20 | 21 | 22 | 23 | 24 | 25 | 26 | 27 | 28 |

March

| 1 | 2 | 3 | 4 | 5 | 6 | 7 | 8 | 9 | 10 | 11 | 12 | 13 | 14 | 15 | 16 | 17 |
| 18 | 19 | 20 | 21 | 22 | 23 | 24 | 25 | 26 | 27 | 28 | 29 | 30 | 31 |

Figure 10.4. *Attendance record in linear format.*

records should be pulled regularly and tracked through the system to ensure that records are current and in their place. The client record, for example, should be tracked to the employee assigned. The personnel record should be checked for proper credentials for the assignment and for evidence of any complaints or compliments regarding the care for that client. The attendance record and other documentation should be evaluated to determine the quality of care being provided.

The accounting records of the employee should be checked to ensure that the plan of care is being followed and that any notes for the employee regarding the client have been documented in the client's files, as they may affect the timing and type of services provided. The signature of the client indicating that the employee is performing the duties should be verified. A final check should be made to see if the services have been billed and collected.

Two procedures are frequently used in verifying documentation. The first is breaking out all the information contained in a schedule by employee in order to confirm that all visits scheduled for that employee were made and verified by the clients. The second is breaking out the information by client in order to see what services a client received throughout the week, and comparing the services received to those authorized in the service orders.

Documentation by Employee

The first step in verifying information by employee is to ensure that there is a time card or cards for every employee on the schedule and that each time card is signed by the client or clients listed. Only those employees who submit time cards should be paid. Since payroll files are usually automated, employees who have not turned in time cards should be flagged in the computer to alert accounting that their paychecks should be held until the time cards are received and verified.

Next, the accounting staff should ensure that the time cards submitted by employees are accurate. They should compare the data on the time cards to the employee's schedule, looking at days and times of service as well as the total number of hours the employee worked. The units recorded (visits or hours) should be compared to the units indicated on the schedule. The information relevant at this stage of accounting operations is whether the number of visits or hours scheduled matches those claimed on the time cards.

When the information on the time cards does not match the schedule, the accounting staff must determine whether there is an error in the time card or in the schedule. It is possible that the employee incorrectly recorded his or her hours of service. In this case, the accounting staff can correct the time card and process the employee's paycheck. It is also possible that the scheduling staff made a change in the schedule that was not recorded or communicated to the accounting department, such as asking an employee to substitute on an extra case because another caregiver was ill. To determine the cause of the discrepancy, the accounting staff must go back to the schedulers.

Documentation by Client

Once the information on the time cards has been verified, the accounting staff must create prebilling reports that summarize the total services provided to each client. The data contained in the schedule (i.e., visits or hours, days and types of service received) are organized so that the data shown can be cross-checked with the service orders to ensure that the services provided are in agreement with those requested or authorized. Discrepancies must be caught as soon as possible, as the agency may have provided service for which it cannot bill a client or third-party payer.

The most important step prior to billing is to compare the prebilling reports to the service orders for each client. Denials of claims by Medicare and Medicaid are a common and costly problem for most home health agencies. These denials can often be reduced with accurate documentation. In this step, the accounting department checks the information from the schedule against the service orders to catch mistakes before the claims are submitted.

In addition, although the reporting requirements of the Health Care Financing Administration, its fiscal intermediaries, and other funding sources are continually changing, the burden is almost always on the home care agency to prove that the claims submitted are reimbursable. An agency must carefully check all claims for reimbursement.

A NOTE ON CONFIDENTIALITY

The scheduling staff must work with a tremendous volume of information daily. Many state health codes regulating home health agencies specify that privacy is a specific right of home care clients. Even when it isn't mandated, confidential treatment of records should be kept in mind by the agency.

Security is an issue in documentation and record keeping. Records may be protected by being referenced by numbers assigned to each client. Using numbers as identifiers ensures that access to computer or hard copy files cannot compromise client privacy. In addition, the agency must ensure that information is maintained separately for each client.

Documentation is a most important part of the tasks performed by the scheduling staff. Recording the services provided, and verifying that they are provided according to the plan of care, are critical for substantiating all billing and payroll claims, as well as ensuring that the client is receiving the type, amount, and level of care authorized and scheduled. Accurate, careful documentation and cross-checking minimize errors in the schedule and ensure that the numerous changes that occur in scheduling are successfully implemented and monitored.

11

An Alternative Scheduling System of Sharing Services

In the current environment of cost containment in health care, purchasers and providers of home health services are faced with increasing pressure to control or reduce the price of their services. However, to develop and retain qualified personnel, particularly when agencies are competing for personnel, it is clear that salaries will have to increase to meet the competition from other service industries. Therefore, creative alternatives for scheduling and delivering services must be developed to reduce costs and maintain quality.

The traditional place to look for a solution to a problem of this nature is in the area of productivity. However, initial efforts to increase worker productivity in home care were abandoned as studies found that productivity increases in this field cannot be achieved. That is, if one assumes that a minimum number of hours of service must be maintained for each case because worker movement between clients increases costs and inefficiency, and that home care is individualized service, few or no productivity gains can be attained.

This dilemma caused most health care planners to abandon the effort to increase productivity in home care until HCR, a proprietary home health agency, reexamined these issues for the Department of Social Services of Monroe County, New York, under a Small Business Innovation Research Grant from the Health Care Financing Administration. By attacking the assumption that home care cost limits were individual and driven by time, a new approach to productivity was developed. The model of Shared Care used the assumption that cost efficiency and productivity increases could be gained by grouping care activities and clients to maximize care, delivering the most critical components of care in a schedule based on the clients' need for the service.

The concept of sharing care was developed in 1981 in Monroe County with a cooperative pilot program of shared services for four severely disabled Medicaid clients. The program was extended to 6 different groups, or "packages," of clients, and over the next 5 years, in the same community, more than 20 different packages were served by numerous agencies learning to implement the system. Shared services have since been provided to groups of up to as many as 30 clients living within an area of over 1 mile, in neighborhoods as well as in apartment buildings or complexes. The packages have included clients requiring different levels of care and funded by various state, federal, and private mechanisms. Throughout each of these packages, the Shared Care model has cut the costs of home care between 29 and 52% (as illustrated in Table 11.1). In each case, cost savings were achieved without any reduction in services provided and, in many instances, quality of care was *improved*.

The Shared Care innovation redefines the traditional personnel assignment plan for the treatment of patients (one client to one worker with minimum units of care, generally 4-hour blocks) to enable greater scheduling flexibility. By grouping clients who live close to one another (e.g., in the same building or on the same block), the time inherent in minimum units of service assigned to low-priority activities is reduced. Travel time is also reduced. That is, in many cases, the staff can successfully assign caregivers to more than one sacrificing quality of care. More importantly, by restructuring the care plan, a caregiver may be with a client more frequently, albeit for shorter intervals, thus offering more coverage; that is, there are shorter periods of no care. This moves home care closer to the model of institutional care, where employees make rounds.

This scheduling system uses a task- rather than a time-based method of organization. That is, scheduling depends on the analysis and timing of required activities rather than on the simple assignment of scheduling units (hours or visits). The staff analyzes the tasks prescribed in the physician's treatment plan or demanded by clients' requirements for personal care and home support. They then group clients in order to schedule workers to perform the needed care for the entire group. The time required to complete each task (based on the task and the client's capabilities) is carefully estimated and, as in more traditional scheduling practices, the relative priority of each task for scheduling is established. Tasks are combined whenever reasonable (such as laundry or grocery shopping, which can be performed for more than one client at the same time) to make the most productive use of the caregiver's time. Professional caregivers and aides are assigned according to task requirements and move among the group of clients as tasks are performed. A care team composed of paraprofessional and professional caregivers, supervisory staff, and scheduling staff then

Table 11.1 Average Costs of Services Under Traditional and Shared Care Scheduling

Package	Geographic Setting	Client Mix	Service Mix	Funding Mechanism	Number of Clients	Cost Before Shared Care	Cost After Shared Care
I	Apartment complex	Elderly, disabled	24-hour personal care	Medicaid	4	$608.09	$288.40
II	High-rise public housing for the elderly	Elderly	Personal care, housekeeping	Private, Title XX, Medicare	31	$114.71	$ 74.14
III	High-rise apartments	Elderly, blind, disabled	Housekeeping	Title XX	11	$ 26.93	$ 26.93
IV	Suburban residential neighbor-hood	Elderly	Personal care, housekeeping	Medicare, Medicaid, Title XX	30	$143.00	$100.50
V	Small apartment complex	Disabled	Personal care, housekeeping	Medicaid, Title XX	5	$199.00	$133.33
VI	Small apartment complex	Disabled, blind, mentally ill	Personal care, housekeeping	Medicaid, Title XX	8	$117.00	$ 75.83

coordinate closely to ensure that the needs of groups of clients are met individually and that the quality of care is maintained.

The concept of sharing care, therefore, is simple. The staff takes advantage of the geographic proximity of a group of clients, itemizes the care plan, estimates the priority of tasks and their completion time, and creates a flexible schedule that eliminates the potential inefficiency created by scheduling long blocks of time with one client. While this is more complicated than scheduling services for one client delivered by one staff member, restructuring the delivery of care creates a health care environment that is better for the client because of increased contacts and therefore fewer periods of no care; better for the home care worker, who stays challenged and active; and better for the agency and payer, which increases productivity.

THE NEED FOR ALTERNATIVE APPROACHES

The concept of shared home health services originated with the growing need for efficient and cost-effective health services because of limited personnel and fiscal resources. It was conceived as a way not only to save money and serve larger numbers of clients, but to better realize the theoretical benefits of institutional care, such as continuity of care, frequent socialization, and round-the-clock accessibility to a variety of health professionals. As it developed, its quality was improved by encouraging workers and clients to take increased responsibility and by delivering needed services throughout an expanded period, thus ensuring fewer intervals when no care was available.

Most home care administrators, like all business owners or managers, would like to increase the productivity and efficiency of their employees. With the strong emphasis on cost containment in the health care field and the implementation of cost-cutting measures such as the prospective payment system, hospital discharge planners and other local referral sources are relying heavily on home health agencies that can accept clients quickly, provide off-hour coverage, and meet frequently changing needs responsively and flexibly.

Unlike the classic example of the productivity gains established in mass production by workers on assembly lines, improving the productivity and efficiency of the home care staff, while carefully monitoring the quality of care provided, is difficult. Health care professionals (nurses and therapists) and paraprofessionals (home health aides, personal care aides, and chore workers) enter a client's home and provide care specified in a plan ordered by a physician. They work largely independently and unsupervised, and the tasks they perform depend on their skill level and may vary from technical medical procedures to light housekeeping chores. In terms of the time required, these tasks vary depending upon the client's level of disability, the layout of the home, and the level of the caregiver.

Managers and schedulers of home care have identified some of the improvements needed in scheduling and delivering services. For example, agencies are generally not reimbursed for the time caregivers spend traveling between clients, although workers are, so managers attempt first to reduce this travel time. Whenever possible, schedulers assign nurses, therapists, or aides to spend blocks of time with clients, so that all tasks can be completed in one visit and travel time between clients reduced. Unfortunately, though this scheduling technique minimizes total travel time, it allows little flexibility for meeting client preferences and needs.

A necessary improvement that has not been achieved is the reduction of unproductive time when a caregiver completes tasks for the client just to fill the remaining time during a visit. This work does not encourage excellence and skill development. Under the hourly billing systems employed by many state Medicaid programs, agencies frequently require that a minimum number of hours of service be provided per client (often 4 hours), regardless of the tasks that need to be performed. Typically, then, a caregiver is scheduled to spend 4 hours with one client, travel to the next home, spend 4 hours with another client, and go home. This can result in payment for idle time or for the completion of tasks not essential to the plan of care.

Workers can accomplish only a set number of tasks in such a time slot that directly contribute to the treatment of the client's health condition. For example, it might be possible to increase the job performance of workers to enable them to complete all required activities in a treatment plan in less than the allotted 4 hours. However, it would not be more productive for them to do so, as they could not beneficially add tasks such as a second bed bath. The result might be an increase in rest or nonproductive time, or time to perform services for which the agency cannot be reimbursed. As resources are reduced, the idea of isolating essential from less essential tasks becomes a necessity.

The problem of idle time is also prevalent in a per-visit billing and reimbursement system. Although there is a greater incentive to provide services efficiently under this system, since each visit is reimbursed in a standard dollar amount regardless of the duration of the visit, there is a strong incentive to provide all care in one block of time because, under Medicare, agencies are only permitted to bill one visit per day. Therefore, under a per-visit billing system such as that of Medicare, workers stay with one client until all tasks are completed. Even if the tasks to be performed would best be provided over the course of a day, the caregiver must complete them in one block of time. The resultant quality is less and the duration of the period when no care is available is the longest.

As a result of these considerations of cost and efficiency, many agencies have found their scheduling constrained by reimbursement regulations and the inefficiencies of inordinate travel time, particularly to difficult-to-reach locations. Therefore, traditional systems for scheduling and delivering home care, whether under hourly or per-visit billing mechanisms, have in some instances reflected the personnel shift and scheduling constraints seen in care provided by hospitals and nursing homes.

In an institution, for example, the needs of the client are subordinated to the structure and regulation of the institutional system, such as nursing shifts and meal distribution. Client care is constrained by the institution's schedule, hence the joke about a client being awakened to take a sleeping pill.

While scheduling in home care is certainly more demand based than institutional care, it is restricted by costs and reimbursement regulations. For example, if a home care worker is assigned for one visit or one 4-hour period and a client needs meals prepared, the caregiver must prepare and serve breakfast and lunch and leave something for dinner. The client does not get meals at the time of his or her preference, but according to scheduling considerations.

THE SHARED CARE SYSTEM

The Shared Care system of providing home health services offers the advantages of institutional care without the restraints. Clients are grouped for scheduling purposes by location and level of care required. Services are provided according to clients' needs and preferences. A care team of professionals and paraprofessionals moves among a group of clients, providing care when the clients need it.

Managers and schedulers achieve these objectives by organizing service delivery by client location, to eliminate unnecessary travel time, and type of care needed, including level of care and job tasks. As mentioned previously, the scheduling staff analyzes the physician's care plan, separates that plan into components of care, priorities (reminding a client to take medication is a time-specific, high-priority task; housekeeping chores are more intermittent, lower-priority tasks), and the client's preferences. To maximize flexibility, the scheduling staff sets up a detailed, highly individualized schedule that is worked into a plan for a group of clients.

The scheduling staff closely estimates the time required to complete components of tasks but leaves enough flexibility in the system so that the health care professional or paraprofessional, who can best gauge the care the client requires, can adjust the schedule as necessary and provide the highest-quality care based on the client's changing needs and preferences and those of the others in the group.

All of the professional and paraprofessional employees involved in delivering services to a group of clients form the Shared Care team. They include:

1. Nurses and therapists, who administer medication and provide medical assistance in the home.

2. Home health aides, personal care aides, homemakers, or chore workers, depending upon a state's regulations and funding mechanisms, who provide assistance with nonmedical tasks.

3. Supervisors, usually required to be registered nurses, who oversee the delivery of care.

4. Schedulers, who plan the delivery of care in close consultation with the clinical staff, who analyze the care tasks.

By scheduling employees to serve a client package, the times of service can be made much more flexible, maximizing this important benefit of home care. Under traditional scheduling systems, for example, a client who needs assistance with ambulation, exercises, personal care, meal preparation, and assistance at bedtime may have the option of 8 hours with a home care worker or a split shift of 4 hours of care in the morning and 4 at night. Under the Shared Care system, employees can enter the client's home three or four times during the day to complete the required tasks.

In addition, the caregiver does not have to be assigned a full block of time when more than one small task must be completed at different times. For example, a diabetic client may require an insulin injection at 8:00 a.m. and a test of the blood sugar level before lunch. A nurse assigned to perform these tasks in a traditional schedule must be in the client's home for nearly 4 hours. Under Shared Care, the nurse can come in the morning to provide the injection, leave to perform another task, such as a dressing change, for another client in the same geographic area, and return before lunch to test the client's blood sugar level.

Similarly, a personal care aide can be scheduled to come in the morning for personal care, prepare lunch at noon, and return in the evening to prepare the client for bed in less than 8 hours. Delivering care in this manner eliminates unnecessary hours without reducing the number of tasks performed or diminishing the quality of care received.

In fact, clients receiving smaller increments of service at more frequent intervals throughout the day receive better care, because the periods in which they are without care or supervision are lessened. Under traditional scheduling systems, an aide or nurse may be scheduled to visit a client for 4 hours a day three times a week. The caregiver is not available to the client at any other time. Under the Shared Care system, the number of consecutive hours a home care worker spends in the client's home may be fewer, but workers are more readily and more frequently accessible.

In addition, the greater frequency of contact with clients in sharing care allows improved monitoring and supervision. While one caregiver serves more than one client at a time, an increased number of home care professionals actually see the client, borrowing the institutional advantage of greater accessibility to health professionals. Under traditional systems, clients see home care workers during the hours of scheduled visits, and see no one at other times. In Shared Care, tasks are split over the course of a day or several days, so that workers enter clients' homes much more frequently. Monitoring of a client's condition is therefore greatly improved.

There is also greater cooperation between the members of the Shared Care team in organizing and delivering care. The home care workers, schedulers, and clinical supervisors communicate much more closely in this system, so that care is comprehensive and coordinated. Additional advantages of sharing care are described below.

BENEFITS OF SHARING CARE

The model Shared Care program, which is described in detail below, clearly demonstrates the advantages of using this alternative scheduling system.

Cost Savings

The most striking aspect of shared services models is the cost savings they realize. Table 11.1 illustrates the average cost per client per week of providing services using traditional and Shared Care programs. For simplicity, figures reflect the cost of home health and personal care services just before and after implementation of the system for each group of clients, ensuring that the changing level of client disability is held constant. Five of the six original Shared Care programs, created as part of the first Shared Care model, resulted in significant cost savings.

The cost savings arise from several aspects of the Shared Care system. Geography and the increased productivity of the staff are two primary considerations. Cost efficiencies are also achieved by combining and consolidating similar tasks performed for clients, such as laundry and grocery shopping. In addition, for larger packages in which several professionals or paraprofessionals care for many clients, greater cost savings are achieved by the separation of job tasks and assignment of the appropriate level of home care worker. In traditional systems, a nurse who performs two or three skilled tasks may also be scheduled to perform less skilled tasks, such as a bed bath, that have to be performed at the same time. In Shared Care packages requiring different levels of care, aides and nurses are assigned tasks that require their level of skill.

Quality of Care

No decrease in costs resulting from an alternative scheduling system would be beneficial if quality of care were reduced. The Shared Care system results in improved quality for both clients and caregivers.

Demand-Based Care

Supervising nurses, knowledgeable about community resources, promoting self-care, and adapting services to clients' needs, are able to provide cost-effective and comprehensive care plans. Clients in the Shared Care system receive care when they need it, and no more (and no less). The system is based entirely on the demands of the client, not on the structure of the system itself. Tasks are completed when they are needed; when workers are finished with a task or set of tasks, they move on to the next client.

Continuity of Care

Perhaps the most important consideration in quality of care, sharing care reduces the hours in which clients have no care at all. Shared Care provides an entirely different psychosocial environment than traditional scheduling systems. Usually clients see a home health caregiver for a specific amount of time, and see no caregivers outside of that time. Fewer hours of no care and increased contact with home care staff help to keep clients, particularly elderly clients, oriented and secure. The psychosocial condition of the client is also aided by the flexibility of the Shared Care system, whereby home care workers can return to the client as frequently as necessary. The more continuous follow-up by caregivers comes closer to the level of supervision available in an institution.

Fostering Independence

In this system, where actual service hours are reduced, clients who are able are encouraged to contribute as much as possible to their own care, fostering their independence and improvement and encouraging them to be aware of other clients in the package and their needs. For example, in the model packages, HCR found that clients in the same buildings or neighborhoods, who tended to know each other, reported on each other's condition and encouraged the aide to finish with them and give special attention to another client. Sharing care encouraged socialization and communication among the clients, encouraged clients to help themselves, and led clients to be aware of the plight of other clients.

While it took clients a little time to get used to the new system, they found this method of care satisfying and rewarding. The clients realized that their home care workers were not scheduled for specific hours of specific days; that the workers would be going in and out of their homes, performing tasks; and that the workers had other clients for whom they were responsible.

More Qualified Workers

Clients in the Shared Care system are served by carefully selected and trained paraprofessionals and professionals. In particular, the system gives paraprofessional aides much greater responsibility. Caring for a group of clients is also more challenging for the aide and requires organizational and time management skills. The home health or personal care aide, under the supervision of management, is responsible for assessing schedule changes and rearranging the priority of tasks as necessary. Thus, motivated aides who seek a full, productive day, rather than plenty of idle time, are attracted to the Shared Care system.

Caregivers benefit greatly by assuming increased responsibility; their jobs are more stimulating and therefore more rewarding than traditional assignments. They learn to deal with a variety of clients, not just one, and they learn to handle emergencies as they arise. From the viewpoint of the agency, the more responsive and responsible a caregiver becomes, the easier it is to run a high-quality home health care program. The ultimate benefit, of course, is improved care for clients.

More Responsive Care

With home care workers already established in a location, new clients can be served immediately by incorporating them into an existing Shared Care package. In addition, short-term schedule changes do not affect th clients as they do in traditional scheduling systems. In the Shared Care system, clients see several different members of a home health agency's staff (whoever is serving on a particular shift or day); therefore, staff absenteeism will not disrupt a client's routine as much in the Shared Care system as in the traditional methods of delivering care. On days when one member of a care team is ill, other members can perform priority tasks with minimal disruption to the client.

THE MODEL SHARED CARE PROGRAM

A description of HCR's experience in developing and implementing the Shared Care model is useful for providing a background and an overview of the Shared Care system. The first two Shared Care packages, created in 1981, are explored here as case studies. While the studies indicate that specific management techniques and resources were required for successful implementation of the system, it should be noted that the description of HCR's experiences is not intended to imply that implementation could only have been achieved by HCR. The system was developed expressly for its replication by different types of agencies across the country.

Package I

The first Shared Care program originated when the Monroe County Department of Social Services was providing home health aide services to four severely disabled Medicaid clients who lived in one apartment complex in Rochester, New York. The combined cost of these services was more than $2,300 per week, a price that the county could no longer continue to pay. In an effort to save money, the county asked HCR to develop a less expensive plan of care.

The kinds of support needed by these clients varied depending on self-care abilities, the availability and cooperation of family members, and the risk of health problems secondary to their compromised medical condition and functional status. The support services delivered to these clients were planned, reviewed, and certified by the referring physician.

A preliminary examination of the needs of these clients showed that although extensive services were required, the number of hours of care that had been provided could be reduced. The scheduling of two clients who required 24-hour service offered the potential for the most reduction. One client had a home health aide throughout the night so that she could be turned every 2 hours. Clearly, this aide could perform other tasks during the shift and still provide the necessary services for this client as long as there were other clients nearby whom the aide could attend in the interim.

By incorporating the services of all four clients in the same building, HCR designed a functional shared services system. The scheduling staff began by analyzing the needs of the clients and determining the job tasks to be performed. The clients, denoted here as client A, client B, client C and client D, all required heavy care. All four also required special attention because of emotional or mental health problems. Client A had suffered a stroke, had congestive heart failure, and was wheelchair bound, incontinent, but alert. She had severe cataracts and suffered from depression. The community health nurse determined that this client needed assistance at various times during the day with required activities for daily living, including full assistance in the morning with personal care, preparation for going to a day care program, light housekeeping, meals, transfers, exercises, preparation for bed, and turning every 2 hours during the night.

The other clients in the package also needed heavy care. Client B had congestive heart failure, and was very obese and a compulsive eater. She was ambulatory with a walker and alert. She required services for meal preparation, supervision with her walker, laundry and light housekeeping, personal care, and preparation for the day care program and for bed. Client C, who relied heavily on aide services, was arthritic and anemic, ambulatory with a walker, and alert. She needed personal care, meal preparation, light housekeeping and laundry, supervision with her walker, and assistance at bedtime. Client D was quadriplegic and an alcoholic. Although she was attended by a licensed practical nurse for 8 hours during the day, she needed an aide's assistance with meal preparation and feeding, light housekeeping and laundry, bedtime preparation, turning throughout the night, toileting, and transfers.

After analyzing the job tasks, the HCR staff estimated the amount of time it would take to perform each task, based on the individual client's level of disability and the time of day or night the tasks had to be performed. Therefore, the average time needed to complete a particular task, such as 15 minutes for a bed bath, was adjusted according to the level of assistance required (e.g., a bed bath can take 15 minutes if a client needs only minor assistance or a full hour if the client requires total help).

Next, for scheduling purposes, the staff assigned priorities to each of the tasks. The top-priority tasks were those that had to be completed at specific times, such as turning client D during the night or preparing the clients for their day care program. The remainder of the tasks were either those that could be completed within certain intervals (such as regular meals) or the lowest-priority tasks that could be completed at any reasonable time within the schedules (such as light housekeeping).

HCR's scheduling staff determined that four aides and a licensed practical nurse could provide services to these four clients who lived in the same apartment house. The staff scheduled the aides to move between the clients, spending 30 minutes to 2 hours at a time with each. The aides would perform the required tasks for each client when they were needed and combine tasks for the four clients where possible, such as doing their laundry or grocery shopping. Thus, unnecessary hours would be eliminated without reducing the number of tasks performed or diminishing the quality of care.

To see how the system worked, it is useful to look at a sample schedule for a home health aide who served this group of clients between 3:00 and 11:00 p.m., shown in Table 11.2. The principles behind the breakdown of time demonstrated here have also been successfully applied to more complicated groups of clients requiring skilled services.

Table 11.2 Sample Home Health Aide Schedule Under the Shared Care System

TIME	CLIENT	TASK
3:00	Client A	Light housekeeping Prepare and serve evening meal Begin laundry for Clients B, C and D
4:30	Client B	Prepare and serve evening meal
5:00	Clients B, C, D Client D	Put laundry in dryers Prepare evening meal and assist with eating Transfer to chair
6:00	Clients B, C, D Client C	Finish laundry Prepare and serve evening meal Eat own meal (brought from home) Supervise exercise with walker
7:00	Client D	Transfer to bed Skin care
8:00	Client A	Assist with toileting Prepare for bed
8:30	Client B	Supervise with walker Prepare for bed
9:30	Client C	Prepare for bed
10:00	Client D	Provide a snack Prepare for bed Empty catheter bag, recording amount
10:50	Client A	Turning

Under a traditional system of providing home care, in one 4-hour period or a visit of comparable length, an aide would have cared for one client. As indicated by the chart, between the hours of 3:00 and 7:00 p.m., all four clients were served their evening meal, according to the time of day they preferred to eat, by one aide. During just 8 hours of service, the aide did laundry for all four clients, prepared all of them for bed, and met their other needs, such as providing skin care to client D, assisting client B with her exercises, and performing housekeeping tasks for client A. The higher-priority tasks (such as turning or transfers, meals, and bed preparation) were provided at the times preferred by the clients, and the lower-priority tasks (such as housekeeping) were scheduled in the remaining time. The clients saw the aide several times throughout her shift. Because the aide stayed only as long as it took to complete tasks, clients were encouraged to contribute as much as possible to their own care.

The Shared Care system also provided the aide with the flexibility to adjust her schedule according to clients' needs. For example, transferring and feeding client D, who required the heaviest care of the four clients in the package, may have taken longer on a particular day than the amount of time allotted to the task. The aide could readjust the schedule so that priority tasks, such as feeding client D, were completed, and rearrange other less important tasks as necessary.

The nursing visits certified by the referring physician were provided on two levels. One level provided intermittent skilled nursing services for direct patient care. These services included periodic catheter changes, injections, and monitoring medications and changes in condition. The second level of nursing care provided direct supervision to the home health aide to ensure continuity and effective delivery of care.

Clearly, this package proved to be successful. The scheduling system based on job tasks allowed the staff to schedule aides flexibly while continuing to meet client needs. Costs decreased dramatically: Assigning one aide to more than one client reduced the number of aide service hours for these clients by 58% and reduced the total cost of providing service by 47% without reducing in any way the quality of care (see Table 11.3). Because the work was

Table 11.3 Comparison of Costs Between Traditional and Shared Care Services: Package I

Service	Hours	Rate Per Hour ($)	Total Cost ($)
		Traditional	
Client A: HHA	56	6.65	372.40
Client B: HHA	128	6.65	851.20
Client C: PCA	12	6.50	78.00
Client D: HHA	168	6.50	1092.00
	364		2393.60
		Shared Care	
Shared HHA	100	9.20	920.00
Traditional HHA	40	6.65	266.00
Traditional PCA	12	6.50	78.00
	152		1264.00

HHA = home health aide; PCA = personal care aide.

more challenging to the aides, worker performance improved as well—an unexpected benefit.

Package II

Since the initial package involved only four clients and one funding mechanism, HCR and Monroe County decided to test the system on a larger scale. The second package was much more complex. It included more than 30 clients from within a very large apartment complex and a few from the surrounding neighborhood. The clients required varying levels of care and services and were funded under different payment mechanisms, including private pay. For these reasons, the package presented greater challenges in scheduling, selecting, and supervising aides and billing, and would serve as a true test of the Shared Care concept on a larger, more complicated scale.

The requirements were influenced by the frequent movement of clients in and out of the package, which caused the scheduling staff to continually revise the schedules. This often required adjusting several clients' hours. In addition, the varying levels of care required and the multiple funding sources made the package problematic.

Job task analysis showed, however, that because most of the clients required only assistance with household tasks, their needs could almost always be met with fewer hours of service than they were receiving. In addition, because of the nature of the tasks performed, smaller assignments of time were often more effective. For example, a client previously scheduled for 4 hours once a week could now receive approximately 2 hours of service twice a week or even 1 hour 4 days a week—a much more sensible schedule for receiving housekeeping or meal preparation services.

Thus, by applying the techniques of job task analysis and by carefully selecting, scheduling, and monitoring the caregivers, HCR made the package a success. The total number of hours provided in the second Shared Care package was 54, a 57% reduction compared with the previous program for these clients (see Table 11.4).

Table 11.4   Comparison of Costs Between Traditional and Shared Care Services: Package II

Service	Hours
Traditional	
Client A: HHA	2
Client B: HHA	2
Client C: PCA	28
Client D: HHA	28
Client E: PCA	12
Client F: PCA	12
Client G: PCA	42
	126
Shared Care Package	
Shared PCA	26
Shared HHA	28
	54

HHA = home health aide; PCA = personal care aide.

Eliminating the 4-hour minimum aide assignment—required at the time by Monroe County home health care providers—played a large part in reducing the number of hours provided.

The second package proved the applicability of the Shared Care model to packages including dozens of clients who:

1. Lived in different geographic locations.
2. Had different levels of disability.
3. Were covered under different reimbursement programs (Medicare, Medicaid, Title XX, and private payment).

RESULTS OF THE PROGRAM

HCR subjected the shared services programs to rigorous quality control tests consisting of on-site review by management staff, as well as interviews with workers, clients, and community health nurses who managed the cases for clients. Community health nurses reported that:

1. Clients demonstrate more independence with shared home care than with traditional home care, which is important in fostering healthy independence.
2. Clients' required activities for daily living are met adequately by the Shared Care employee, with more options for flexibility.
3. Tasks are completed in appropriate time frames; clients' unscheduled needs can more easily be met by the shared employee, because the services are more flexible and employee travel is minimized.
4. Clients' contact with health care personnel is increased even though hours of service are reduced.
5. In a shared care plan, continuity of care is as good as or better than that under traditional plans.
6. The quality of care is as good as or better than traditionally scheduled home care.

PARAMETERS OF THE SYSTEM

Shared Care systems, even when fully operational, are never likely to completely replace traditional one-on-one assignments; there will always be clients whose need for care or whose place of residence requires that their home health worker not serve any other clients. Certainly, in rural areas, where a "short" distance among clients may be 30 miles, the implementation of this system is not feasible.

In determining the replicability of the shared services models in different circumstances and communities, the following parameters were identified:

1. *Geographic parameters.* There must be at least two clients who live reasonably close together and who together require at least 4 hours of care on the same days of the week.

2. *Client disability parameters.* Most individuals for whom home health care is appropriate can be placed in a Shared Care program; those who, because of their medical condition, require constant monitoring or extremely rigid structures are not usually appropriate clients.

3. *Referral parameters.* The development of a shared care package may be done within the home health agency itself, where clients are grouped by the scheduling manager, by local/state health or social services departments, or by hospital case managers. The more centralized the referral process, the greater the efficiency of the model.

4. *Reimbursement parameters.* Agencies may be reimbursed by Medicare, Medicaid, or Title XX, or paid privately for shared services, whether they are billed on a per-hour or per-visit basis, as long as traditional definitions of a visit or minimum blocks of service are waived by the provider agency.

5. *Agency management parameters.* The provider agency must be willing to commit additional management hours and dollars than were required under traditional delivery systems.

6. *Job task analysis.* Clients must be assessed and workers scheduled on the basis of tasks to be performed, not units of time.

7. *Special selection and training of the Shared Care worker.*

The caregiver must possess strong occupational skills and exceptional organizational, judgment, and interpersonal skills to work in the Shared Care system, because added coordination is required between workers and clients. Special orientation and training is necessary in time and crisis management skills.

IMPLEMENTING A SHARED CARE SCHEDULE

The techniques required for implementing Shared Care are fundamentally the same as those employed in traditional scheduling systems. However, significantly greater management resources are required to ensure the level of success that will expand the agency's caseload while saving the agency, funding sources, and, in many cases, clients, money and increasing the quality of care.

To implement the Shared Care system, a home health agency must commit resources to training its scheduling staff and care teams, developing additional monitoring and supervisory systems, and selecting a staff to work within the system. In addition, the agency must work with local referral agencies and third-party payers, who must understand this method of providing care so that referral procedures can be restructured and the method of billing for Shared Care services accepted and properly audited. Detailed guidelines on documenting and billing for shared services are presented later in this chapter.

For the managers of a home health agency, scheduling and monitoring the delivery of services are more complex, but creating care teams of professionals and paraprofessionals makes rescheduling for new clients or changes in personnel simpler. With several clients receiving services from a home health agency in the same apartment building or neighborhood, supervision of the delivery of services is facilitated and improved, as a supervising nurse need only go to one location or neighborhood to supervise an entire team of caregivers serving many clients. One case manager and one supervising nurse can oversee the provision of care to a group of clients, reducing the travel time required for supervisory visits and ensuring continuity of care. Procedures for monitoring shared services are discussed in the next section.

Selecting a qualified staff to deliver shared services requires a special effort. The most important components of the Shared Care system are the workers who deliver services. In large home health agencies that deliver services under more conventional systems, agency managers may be far removed from the caregivers who serve the clients. In the Shared Care system, those who provide care take on increased importance as key members of the care team composed of management staff, scheduling staff, supervisory nurses, therapists, nurses, and aides. The workers providing services directly influence the way in which an agency implements or modifies the mechanics of the Shared Care system. It is therefore critical that managers pay close attention to the employees who are placed in Shared Care packages and select workers for multiclient assignments carefully.

Employees who work within the Shared Care system carry a great deal of responsibility. The Shared Care program differs from institutional care in that employees provide services in a demand-based, flexible system which serves several clients in a residential setting during short periods of time. Because a member of a care team may be responsible for numerous clients within a package, he or she must manage time, tasks, and functions and assume greater responsibility for communicating with clients to monitor their needs. The system also requires very close communication between services staff and management staff and requires workers to adjust their schedules upon direction from the agency to accommodate the many changes that may occur daily. This system of home health care, which is more complex than the usual assignment of staff members to one client for a fixed period of time, greatly increases the responsibilities of the employees.

To work well in Shared Care, an employee must be good at his or her job to begin with, since the care-sharing model builds on skills already mastered. The Shared Care program also demands that workers possess excellent technical skills and great efficiency. Employees who deliver services to many different clients in a specific amount of the time must not only perform each required task expertly but must also be productive and use their time wisely. Assuming that there will be delays and contingencies as a matter of course, Shared Care employees must be able to plan ahead and speed up the completion of their tasks whenever possible. They must be able to evaluate and reevaluate the priority of tasks and adjust the complexity of tasks (such as simplifying a menu) to use their time wisely, and adjust their schedules in the event of a disruption. These qualities are representative of those which distinguish employees who work best within a Shared Care system and indicate the need for a special selection process.

Care sharing does not involve changes in the type of care provided or the kinds of services reimbursed, but rather in the plan under which these services are delivered. As with traditional methods of home care, services provided under a Shared Care arrangement are based on a comprehensive program of care developed by a physician. The physician's care plan is the basic tool of this management technique, governing the scheduling of tasks, the assignment of the home health care team, the monitoring of services by registered nurses, and billing for all services provided.

MONITORING IN A SHARED CARE SYSTEM

Some scheduling systems afford employees greater independence in serving their clients, such as the Shared Care system, in which employees move among clients in the performance of job tasks according to a schedule which has more than usual flexibility in the times established for care. Accordingly, the level of monitoring required to ensure that the schedule is effective and efficient and that the needs of the clients are being met is increased. Since the Shared Care system is highly management intensive, it will be used as an example of enhanced monitoring practices.

Employees in the Shared Care system work under a highly demanding schedule for clients whose conditions vary daily. The purpose of the monitoring procedures for shared aides is threefold: to keep abreast of clients' conditions, to ensure that the employee's schedule is properly structured, and to facilitate communication between the clients, the care team, and the supervisory staff.

Because the simplest standard against which worker performance and client satisfaction can be measured in scheduling—time spent with the client—is inapplicable in Shared Care, more sophisticated measurement systems are needed. This is because, since less productive time is reduced, the specific time spent with the client varies; only the tasks performed remain the same.

To measure the quality of care provided, the client must be the ultimate standard. It is useful, while scheduling, to go back to the treatment goals defined for the client in the care plan, such as increasing functional ability during a rehabilitation period, and compare them with the client's present functional level. Similarly, from the employee's perspective, the degree of job satisfaction attained in terms of his or her own goals can indicate the success of long-term assignments.

It is extremely helpful if specific, realistic goals for each client in a Shared Care package are defined. The quality of care can then be measured against these goals, which will also provide focal points for supervisors to discuss client and worker satisfaction with each caregiver assigned to the group. Goals identified may include both short- and long-term objectives, such as increased functioning, increased level of comfort, pain control, control of debilitating conditions and diseases, maintenance of physical activity and mental activity, increased participation in care, and greater independence.

In Shared Care, the purpose of monitoring becomes not only ensuring that quality care is delivered but also assessing the structure of the employees' schedules for each group of clients and noting any adjustments that need to be made. Monitoring should also include a continuous effort to increase productivity and quality of care. Thus, more frequent home visits are required. In addition, the management staff needs to phone workers and clients frequently in order to monitor changes in workers' routines and to ensure that schedules are completed.

To illustrate these concepts, it is useful to refer to the example of a client package used earlier. The goals for client A, the stroke victim who was wheelchair bound, incontinent, and suffered from cataracts and depression, included prevention of bed sores and other infections that could result from decreased mobility due to her stroke; continued activity in the day care program; and improved mental outlook. The goals for client B, who suffered from congestive heart failure and obesity, included weight loss, increased mobility, and continued participation in day care. These goals are extremely helpful in refining schedules to ensure that the tasks provided are done in the most beneficial way.

For example, on some mornings, client A, usually an early riser, did not want to wake up and get ready early enough for the aide to prepare her for day care and have enough time to help the next client, client B, get ready. On these mornings, client A felt that she was being rushed and declined to go to day care at all. On these occasions, she was generally quite depressed by the end of the day. Because participation in day care and improvement in mental health had been identified as treatment goals when the plan of care was developed, the home health aide providing care on Monday, Wednesday, and Friday mornings brought this situation to the attention of the supervising nurse assigned to her care team.

After reviewing the problem, the nurse suggested that on mornings when client A appeared sluggish, the aide should try moving on to client B, who was also an early riser and quite flexible. Rather than prodding client A to get out of bed on these mornings, the home health aide would instead merely tell her that she would be back and not to worry about getting ready in time for day care. The approach worked; when she did not feel locked into a rigid system, client A felt less rushed and missed fewer sessions of day care as a result.

Supervisory visits under the Shared Care system are conducted more frequently but require less travel time because clients are grouped geographically. In order to perform home visits, supervisors must know the schedule of each worker providing services in a package. Because of the daily variation in the schedules of care providers, the supervising nurse cannot be formally scheduled to meet the employee with a particular client at an exact time. Schedulers must therefore familiarize the clinical supervisors with employees' schedules so that they can perform supervisory visits at any time. It is helpful for the staff to use a geographic layout of the package on which the movement of each caregiver is diagrammed.

Close monitoring of package assignments is most necessary when employees first begin delivering care within this system to ensure that they have been scheduled correctly and to guarantee that the client fully understands this form of care. Although the shared services arrangements may have been explained beforehand, clients who have received care under traditional methods of delivery are accustomed to having workers arrive at an exact time and remain for a given number of hours or until all tasks are completed. Thus, increased supervision serves to reassure the clients and ensure that their questions and concerns are addressed.

Closer monitoring under alternative scheduling systems also allows employees to ask questions and receive additional support. This ensures that fewer difficulties will arise unexpectedly.

Monitoring ensures that the goals of a schedule for quality of care, appropriateness, and efficiency are met. Services are monitored to see that a smooth, stable, and efficient schedule has been achieved.

RECORD KEEPING AND BILLING FOR SHARED CARE

To be reimbursed for services delivered under an alternative scheduling system such as Shared Care, the agency must work with the funding agency or fiscal intermediary to establish procedures for billing and documenting the delivery of care. The agency can follow a few simple guidelines in working with intermediaries or referral sources to establish a Shared Care program. As explained earlier, fiscal intermediaries must redefine a visit in order for agencies to implement a Shared Care system, since caregivers perform shorter but much more frequent visits, entering the client's home several times a day to perform necessary tasks. The agency must reach an agreement with the third-party payer to redefine the visit and evaluate the agency's claims for reimbursement not on the basis of entry into the home but on the basis of tasks performed.

It is recommended that the agency propose to the fiscal intermediary a pilot project of one small Shared Care package to demonstrate the feasibility and cost savings that can be achieved. The agency must negotiate with the intermediary a daily or weekly rate for each group of clients to be served with Shared Care based on the levels of care required, travel expenses, and other factors influencing the cost of delivering services. The agency should also agree to demonstrate, through the pilot project, continued compliance with all regulations governing the provision of home care.

Ensuring compliance with state regulations for home health care generally means ensuring that the number of hours or visits billed equals the number provided. Under the Shared Care system, where service is based on job tasks or activities rather than a set number of hours or visits, monitoring compliance means ensuring that all tasks specified in the plan of care are completed for the client.

The key measures of compliance in a system of sharing staff are whether the services ordered are actually provided and whether the amount billed for those services is the amount agreed upon by the funding source and the home care agency. Auditors must determine if the services required by the client, as delineated in the care plan, were delivered. They must do so by comparing the care plan to the employee's time card, signed by the client, that lists every activity completed.

The theory behind reporting and billing procedures for Shared Care is simple. A record of activities or job tasks performed by an employee for a group of clients must be converted into a format (e.g., units of hours or visits) which follows the procedures and formats established by federal, state, and local authorities. Data regarding services to be provided are derived from the service orders and treatment plans, and a record of services delivered is derived from time cards submitted by personnel. The data are collated, audited, broken out, and reorganized into a format consistent with current reimbursement procedures.

In order to process billing for Shared Care services, the health care provider must follow a series of specific steps to ensure that service delivery is verifiable through an audit and that billing follows established procedures and formats.

Data Records

The first step in accounting for employees' time is the preparation of a preliminary aggregate spreadsheet for all clients in a Shared Care package. The spreadsheet shows the number of units (hours or visits) authorized for each Shared Care client from the service order, care plan, or caregivers' schedules. Total units of service authorized for all clients in a package will represent the billing at the end of the period if all services are delivered as planned. The compilation of data on clients and units of service into one spreadsheet allows the accounting department to have a theoretical picture of the entire Shared Care package. Figure 11.1 shows a sample spreadsheet for services ordered for the four clients described earlier.

Agencies must construct this spreadsheet regardless of whether they are under hourly or per-visit billing systems. To convert this figure to visits, an agency will have to develop an equation to be approved by the third-party payer. Due to the nature of Shared Care services, the agency may want to bill one visit for every 3 or 4 hours of service, for example, regardless of the increments in which care was delivered or even if services were provided on different days.

Client names run across the top and the days of the week down the side. The number of hours of service per day is entered for each

SPREADSHEET FOR SERVICES ORDERED

Client	A	B	C	D
Monday	7	3	4	13.5
Tuesday	8.5	3.5	4	11.5
Wednesday	7	3	4	13.5
Thursday	8.5	3.5	4	11.5
Friday	7	3	4	13.5
Totals	38	16	20	63.5

Total for package _____ 137.5

Figure 11.1. Spreadsheet for services ordered under the Shared Care scheduling system.

client, and the individual weekly totals are combined into a total number for the entire package. This format, which shows hours of service on a daily basis, is adjustable, as the format is determined by the provider agency's regular accounting system. If the reimbursing agency or third-party payer must have a daily record of service, units (hours or visits) can be placed as they are here; if units must be logged in a weekly format (e.g., three visits per week), the spreadsheet can be developed in that format as well.

This data record represents the operation of the Shared Care system if no variations occur in employees' schedules. For accounting purposes, units of time are assigned to each client, even though the services provided through Shared Care do not follow such a schedule exactly. For example, the service authorized for client A is for 38 hours of care during the week, broken into periods as brief as 15 minutes. Although the home health agency has reached an agreement with the third-party payer to provide care by sharing staff, the third-party payer's computerized system may only accept bills for service provided in increments of no fewer than 4 hours of care. In this case, the bill for services will not reflect the way in which care was actually delivered. This record is developed according to an established agreement with the third-party payer to translate actual service delivery in a Shared Care system into the traditional billing format. Nevertheless, the sheet sets a pattern of hours that will be necessary for billing.

Time cards in Shared Care serve the same function as in more traditional scheduling systems: They are records of the time an employee spends with a client. When different types of systems are used, employees record all hours worked, including Shared Care hours, substitute hours, traditional hours, or extra assignments, on one time card.

Each day, the caregiver records the time spent with each client; if tasks were performed for a client three times in one day, the service is recorded each time. Time in and out, and the number of hours spent performing the services, are logged. There must also be a column on the time card for a client signature; the signature represents the client's verification that services were provided.

In many cases, employee time cards are not completed in blocks of time (their schedules are oriented by tasks, not by hours). Time cards are an approximate representation of service delivery. The auditing of these cards and the subsequent billing therefore rely on the use of statistical averages, since visits are of no specified length and the amount of time needed to perform a task may vary. Most often, employees provide rough estimates of Shared Care hours; in other instances, the responsibility for translating tasks completed to billing hours lies with the accountants. That is, services provided without schedule changes may be recorded by the employee as completed between 7:00 a.m. and 3:00 p.m., and the accountant, using the employee's schedule, divides the day into billable hours by the tasks performed. Billable visits are similarly derived, using an equation translating service hours provided to visits, either established through an agreement with the third-party payer or developed by the home health agency.

Data Reorganization

The next step in the reporting procedure is the reorganization of data from the time cards. The data are broken out into total hours, total shared hours, and the number of hours in which one employee substituted for another. The Shared Care hours for each client are taken from the time cards and put into a second spreadsheet (see Figure 11.2). On this record, the hours of service for a group of clients are logged. The clients' names are at the top, the days of the week are down the side, and the data show which hours were provided by which employees (here employees are represented by numbers). The totals for each client are at the bottom of the page, along with a gross total of hours that were provided to the entire package.

It is at this point that the delivery of services is compared to the theoretical delivery mapped out in the first spreadsheet, either from employees' schedules or according to the billing format of the third-party payer. The amount of service provided in the package is matched with the care plan for the Shared Care package. As mentioned above, units of service for each client are billed using a statistical average, since the amount of time needed to complete a task may vary slightly. An employee's schedule will also vary, but the same tasks are completed. Therefore, the number of hours or visits billed is averaged.

The use of statistical averages means that the delivery of services

SPREADSHEET FOR SERVICES PROVIDED

Client:	A Aide/Hours		B Aide/Hours		C Aide/Hours		D Aide/Hours	
Monday	#1	1	#1	1	#1	2		
	#2	.5	#2	.5	#2	.5	#2	5
	LPN	.5					LPN	1.5
	#3	1	#3	1.5	#3	1.5	#3	3
	#4	4					#4	4
Tuesday	#1	3	#1	2	#1	1.5	#1	1
					#2	1	#2	2
	LPN	.5					LPN	1.5
	#3	1	#3	1.5	#3	1.5	#3	3
	#4	4					#4	4
Wednesday	#1	1	#1	1	#1	2	#1	5
	#2	.5	#2	.5	#2	.5	#2	5
	LPN	.5					LPN	1.5
	#3	1	#3	1.5	#3	1.5	#3	3
	#4	4					#4	4
Thursday	#1	3	#1	2	#1	1.5	#1	1
					#2	1	#2	2
	LPN	.5					LPN	1.5
	#3	1	#3	1.5	#3	1.5	#3	3
	#4	4					#4	4
Friday	#1	1	#1	1	#1	2		
	#2	.5	#2	.5	#2	.5	#2	5
	LPN	.5					LPN	1.5
	#3	1	#3	1.5	#3	1.5	#3	3
	#4	4					#4	4
Total/Client		38		16		20		63.5

Total for package _____ 137.5

Figure 11.2. Spreadsheet for services provided under the Shared Care scheduling system.

in units of time may not match the care plan for an individual client. If the client has received more units of care in this billing period, it is assumed that at another time he or she will receive fewer units in another period. Any consistent variance in care provided is detected early and a change in the employee's schedule is authorized. Therefore, if the total amount of services for the entire package matches on both spreadsheets, it is assumed that service was delivered as planned for all clients and the amounts laid out in the care plan are billed, as is the case in our example, where the 126 hours of service ordered were provided.

If the gross totals from the two spreadsheets do not match, the package as a whole did not receive the care authorized. When this occurs, the discrepancy must be investigated by comparing the total hours or visits authorized for each client in the package to the total units provided each client to determine whether or not a client's bill must be adjusted. The first possible reason for the discrepancy is human error (e.g., an employee's mistake in recording his or her hours). In this case, the error is corrected on the card and on the spreadsheet, and the package is billed as planned.

The second possibility is that services were not delivered according to the treatment plan. Any number of circumstances can bring about a change in services; for example, a client may be hospitalized for several days, in which case he or she would not have received services at home. This would affect the total care provided to the package. If the discrepancy is due to an actual difference in service delivery, the agency must determine how much care the client received and why it differed from the treatment plan. If a client received fewer services than authorized because of hospitalization, for example, his or her bill must be reduced and the rest of the package billed as usual.

If the gross total is greater than the number of services laid out in the treatment plan, the agency must identify which client received additional care. If additional care was provided a client in an emergency, those services are billable. If the extra hours were unwarranted or the employee was unauthorized to provide extra care, the agency must determine whether the client can be legitimately billed. If not, the agency must absorb the cost of the extra services.

Monitoring Compliance with State and Federal Regulations

Regardless of whether a home health agency is billing for Shared Care services by visit or by hours, it must still schedule and record activities by hour, translating that time into visits if necessary. Fiscal intermediaries reviewing Medicare claims may still request a breakdown of activities by level of care by hour. The procedures used by government agencies and fiscal intermediaries to ensure that the treatment plan was implemented will differ under per-visit and hourly billing systems. They will both, however, compare the tasks specified in the treatment plan to those on the activity sheets to ensure that the appropriate care was provided. Procedures for ensuring that home health agencies are assigning employees who have completed the appropriate training and have passed all physical examinations are no different under the Shared Care system than under the traditional systems of providing home health services.

Per-Visit Billing

Home health agencies providing care under a traditional per-visit billing system are charging third-party payers for a visit each time an employee providing care enters the client's home. The duration of the visit varies depending upon the time required to complete all tasks; therefore, agencies are accustomed to demonstrating that the care plan was followed based on completion of tasks rather than the provision of a specified number of hours of care. Regardless of whether the visit was billed to Medicaid, Medicare, or another program using per-visit billing, the monitoring agency can ensure that all tasks were completed for each client by analyzing a record of the home health agency's activity sheet signed by both the employee and the client for each billing period.

Ensuring that the home health agency is not billing for too many visits requires that the claims reviewer, whether from a fiscal intermediary or a government agency overseeing Medicaid reimbursement, understand that a visit is not billed each time the professional or paraprofessional enters the client's home. The fiscal intermediary or third-party payer may want to develop an equation of the number of average hours that constitute a visit, or may redefine the visit with the understanding that no more than one visit can be charged each day. Regardless of the agreement, the claims reviewer must understand that the number of visits charged for each client does not represent the same form of care as that delivered under the traditional definition of a visit.

Hourly Billing Systems

Ensuring that proper care was provided under an hourly billing system is more complex. Reviewers in this system are accustomed to comparing a number of hours of care authorized for a client to the number of hours of care provided a client. The government agency overseeing the referral of clients and the reimbursement for services to a home health agency using a Shared Care system may choose to implement stricter controls and more frequent record reviews than under traditional systems to ensure that adequate care is provided.

Officials monitoring care in this system must have a thorough knowledge of the way care is delivered. The home health agency is now billing the statistical average of hours of care provided; slight variances in the hours of care provided in a given billing period may not be reflected on the employee's time card. Reviewing officials will have to refer to the activity sheets to ensure that all tasks were completed for each client, but this document does not show the hours of care provided. Persons reviewing an agency's documentation will no longer be able to compare the hours of care authorized for the client to a time card to determine if exactly that amount of care was delivered. Rather, records must now be analyzed *by package*, with the total number of hours authorized for that package compared to the spreadsheet totaling the care provided that package.

Generally, if a home health agency's bills conform to a government agency's computerized system for reimbursement, those bills will not accurately reflect the method by which care was actually delivered. For example, most hourly billing for traditional services is based on care authorized for blocks of time, such as 4 hours on Tuesday and Thursday. The bill for Shared Care services will be formatted this way despite the fact that the 8 hours of care were actually provided over 4 days that week in increments totaling 2 hours each day. Again, agencies billing by visit will have to develop a method for converting these hours to visits based on their costs. In such a conversion, if the agency provided 8 hours of service and billed a visit for every 4 hours, two visits would be billed despite the fact that the aide, nurse, or therapist entered the client's home four times. Reviewers of an agency's documentation must clearly understand that clients must be grouped by package in order to compare bills to time cards.

In Shared Care, as in more traditional scheduling systems, the information posted to the records after a schedule is designed and implemented is a critical component of scheduling. The verification of services scheduled and provided ensures not only regulatory compliance but also the best and most consistent quality of care.

The management of home care in a way that reduces the costs of the service while maintaining or increasing the quality of care is a primary issue facing practitioners and directors of home care agencies. The Shared Care system of home health reduces patient care costs while improving the plan of care through coordination between skilled workers and paraprofessionals. Reductions in travel time reduce agency administrative costs related to transportation, costs which do not contribute to quality and clinical issues. Coordination among clients and increased client contacts foster independence and help reduce isolation. The careful and deliberate modification of an agency's management practices toward sharing care will allow the agency to be more competitive and offer the highest quality of care.

Index

Absenteeism, 159, 214–215, 233.
    See also Attendance records
Accounting records, 204–205, 208,
    214, 215, 218–219, 220, 251
Activities to be performed:
  analyzing, 32, 80–87, 235, 239,
    241
  assessing blocks of time for,
    82–83
  determining, 9–11
  prioritizing, 82, 235
  scheduling blocks of time and,
    30–31
  Shared Care system and,
    223–225, 228–231, 235–236,
    240, 248
Activity level of client, 76–77
Activity sheets, 54, 77, 78, 186, 188,
    203
Adjusting schedule, 152–154,
    195–197
  documentation for, 205, 208–210

Administrative supervision to
    monitor schedule, 183, 191,
    193
Allowance fraction, 19
Appearance, employee's, 104, 112,
    187
Assembly line, 5, 9
Assigning personnel, *see* Personnel
    assignment
Attendance records, 112, 142, 146,
    159, 204, 214–215
  adjusting schedule based on, 196
  in calendar format, 216
  information learned from, 159,
    188, 215
  in linear format, 217
  monitoring schedule with, 188
Attitude barriers to
    communication, 65–66
  neutralizing, 70–71
Audience, gearing communication
    to, 67–68

Audits:
  internal, 215-218
  for Shared Care system, 248, 251
Audit trail, 52
Automation of scheduling, *see*
  Computer-assisted scheduling
  system
Availability of appropriate
  caregivers, 39-40, 123-124
Availability calendar, 84-85, 86,
  204
Availability of client or family,
  32-33, 79, 80, 84-85

Backing up computer records, 180,
  205-206
Biases as barriers to
  communication, 65-66
  neutralizing, 70-71
Billing function, 178, 179, 219, 220,
  226
  hourly billing system, *see* Hourly
    billing systems
  per-visit billing system, 19, 227,
    254
  for Shared Care system, 247-256
Billing units, *see* Units of service
  (billing units)
Body language, 58
Breakeven point, 14

Calendars, 142
  availability, 84-85, 86, 204
  supervisory visit, 156
Card index, 140-141
Care plans, 30, 31-32, 35, 54, 196,
  203, 244, 245, 248
  responsibility for formulating, 75
  updating, 185-191
Caring qualities, 112, 117
Carrying costs, 12-13
Change in Service Form, 208-210
Changing the schedule, 152-154,
  195-197. *See also* Monitoring
  the schedule

documentation for, 205, 208-210
Channels for communication,
  59-61
Checking the schedule, 151-152
Classification of data, computer,
  171-172
Client condition:
  evaluating, with supervisory
    visits, 184-186, 193
  feedback on, 192-193
  monitoring under Shared Care,
    220, 244-246
  record of changes, 203
Client data sheet, 203, 206
Client-employee relationship:
  adjusting schedule for
    unsuccessful, 195-197
  evaluating the, 187-188, 193
Client needs:
  checklist, 77, 78
  evaluating, 75-78
  medical and therapeutic, 23, 28,
    29-32, 76-77
  personnel selection and,
    121-123
  psychosocial, 35-36, 77-79
  Shared Care parameters, 241
Client preferences, 34, 79, 80,
  85-86, 128-129
Client roster, 208
Client summary sheet, 80, 81
Clinical supervision to monitor
  schedule, 182-183, 191, 193
Closing out current computer
  schedule, 180
Commendations of employees,
  documentation of, 204
Communication, 46-72
  accuracy, 58
  case study, 47-48
  channels for, 59-61
  among clients in Shared Care,
    232
  common problems in, 63-66
  frequency, 62-63

importance, to scheduling staff.
46–48
improving methods, 66–71
as method of reassurance, 47
with employee's office, 112
proper forms, 61–62
quality, 58
round-the-clock, 71–72
as two-way process, 46, 58
types, 48–58
verbal, 49–52, 61–62
visual, 57–58
written, 52–57, 58, 62, 206
Communication skills, employee,
100, 104, 105, 117
Community services, *see* Outside
support system, availability of
Company allowance fraction, 19
Company policies and procedures,
56, 61, 105
assessing compliance with, 187
on computer documentation,
205
for supervisory visits, 184
Complaints, 114
documentation, 203
investigating, 156
logging, 146
resolving, 51, 52
Completion of assigned tasks, 112
evaluating, 186
Computer-assisted scheduling
system, 162–180. *See also*
Manual scheduling
advantages, 163
anticipated growth of agency and,
165
backing up records, 180,
205–206
capabilities, 171–175
confidentiality issue, 180
daily use, 177–180
developing system of, 164–170
disadvantages, 163–164
evaluation, 170

feasibility, 164–165
geography as matching factor
and, 38, 126
implementation, 169–170
integration, 168
purchasing, 167–168
reports produced, 165–166, 178
security, 168–169
staff commitment, 175–177
tasks to be performed, 166–167
training in use, 177
Computer-produced records, 53
Confidentiality of records, 53, 180,
212, 219–220
Continuing service, evaluating
client's need for, 185–186
Continuity of care, 225
scheduling of personnel and, 37,
39, 40, 123
in Shared Care system, 231–232,
240
Contribution margin per unit, 14
Control systems, computer, 175,
179–180
Cost/benefit analysis, 166
Cost effectiveness:
of computer-assisted scheduling,
162
scheduling and, 23, 124, 154
of Shared Care system, 222, 223,
224, 230–231, 237–238, 239
of supervisory visits, 157
Cost of travel, 37
Cost/volume analysis, 13–14
Creating the schedule, 148–151
handling employee shortages,
151
manually, 148–151
one-time assignments, 150
permanent assignments,
149–150
temporary assignments, 150
Credentials, employee, 95–97, 204
Cross-checking schedule, 151–152
Cultural considerations, 38, 39

Cultural considerations
(*Continued*)
special skills, 103–104, 128
Cycle time, 10

Day care services, 35
Dedication, 116
Demand-based care, 231, 243
Documentation, 52–53, 202–220.
*See also specific forms of
documentation*
as aid in anticipating scheduling
problems, 159
computer system, 177, 205–206
confidentiality, 212, 219–220
record keeping, 203–205
requirements for, 192–193, 203,
207, 210, 219
reviewing, to monitor schedule,
188
for Shared Care system, 247–256
tools for, 205–215
verification of, 215–219
Downward communication, 59
Duration of case as scheduling
factor, 27

Economic feasibility of computer-
based scheduling system, 165
Emergency situations:
miscommunication in, 64–65
round-the-clock message system
for, 72
Emotional needs, *see* Psychosocial
needs of client
Employee data record, 207–208
Employee preferences, *see*
Preferences of employees
Ethnic considerations, 38, 39
special skills, 103–104, 128
Evaluating a computer scheduling
system, 170
Evaluating personnel, *see*
Personnel evaluation
Experience of employee, 97–98

Face-to-face communication,
49–50, 51, 52, 67
Factors in scheduling, 22–42
Family members, 22–23
availability, 33, 80
degree of support from, 34–35,
79, 87–88
evaluation of client's
psychosocial needs with aid, 79
feedback from, during
supervisory visits, 185
preferences, 33–34, 80, 85–86
psychosocial needs, 36, 87
Favoritism, 132
Feedback, 69–70, 192–193. *See
also* Monitoring the schedule
on on-the-job performance,
102–103, 113–114, 156–157,
187
from peers, 109–110, 114,
188–189
during supervisory visits, 185,
187
Files, computer-generated,
173–174
Fixed costs, 14
Fixed-position layout, 6, 7, 8–9, 10
Flexibility of computer scheduling
system, 175
Flexibility of employee, 104, 115
Flexibility of scheduling, 22, 24, 31
Flexibility of Shared Care system,
237, 243
Follow-up communication, 70
Ford, Henry, 5
Funding source, 124, 219
evaluating need for continuing
service for, 185–186
frequency of supervisory visits
and, 154–155, 190
scheduling constrictions, 83, 90
selection of computer scheduling
system and, 166
Shared Care billing and record
keeping and, 247–248,

253-256
Shared Care parameters and, 241

Gantt, Henry, 5
Geography, 37-39, 40, 107
  ethnicity and culture, 38, 39
  neighborhood services, 38-39
  selecting personnel, 124-126
  Shared Care and, 223, 225, 231,
    241, 246
  supervisory visit assignment, 157
  travel requirements, 15-16,
    37-38, 124-125, 157, 223, 226,
    227, 246
Grouping tasks to be performed, 88
Group interviews, 101
Growth of health care agency,
  anticipated, 165

HCR, 222, 232
  model Shared Care programs,
    222-223, 233-240
Health Care Financing
  Administration, 219, 222
Home environment:
  assessing the, 79, 186-187
  as matching consideration, 42,
    105, 128
Home visit report, 193-194
Home visits, *see* Initial home visit;
  On-site supervision
Honesty, employee's, 104
Hourly billing systems, 226-227
  Shared Care systems and,
    255-256
  units of service (billing units), 30,
    82-83, 218, 250, 251-252, 255

Idle time, 19, 227, 233
Implementation of computer
  scheduling system, 169-170
Implementation of a Shared Care
  schedule, 242-244
Independence, fostering client,
  232, 240

Independent work skills, 100
Index cards, 140-141
Informal communication to
  monitor schedule, 189
Information:
  scheduling, defined, 203
  trickle-down effect, 64
  vague or incomplete, 63-64
Initial home visit, 190, 194
  evaluating a client's needs at,
    75-80
Inputting data into computer, 179
Institutional care, 227
Insurance coverage, 90
Interests and hobbies as matching
  consideration, 42, 127, 128
Interpersonal skills, 104, 105
  evaluating caregiver's, 103,
    108-109, 117
Interviews, personal, of new
  employees, 100-101, 105-106
Inventory management theory,
  11-13

Job task analysis, *see* Activities to
  be performed, analysis of
Job tasks, *see* Activities to be
  performed

Language problems, 65
Learning curve effect, 10, 11
Ledgers, 142-144
Linear programming techniques,
  14-15
Lines of communication,
  establishing, 66-67
Linguistic skills, 103-104, 128
Listening skills, 68-69
Lists for manual scheduling,
  144-145
Logs, 145
  of substitute assignments, 153
  supervisory visit, 155-156
  telephone, 145-146, 152,
    209

Managing supervisory visits, 16–20
Manual scheduling, 140–159. *See also* Computer-assisted scheduling system
anticipating problems, 158–159
attendance records for, 146
card index for, 140–141
changing the schedule, 152–154
checking schedule, 151–152
creating schedule, 148–151
lists for, 144–145
logs for, 145–146, 152, 153, 155–156
maps for, 141–142
matrices for, 142–144, 146–147, 148, 151–152
organizing the schedule, 146–148
scheduling tools, 140–146
of supervisory visits, 154–158
switching to computer-assisted system, 169–170
Maps, 38, 126, 141–142
Marketing niche of agency, 27
Matrices, 142–144, 146–147, 148, 151–152, 176, 177
Maturity, 104, 105, 107
Maximization, 14–15
Medicaid, 27, 32, 155, 190, 219, 226
Medicare, 27, 32, 47, 84, 154, 185–186, 190, 219, 227, 253
Memoranda, 55–56
Minimization, 14
Mismatches, avoiding obvious, 129, 130
Monitoring the schedule, 182–194. *See also* Changing schedule; Monitoring in a Shared Care system
administrative supervision, 183
clinical supervision, 182–183
with off-site supervision, 188–189
with on-site supervision, 183–188

organizing a system for, 190–194
supportive approach to, 192
Monitoring in Shared Care system, 244–247, 248. *See also* Monitoring the schedule
Motivation, employee, 100, 104, 105, 107, 108, 116–117

New clients, frequency of monitoring, 191–192
New employees, 179
assignment, 131, 150–151
evaluating, *see* Personnel evaluation
frequency of monitoring, 191–192
recruiting, 151
Newsletters, 56–57

Off-site supervision, 188–189
by informal communication, 189
by peer review, 188–189
by reviewing documentation, 188
by telephone contact, 189
One-time assignments, 150
On-line scheduling, 174
On-site supervision, 183–188
assigning, 156–158
charting and logging, 155–156
to evaluate client condition, 184–186, 193
to evaluate client–employee relationship, 187–188
to evaluate completion of tasks, 186
to evaluate personnel, 102–103, 112–113, 155–156, 184, 186–188, 193
to evaluate quality of work, 186–187
frequency, 154–155, 190–193, 246
goals, 183
home visit report, 193–194
managing, 16–20

scheduling, 154–158, 194
in Shared Care system, 244–247
steps in monitoring the
assignment, 184
Operational feasibility of computer-
based scheduling system,
164–165
Operations management theory,
5–6
application, to home health care
services, 5, 7–20
Ordering costs, 12–13
Organizing schedule, 146–148
difficult cases first, 147–148
manually, 146–148
matrices for, 146–147, 148
Organizing system to monitor
schedule, 190–194
frequency of monitoring,
154–155, 190–193
scheduling supervisory visits,
154–158, 194
staff responsibilities, 193–194
Orientation period, evaluating
personnel during, 101–102,
106–108
Outpatient medical services or
treatments, 35
Outside support system,
availability of, 34–35, 79, 80, 86

Part-time employees, 151, 158
Patient care records, 203–204
Payroll, 175, 178, 179, 218, 220
Peers, evaluation by, 109–110, 114,
188–189
Permanent assignments, 26–27,
132, 149–150
Personal interviews of new
employees, 100–101, 105–106
Personality:
evaluating, at supervisory visit,
187
as matching consideration, 41,
42, 128

Personal qualities of personnel,
evaluating, 103, 104–111,
112–117
Personnel assignment, 120, 121,
130–135
achieving balance, 131
agency approach to, 121
favoritism, 132
of new employees, 131
permanent, 26–27, 132, 149–150
substitute, 133–134, 151, 153
for supervisory visits, 156–158
team approach, 131–132
temporary, 26, 27, 132–133, 150
Personnel evaluation, 94–118
on a continual basis, 111–118
credentials, 95–97
feedback on on-the-job
performance, 102–103,
113–114, 156–157, 187
observation during training or
orientation, 101–102, 106–110
personal interviews, 100–101,
105–106
of personal qualities, 103,
104–111, 112–117
recommendations from previous
employers, 99–100, 110–111
of skill levels, 95–104
specialized abilities, 103–104
through supervisory visits, *see*
On-site supervision
years and type of experience,
97–98
Personnel factors in scheduling
home health care, 27, 28–29,
36–42
availability of appropriate
caregiver, 39–40
employee preferences, 40
geography, 37–39
service needs, 36–37
special factors, 40–42
Personnel files, 204, 207–208. *See
also specific files, e.g.,*

Personnel files (*Continued*)
Attendance records; Employee
data record
Personnel selection, 120-130,
134-135
availability and, 123-124
employee preferences and,
126-127
geography and, 124-126
other considerations, 129-130
service needs and, 121-123
special factors, 127-129
Per-visit billing, 19, 227
Shared Care system and, 254
Pets, 42, 105, 128
Physical barriers to
communication, 65
Physician Report, 207
Physician's orders, 30, 207, 217,
219, 244
Plan of care, *see* Care plans
Policy, *see* Company policies and
procedures
Prebilling reports, 219
Preemployment documents, 55,
204
Preferences of client or family,
33-34, 79, 80, 85-86, 128-129
Preferences of employees, 40, 104,
105, 125, 126-127
Previous matches, feedback from,
129, 130
Process layout, 8
Production management theory,
5-6
application, to home health care
services, 4, 5, 7-20
Productive time, 10
Productivity, 222, 225-227, 231,
245
Product layout, 8, 9
Profitability, 13-14, 26
Psychosocial needs of client, 35-36,
77-79, 86-87
Shared Care system and, 232

Punctuality, 100, 106, 109, 112,
159, 187. *See also* Tardiness
documentation of, 204
Purchasing a computer scheduling
system, 167-168

Real time processing of
information, 174
Recommendations, employee,
99-100, 110-111
Record keeping, 52-53, 203-205.
See also Documentation;
specific types of records
for Shared Care system, 247-256
Recruiting personnel, 151
References, employee, 99-100,
110-111
Referrals of new clients, 50, 151
Shared Care parameters for, 241
Reports produced by computer
scheduling system, 165-166,
178
Responsibility, ability to handle,
115, 116, 232-233
Revising the schedule, 152-154

Schedules, 5, 54
Scheduling chart, 87, 88
Scheduling home health care:
assigning personnel, *see*
Personnel assignment
changing the schedule, 152-154,
195-197
communication's role in, *see*
Communication
by computer, *see* Computer-
assisted scheduling system
documentation for, *see*
Documentation
evaluating personnel, *see*
Personnel evaluation
factors in, 22-42
flexibility in, 22, 24, 31
management theory applied to,
6-20

manually, *see* Manual scheduling
monitoring the schedule, *see* Monitoring the schedule
primary considerations in, 23-24
selecting personnel, *see* Personnel selection
for Shared Care, *see* Sharing services
strategy for, 24
Scheduling plan, 24-27
  criteria for prioritizing cases, 25-27
  desired mix of clients and, 27
  duration of coverage and, 27
  profitability and, 26
  total hours of coverage or number of visits made and, 25-26
  type of case and, 26-27
  urgency of case and, 25
Scheduling staff, 24-25
  commitment to computer scheduling system, 175-177
  monitoring responsibilities of, 193-194
Searching function, computer, 172-173, 176
Security:
  of computer scheduling system, 168-169
  of documentation, 220
Selecting personnel, *see* Personnel selection
Self-confidence, employee, 116, 129
Sequencing of operations, methods for, 5, 9-10
Service authorization form, 90-91
Shared Care, 23, 222-223, 228-256. *See also* Sharing services
  results, 240
Sharing services, 23, 222-256
  advantages, 228-233
  cost-effectiveness, 222, 223, 224, 230-231, 237-238, 239
  how it works, 228-230
  implementing a schedule for, 242-244
  model Shared Care program, 222-223, 233-240
  monitoring, 244-247
  needs for, 225-228
  origins, 225
  parameters, 241-242
  pilot programs, 222-223, 233-240
  record keeping and billing, 247-256
  results, 240
  as task-based, 223
Skill levels of personnel:
  evaluating, 95-104
  for Shared Care system, 241-242, 243-244
Smoking, 42, 105, 128
Social needs, *see* Psychosocial needs of clients
Software, *see* Computer-assisted scheduling system
Software vendors, 167, 168
Sorting of data, computer, 172
Spreadsheets:
  for services ordered under Shared Care scheduling system, 248-250, 252-253
  for services provided under Shared Care scheduling system, 251-253
Stockout, 13
Substitute assignments, 133-134, 151, 153
Suggestion surveys, 57
Summary sheet, client, 80, 81
Supervisory visit log, 155-158
Supervisory visits, *see* On-site supervision
Surveys, 57

Talents of employee, considering special, in matching process, 41

Tardiness, 159, 214–215. *See also* Punctuality

Tasks to be performed, *see* Activities to be performed

Team approach, 131–132

Technical feasibility of computer-based scheduling system, 164

Telephone communication, 49, 50–51, 66–67, 72
to monitor schedule, 189, 245

Telephone logs, 145–146, 152, 209

Temporary assignments, 26, 27, 132–133, 150

Termination documents, 204

Time cards or sheets, 55, 204–205, 210–214, 218, 219
for Shared Care system, 248, 250–251, 255
simple, 210, 211
two-sided, 212, 213–214

Time constraints, communication hindered by, 65

Time management skills, employee's, 104, 115

Time-specific tasks, 32

Times of service, determining, 27, 28–38, 74–91. *See also* Sharing services
analyzing activities, 80–87
assigning days and times, 87–91
availability of client or family, 32–33, 79, 80, 84–85
availability of outside support, 34–35, 79, 80, 86
evaluating service needs, 29–32, 75–80
preferences of client or family, 33–34, 79, 80, 85, 86
psychosocial needs of client, 35–36, 77–79, 86–87

Time spent communicating, 71

Title XIX, *see* Medicaid

Tracking schedule changes, 51

Training period:
evaluating personnel during, 101–102, 108–110
for Shared Care personnel, 242

Training scheduling staff to use computer system, 177

Transactions performed by computer scheduling system, 171

Travel requirements, 15–16, 17, 37–38, 124–125, 157, 226, 227
Shared Care and, 223, 246

Trickle-down effect in communication, 64

Units of service (billing units), 30, 82–83, 218, 250, 251–252, 255

Updating information by computer, 174, 205

Upward communication, 59

User friendly software, 168

Variable costs, 14
per unit, 14

Verbal communication, 49–52, 61–62
advantages, 49
for case coverage, 50–51
for complaint resolution, 51, 52
for evaluating process, 51
for monitoring schedules, 52
for receipts of referrals, 50
for tracking changes, 51

Verifying documentation, 215–219
documentation by client, 219
documentation by employee, 218–219
internal audits, 215–218

Verifying schedule, records for, *see* Attendance records; Time cards or sheets

Visits, defined, 30

Visual communication, 57–58

Vocabulary, lack of understanding,
 65

Whitney, Eli, 5
Work sampling, 18-19
Written communication, 52-57, 62,
 206
 activity sheets, 54
 advantages of, 53
 care plans, 54

company policies and
 procedures, 56
memoranda, 55-56
newsletters, 56-57
preemployment documents,
 55
schedules, 54
suggestion surveys, 57
time cards, 55
types, 54-57